ISBN 0-8373-4709-2
C-4709

CAREER EXAMINATION SERIES

This is your
PASSBOOK® for...

Supervising Emergency Services Dispatcher

Test Preparation Study Guide
Questions & Answers

NATIONAL LEARNING CORPORATION®

PASSBOOK®

NOTICE

PASSBOOK® SERIES

THE *PASSBOOK® SERIES* has been created to prepare applicants and candidates for the ultimate academic battlefield – the examination room.

At some time in our lives, each and every one of us may be required to take an examination – for validation, matriculation, admission, qualification, registration, certification, or licensure.

Based on the assumption that every applicant or candidate has met the basic formal educational standards, has taken the required number of courses, and read the necessary texts, the *PASSBOOK® SERIES* furnishes the one special preparation which may assure passing with confidence, instead of failing with insecurity. Examination questions – together with answers – are furnished as the basic vehicle for study so that the mysteries of the examination and its compounding difficulties may be eliminated or diminished by a sure method.

This book is meant to help you pass your examination provided that you qualify and are serious in your objective.

The entire field is reviewed through the huge store of content information which is succinctly presented through a provocative and challenging approach – the question-and-answer method.

A climate of success is established by furnishing the correct answers at the end of each test.

You soon learn to recognize types of questions, forms of questions, and patterns of questioning. You may even begin to anticipate expected outcomes.

You perceive that many questions are repeated or adapted so that you can gain acute insights, which may enable you to score many sure points.

You learn how to confront new questions, or types of questions, and to attack them confidently and work out the correct answers.

You note objectives and emphases, and recognize pitfalls and dangers, so that you may make positive educational adjustments.

Moreover, you are kept fully informed in relation to new concepts, methods, practices, and directions in the field.

You discover that you are actually taking the examination all the time: you are preparing for the examination by "taking" an examination, not by reading extraneous and/or supererogatory textbooks.

In short, this PASSBOOK®, used directedly, should be an important factor in helping you to pass your test.

SUPERVISING EMERENCY SERVICES DISPATCHER

DUTIES:

   This position exists in the public safety communications center and involves supervising the activities of subordinate Emergency Service Dispatchers during an assigned shift at the Center. Under the general supervision of the administrator, an employee in this class oversees the processing and dispatch of emergency and non-emergency telephone calls from the public for police, fire and emergency medical services, emergency medical service pre-arrival instruction as required, the efficient relay of information to public safety units, and the dispatch of personnel and equipment. Employee will render assistance in answering questions posed by dispatchers on duty relative to equipment, policies and procedures. Employee may also, on occasion, be required to work as a dispatcher. Employee will be responsible for training, development and evaluation of subordinate staff. While on duty, the employee may also be required to monitor activities of maintenance and technical support personnel or other contractual agents servicing the center and associated equipment. This job involves an unusual working environment of high stress dealing with life and death situations. The ability to remain calm, polite, and patient in strenuous and often exorbitant situations is basic character requirements for the person who holds this job. Shift work may be required. Extensive background in the use of computers is strongly recommended.

SUBJECTS OF EXAMINATION:

The written test designed to evaluate knowledge, skills and/or abilities in the following areas:

1. **Coding/decoding information**: These questions test for the ability to follow a set of coding rules. Some questions will require you to code information by converting certain information into letters or numbers. Other questions will require you to decode information by determining if the information that has already been converted into letters or numbers is correct. Complete directions will be provided; no previous knowledge of or training in any coding system is required.

2. **Retaining and comprehending spoken information from calls for emergency services**: These questions test for your ability to retain specific information that is heard in calls for emergency service, such as a street address, or to comprehend spoken information from emergency service calls, such as determining the location of a site in relation to landmarks. Simulated 911 calls will be played on audio CD. Immediately following each call, candidates are given audio instructions identifying which questions they are to answer within the test booklet. The questions that candidates are directed to answer for each simulated call will not be in sequential order. Candidates will need to retain and comprehend the information and instruction provided in this portion of the test to respond appropriately to the questions asked and to determine which questions to answer. The time allotted to answer these questions will be limited. At the end of each answer period, the CD will automatically play the next call. Note paper will be provided. Candidates will be permitted to take notes and to refer to them when answering the questions.

3. **Office record keeping**: These questions test your ability to perform common office record keeping tasks. The test consists of two or more "sets" of questions, each set concerning a different problem. Typical record keeping problems might involve the organization or collation of data from several sources; scheduling; maintaining a record system using running balances; or completion of a table summarizing data using totals, subtotals, averages and percents. You should bring with you a hand-held battery- or solar-powered calculator for use on this test. You will not be permitted to use the calculator function of your cell phone.

4. **Radio operations and dispatching procedures**: These questions test for knowledge of two-way radio systems and operations, and may cover dispatching procedures when appropriate.

5. **Supervision and training**: These questions test for the knowledge required by a supervisor to set goals, plan and organize work, train workers in how to do their jobs, and direct workers towards meeting established goals. The supervisory questions cover such areas as assigning and reviewing work, evaluating performance, maintaining work quality, motivating employees, increasing efficiency, and dealing with problems that may arise on the job. The training questions cover such areas as determining the necessity for training, selecting appropriate training methods, and evaluating the effectiveness of training.

6. **Understanding and interpreting written material**: These questions test how well you comprehend written material. You will be provided with brief reading selections and will be asked questions about the selections. All the information required to answer the questions will be presented in the selections; you will not be required to have any special knowledge relating to the subject areas of the selections.

HOW TO TAKE A TEST

I. YOU MUST PASS AN EXAMINATION

A. WHAT EVERY CANDIDATE SHOULD KNOW

Examination applicants often ask us for help in preparing for the written test. What can I study in advance? What kinds of questions will be asked? How will the test be given? How will the papers be graded?

As an applicant for a civil service examination, you may be wondering about some of these things. Our purpose here is to suggest effective methods of advance study and to describe civil service examinations.

Your chances for success on this examination can be increased if you know how to prepare. Those "pre-examination jitters" can be reduced if you know what to expect. You can even experience an adventure in good citizenship if you know why civil service exams are given.

B. WHY ARE CIVIL SERVICE EXAMINATIONS GIVEN?

Civil service examinations are important to you in two ways. As a citizen, you want public jobs filled by employees who know how to do their work. As a job seeker, you want a fair chance to compete for that job on an equal footing with other candidates. The best-known means of accomplishing this two-fold goal is the competitive examination.

Exams are widely publicized throughout the nation. They may be administered for jobs in federal, state, city, municipal, town or village governments or agencies.

Any citizen may apply, with some limitations, such as the age or residence of applicants. Your experience and education may be reviewed to see whether you meet the requirements for the particular examination. When these requirements exist, they are reasonable and applied consistently to all applicants. Thus, a competitive examination may cause you some uneasiness now, but it is your privilege and safeguard.

C. HOW ARE CIVIL SERVICE EXAMS DEVELOPED?

Examinations are carefully written by trained technicians who are specialists in the field known as "psychological measurement," in consultation with recognized authorities in the field of work that the test will cover. These experts recommend the subject matter areas or skills to be tested; only those knowledges or skills important to your success on the job are included. The most reliable books and source materials available are used as references. Together, the experts and technicians judge the difficulty level of the questions.

Test technicians know how to phrase questions so that the problem is clearly stated. Their ethics do not permit "trick" or "catch" questions. Questions may have been tried out on sample groups, or subjected to statistical analysis, to determine their usefulness.

Written tests are often used in combination with performance tests, ratings of training and experience, and oral interviews. All of these measures combine to form the best-known means of finding the right person for the right job.

II. HOW TO PASS THE WRITTEN TEST

A. NATURE OF THE EXAMINATION

To prepare intelligently for civil service examinations, you should know how they differ from school examinations you have taken. In school you were assigned certain definite pages to read or subjects to cover. The examination questions were quite detailed and usually emphasized memory. Civil service exams, on the other hand, try to discover your present ability to perform the duties of a position, plus your potentiality to learn these duties. In other words, a civil service exam attempts to predict how successful you will be. Questions cover such a broad area that they cannot be as minute and detailed as school exam questions.

In the public service similar kinds of work, or positions, are grouped together in one "class." This process is known as *position-classification*. All the positions in a class are paid according to the salary range for that class. One class title covers all of these positions, and they are all tested by the same examination.

B. FOUR BASIC STEPS

1) Study the announcement

How, then, can you know what subjects to study? Our best answer is: "Learn as much as possible about the class of positions for which you've applied." The exam will test the knowledge, skills and abilities needed to do the work.

Your most valuable source of information about the position you want is the official exam announcement. This announcement lists the training and experience qualifications. Check these standards and apply only if you come reasonably close to meeting them.

The brief description of the position in the examination announcement offers some clues to the subjects which will be tested. Think about the job itself. Review the duties in your mind. Can you perform them, or are there some in which you are rusty? Fill in the blank spots in your preparation.

Many jurisdictions preview the written test in the exam announcement by including a section called "Knowledge and Abilities Required," "Scope of the Examination," or some similar heading. Here you will find out specifically what fields will be tested.

2) Review your own background

Once you learn in general what the position is all about, and what you need to know to do the work, ask yourself which subjects you already know fairly well and which need improvement. You may wonder whether to concentrate on improving your strong areas or on building some background in your fields of weakness. When the announcement has specified "some knowledge" or "considerable knowledge," or has used adjectives like "beginning principles of…" or "advanced … methods," you can get a clue as to the number and difficulty of questions to be asked in any given field. More questions, and hence broader coverage, would be included for those subjects which are more important in the work. Now weigh your strengths and weaknesses against the job requirements and prepare accordingly.

3) Determine the level of the position

Another way to tell how intensively you should prepare is to understand the level of the job for which you are applying. Is it the entering level? In other words, is this the position in which beginners in a field of work are hired? Or is it an intermediate or advanced level? Sometimes this is indicated by such words as "Junior" or "Senior" in the class title. Other jurisdictions use Roman numerals to designate the level – Clerk I, Clerk II, for example. The word "Supervisor" sometimes appears in the title. If the level is not indicated by the title, check the description of duties. Will you be working under very close supervision, or will you have responsibility for independent decisions in this work?

4) Choose appropriate study materials

Now that you know the subjects to be examined and the relative amount of each subject to be covered, you can choose suitable study materials. For beginning level jobs, or even advanced ones, if you have a pronounced weakness in some aspect of your training, read a modern, standard textbook in that field. Be sure it is up to date and has general coverage. Such books are normally available at your library, and the librarian will be glad to help you locate one. For entry-level positions, questions of appropriate difficulty are chosen – neither highly advanced questions, nor those too simple. Such questions require careful thought but not advanced training.

If the position for which you are applying is technical or advanced, you will read more advanced, specialized material. If you are already familiar with the basic principles of your field, elementary textbooks would waste your time. Concentrate on advanced textbooks and technical periodicals. Think through the concepts and review difficult problems in your field.

These are all general sources. You can get more ideas on your own initiative, following these leads. For example, training manuals and publications of the government agency which employs workers in your field can be useful, particularly for technical and professional positions. A letter or visit to the government department involved may result in more specific study suggestions, and certainly will provide you with a more definite idea of the exact nature of the position you are seeking.

III. KINDS OF TESTS

Tests are used for purposes other than measuring knowledge and ability to perform specified duties. For some positions, it is equally important to test ability to make adjustments to new situations or to profit from training. In others, basic mental abilities not dependent on information are essential. Questions which test these things may not appear as pertinent to the duties of the position as those which test for knowledge and information. Yet they are often highly important parts of a fair examination. For very general questions, it is almost impossible to help you direct your study efforts. What we can do is to point out some of the more common of these general abilities needed in public service positions and describe some typical questions.

1) General information

Broad, general information has been found useful for predicting job success in some kinds of work. This is tested in a variety of ways, from vocabulary lists to questions about current events. Basic background in some field of work, such as sociology or economics, may be sampled in a group of questions. Often these are principles which have become familiar to most persons through exposure rather than through formal training. It is difficult to advise you how to study for these questions; being alert to the world around you is our best suggestion.

2) Verbal ability

An example of an ability needed in many positions is verbal or language ability. Verbal ability is, in brief, the ability to use and understand words. Vocabulary and grammar tests are typical measures of this ability. Reading comprehension or paragraph interpretation questions are common in many kinds of civil service tests. You are given a paragraph of written material and asked to find its central meaning.

3) Numerical ability

Number skills can be tested by the familiar arithmetic problem, by checking paired lists of numbers to see which are alike and which are different, or by interpreting charts and graphs. In the latter test, a graph may be printed in the test booklet which you are asked to use as the basis for answering questions.

4) Observation

A popular test for law-enforcement positions is the observation test. A picture is shown to you for several minutes, then taken away. Questions about the picture test your ability to observe both details and larger elements.

5) Following directions

In many positions in the public service, the employee must be able to carry out written instructions dependably and accurately. You may be given a chart with several columns, each column listing a variety of information. The questions require you to carry out directions involving the information given in the chart.

6) Skills and aptitudes

Performance tests effectively measure some manual skills and aptitudes. When the skill is one in which you are trained, such as typing or shorthand, you can practice. These tests are often very much like those given in business school or high school courses. For many of the other skills and aptitudes, however, no short-time preparation can be made. Skills and abilities natural to you or that you have developed throughout your lifetime are being tested.

Many of the general questions just described provide all the data needed to answer the questions and ask you to use your reasoning ability to find the answers. Your best preparation for these tests, as well as for tests of facts and ideas, is to be at your physical and mental best. You, no doubt, have your own methods of getting into an exam-taking mood and keeping "in shape." The next section lists some ideas on this subject.

IV. KINDS OF QUESTIONS

Only rarely is the "essay" question, which you answer in narrative form, used in civil service tests. Civil service tests are usually of the short-answer type. Full instructions for answering these questions will be given to you at the examination. But in case this is your first experience with short-answer questions and separate answer sheets, here is what you need to know:

1) Multiple-choice Questions

Most popular of the short-answer questions is the "multiple choice" or "best answer" question. It can be used, for example, to test for factual knowledge, ability to solve problems or judgment in meeting situations found at work.

A multiple-choice question is normally one of three types—

- It can begin with an incomplete statement followed by several possible endings. You are to find the one ending which *best* completes the statement, although some of the others may not be entirely wrong.
- It can also be a complete statement in the form of a question which is answered by choosing one of the statements listed.

- It can be in the form of a problem – again you select the best answer.

Here is an example of a multiple-choice question with a discussion which should give you some clues as to the method for choosing the right answer:

When an employee has a complaint about his assignment, the action which will *best* help him overcome his difficulty is to
- A. discuss his difficulty with his coworkers
- B. take the problem to the head of the organization
- C. take the problem to the person who gave him the assignment
- D. say nothing to anyone about his complaint

In answering this question, you should study each of the choices to find which is best. Consider choice "A" – Certainly an employee may discuss his complaint with fellow employees, but no change or improvement can result, and the complaint remains unresolved. Choice "B" is a poor choice since the head of the organization probably does not know what assignment you have been given, and taking your problem to him is known as "going over the head" of the supervisor. The supervisor, or person who made the assignment, is the person who can clarify it or correct any injustice. Choice "C" is, therefore, correct. To say nothing, as in choice "D," is unwise. Supervisors have and interest in knowing the problems employees are facing, and the employee is seeking a solution to his problem.

2) True/False Questions

The "true/false" or "right/wrong" form of question is sometimes used. Here a complete statement is given. Your job is to decide whether the statement is right or wrong.

SAMPLE: A roaming cell-phone call to a nearby city costs less than a non-roaming call to a distant city.

This statement is wrong, or false, since roaming calls are more expensive.

This is not a complete list of all possible question forms, although most of the others are variations of these common types. You will always get complete directions for answering questions. Be sure you understand *how* to mark your answers – ask questions until you do.

V. RECORDING YOUR ANSWERS

Computer terminals are used more and more today for many different kinds of exams.

For an examination with very few applicants, you may be told to record your answers in the test booklet itself. Separate answer sheets are much more common. If this separate answer sheet is to be scored by machine – and this is often the case – it is highly important that you mark your answers correctly in order to get credit.

An electronic scoring machine is often used in civil service offices because of the speed with which papers can be scored. Machine-scored answer sheets must be marked with a pencil, which will be given to you. This pencil has a high graphite content which responds to the electronic scoring machine. As a matter of fact, stray dots may register as answers, so do not let your pencil rest on the answer sheet while you are pondering the correct answer. Also, if your pencil lead breaks or is otherwise defective, ask for another.

Since the answer sheet will be dropped in a slot in the scoring machine, be careful not to bend the corners or get the paper crumpled.

The answer sheet normally has five vertical columns of numbers, with 30 numbers to a column. These numbers correspond to the question numbers in your test booklet. After each number, going across the page are four or five pairs of dotted lines. These short dotted lines have small letters or numbers above them. The first two pairs may also have a "T" or "F" above the letters. This indicates that the first two pairs only are to be used if the questions are of the true-false type. If the questions are multiple choice, disregard the "T" and "F" and pay attention only to the small letters or numbers.

Answer your questions in the manner of the sample that follows:

32. The largest city in the United States is
   A. Washington, D.C.
   B. New York City
   C. Chicago
   D. Detroit
   E. San Francisco

1) Choose the answer you think is best. (New York City is the largest, so "B" is correct.)
2) Find the row of dotted lines numbered the same as the question you are answering. (Find row number 32)
3) Find the pair of dotted lines corresponding to the answer. (Find the pair of lines under the mark "B.")
4) Make a solid black mark between the dotted lines.

VI. BEFORE THE TEST

Common sense will help you find procedures to follow to get ready for an examination. Too many of us, however, overlook these sensible measures. Indeed, nervousness and fatigue have been found to be the most serious reasons why applicants fail to do their best on civil service tests. Here is a list of reminders:

- Begin your preparation early – Don't wait until the last minute to go scurrying around for books and materials or to find out what the position is all about.
- Prepare continuously – An hour a night for a week is better than an all-night cram session. This has been definitely established. What is more, a night a week for a month will return better dividends than crowding your study into a shorter period of time.
- Locate the place of the exam – You have been sent a notice telling you when and where to report for the examination. If the location is in a different town or otherwise unfamiliar to you, it would be well to inquire the best route and learn something about the building.
- Relax the night before the test – Allow your mind to rest. Do not study at all that night. Plan some mild recreation or diversion; then go to bed early and get a good night's sleep.
- Get up early enough to make a leisurely trip to the place for the test – This way unforeseen events, traffic snarls, unfamiliar buildings, etc. will not upset you.
- Dress comfortably – A written test is not a fashion show. You will be known by number and not by name, so wear something comfortable.

- Leave excess paraphernalia at home – Shopping bags and odd bundles will get in your way. You need bring only the items mentioned in the official notice you received; usually everything you need is provided. Do not bring reference books to the exam. They will only confuse those last minutes and be taken away from you when in the test room.
- Arrive somewhat ahead of time – If because of transportation schedules you must get there very early, bring a newspaper or magazine to take your mind off yourself while waiting.
- Locate the examination room – When you have found the proper room, you will be directed to the seat or part of the room where you will sit. Sometimes you are given a sheet of instructions to read while you are waiting. Do not fill out any forms until you are told to do so; just read them and be prepared.
- Relax and prepare to listen to the instructions
- If you have any physical problem that may keep you from doing your best, be sure to tell the test administrator. If you are sick or in poor health, you really cannot do your best on the exam. You can come back and take the test some other time.

VII. AT THE TEST

The day of the test is here and you have the test booklet in your hand. The temptation to get going is very strong. Caution! There is more to success than knowing the right answers. You must know how to identify your papers and understand variations in the type of short-answer question used in this particular examination. Follow these suggestions for maximum results from your efforts:

1) Cooperate with the monitor
The test administrator has a duty to create a situation in which you can be as much at ease as possible. He will give instructions, tell you when to begin, check to see that you are marking your answer sheet correctly, and so on. He is not there to guard you, although he will see that your competitors do not take unfair advantage. He wants to help you do your best.

2) Listen to all instructions
Don't jump the gun! Wait until you understand all directions. In most civil service tests you get more time than you need to answer the questions. So don't be in a hurry. Read each word of instructions until you clearly understand the meaning. Study the examples, listen to all announcements and follow directions. Ask questions if you do not understand what to do.

3) Identify your papers
Civil service exams are usually identified by number only. You will be assigned a number; you must not put your name on your test papers. Be sure to copy your number correctly. Since more than one exam may be given, copy your exact examination title.

4) Plan your time
Unless you are told that a test is a "speed" or "rate of work" test, speed itself is usually not important. Time enough to answer all the questions will be provided, but this does not mean that you have all day. An overall time limit has been set. Divide the total time (in minutes) by the number of questions to determine the approximate time you have for each question.

5) Do not linger over difficult questions

If you come across a difficult question, mark it with a paper clip (useful to have along) and come back to it when you have been through the booklet. One caution if you do this – be sure to skip a number on your answer sheet as well. Check often to be sure that you have not lost your place and that you are marking in the row numbered the same as the question you are answering.

6) Read the questions

Be sure you know what the question asks! Many capable people are unsuccessful because they failed to *read* the questions correctly.

7) Answer all questions

Unless you have been instructed that a penalty will be deducted for incorrect answers, it is better to guess than to omit a question.

8) Speed tests

It is often better NOT to guess on speed tests. It has been found that on timed tests people are tempted to spend the last few seconds before time is called in marking answers at random – without even reading them – in the hope of picking up a few extra points. To discourage this practice, the instructions may warn you that your score will be "corrected" for guessing. That is, a penalty will be applied. The incorrect answers will be deducted from the correct ones, or some other penalty formula will be used.

9) Review your answers

If you finish before time is called, go back to the questions you guessed or omitted to give them further thought. Review other answers if you have time.

10) Return your test materials

If you are ready to leave before others have finished or time is called, take ALL your materials to the monitor and leave quietly. Never take any test material with you. The monitor can discover whose papers are not complete, and taking a test booklet may be grounds for disqualification.

VIII. EXAMINATION TECHNIQUES

1) Read the general instructions carefully. These are usually printed on the first page of the exam booklet. As a rule, these instructions refer to the timing of the examination; the fact that you should not start work until the signal and must stop work at a signal, etc. If there are any *special* instructions, such as a choice of questions to be answered, make sure that you note this instruction carefully.

2) When you are ready to start work on the examination, that is as soon as the signal has been given, read the instructions to each question booklet, underline any key words or phrases, such as *least, best, outline, describe* and the like. In this way you will tend to answer as requested rather than discover on reviewing your paper that you *listed without describing*, that you selected the *worst* choice rather than the *best* choice, etc.

3) If the examination is of the objective or multiple-choice type – that is, each question will also give a series of possible answers: A, B, C or D, and you are called upon to select the best answer and write the letter next to that answer on your answer paper – it is advisable to start answering each question in turn. There may be anywhere from 50 to 100 such questions in the three or four hours allotted and you can see how much time would be taken if you read through all the questions before beginning to answer any. Furthermore, if you come across a question or group of questions which you know would be difficult to answer, it would undoubtedly affect your handling of all the other questions.

4) If the examination is of the essay type and contains but a few questions, it is a moot point as to whether you should read all the questions before starting to answer any one. Of course, if you are given a choice – say five out of seven and the like – then it is essential to read all the questions so you can eliminate the two that are most difficult. If, however, you are asked to answer all the questions, there may be danger in trying to answer the easiest one first because you may find that you will spend too much time on it. The best technique is to answer the first question, then proceed to the second, etc.

5) Time your answers. Before the exam begins, write down the time it started, then add the time allowed for the examination and write down the time it must be completed, then divide the time available somewhat as follows:
   - If 3-1/2 hours are allowed, that would be 210 minutes. If you have 80 objective-type questions, that would be an average of 2-1/2 minutes per question. Allow yourself no more than 2 minutes per question, or a total of 160 minutes, which will permit about 50 minutes to review.
   - If for the time allotment of 210 minutes there are 7 essay questions to answer, that would average about 30 minutes a question. Give yourself only 25 minutes per question so that you have about 35 minutes to review.

6) The most important instruction is to *read each question* and make sure you know what is wanted. The second most important instruction is to *time yourself properly* so that you answer every question. The third most important instruction is to *answer every question*. Guess if you have to but include something for each question. Remember that you will receive no credit for a blank and will probably receive some credit if you write something in answer to an essay question. If you guess a letter – say "B" for a multiple-choice question – you may have guessed right. If you leave a blank as an answer to a multiple-choice question, the examiners may respect your feelings but it will not add a point to your score. Some exams may penalize you for wrong answers, so in such cases *only*, you may not want to guess unless you have some basis for your answer.

7) Suggestions
   a. Objective-type questions
      1. Examine the question booklet for proper sequence of pages and questions
      2. Read all instructions carefully
      3. Skip any question which seems too difficult; return to it after all other questions have been answered
      4. Apportion your time properly; do not spend too much time on any single question or group of questions

5. Note and underline key words – *all, most, fewest, least, best, worst, same, opposite,* etc.
6. Pay particular attention to negatives
7. Note unusual option, e.g., unduly long, short, complex, different or similar in content to the body of the question
8. Observe the use of "hedging" words – *probably, may, most likely,* etc.
9. Make sure that your answer is put next to the same number as the question
10. Do not second-guess unless you have good reason to believe the second answer is definitely more correct
11. Cross out original answer if you decide another answer is more accurate; do not erase until you are ready to hand your paper in
12. Answer all questions; guess unless instructed otherwise
13. Leave time for review

b. Essay questions
  1. Read each question carefully
  2. Determine exactly what is wanted. Underline key words or phrases.
  3. Decide on outline or paragraph answer
  4. Include many different points and elements unless asked to develop any one or two points or elements
  5. Show impartiality by giving pros and cons unless directed to select one side only
  6. Make and write down any assumptions you find necessary to answer the questions
  7. Watch your English, grammar, punctuation and choice of words
  8. Time your answers; don't crowd material

8) Answering the essay question

Most essay questions can be answered by framing the specific response around several key words or ideas. Here are a few such key words or ideas:

M's: manpower, materials, methods, money, management
P's: purpose, program, policy, plan, procedure, practice, problems, pitfalls, personnel, public relations
  a. Six basic steps in handling problems:
    1. Preliminary plan and background development
    2. Collect information, data and facts
    3. Analyze and interpret information, data and facts
    4. Analyze and develop solutions as well as make recommendations
    5. Prepare report and sell recommendations
    6. Install recommendations and follow up effectiveness

  b. Pitfalls to avoid
    1. *Taking things for granted* – A statement of the situation does not necessarily imply that each of the elements is necessarily true; for example, a complaint may be invalid and biased so that all that can be taken for granted is that a complaint has been registered

2. *Considering only one side of a situation* – Wherever possible, indicate several alternatives and then point out the reasons you selected the best one
3. *Failing to indicate follow up* – Whenever your answer indicates action on your part, make certain that you will take proper follow-up action to see how successful your recommendations, procedures or actions turn out to be
4. *Taking too long in answering any single question* – Remember to time your answers properly

IX. AFTER THE TEST

Scoring procedures differ in detail among civil service jurisdictions although the general principles are the same. Whether the papers are hand-scored or graded by machine we have described, they are nearly always graded by number. That is, the person who marks the paper knows only the number – never the name – of the applicant. Not until all the papers have been graded will they be matched with names. If other tests, such as training and experience or oral interview ratings have been given, scores will be combined. Different parts of the examination usually have different weights. For example, the written test might count 60 percent of the final grade, and a rating of training and experience 40 percent. In many jurisdictions, veterans will have a certain number of points added to their grades.

After the final grade has been determined, the names are placed in grade order and an eligible list is established. There are various methods for resolving ties between those who get the same final grade – probably the most common is to place first the name of the person whose application was received first. Job offers are made from the eligible list in the order the names appear on it. You will be notified of your grade and your rank as soon as all these computations have been made. This will be done as rapidly as possible.

People who are found to meet the requirements in the announcement are called "eligibles." Their names are put on a list of eligible candidates. An eligible's chances of getting a job depend on how high he stands on this list and how fast agencies are filling jobs from the list.

When a job is to be filled from a list of eligibles, the agency asks for the names of people on the list of eligibles for that job. When the civil service commission receives this request, it sends to the agency the names of the three people highest on this list. Or, if the job to be filled has specialized requirements, the office sends the agency the names of the top three persons who meet these requirements from the general list.

The appointing officer makes a choice from among the three people whose names were sent to him. If the selected person accepts the appointment, the names of the others are put back on the list to be considered for future openings.

That is the rule in hiring from all kinds of eligible lists, whether they are for typist, carpenter, chemist, or something else. For every vacancy, the appointing officer has his choice of any one of the top three eligibles on the list. This explains why the person whose name is on top of the list sometimes does not get an appointment when some of the persons lower on the list do. If the appointing officer chooses the second or third eligible, the No. 1 eligible does not get a job at once, but stays on the list until he is appointed or the list is terminated.

X. HOW TO PASS THE INTERVIEW TEST

The examination for which you applied requires an oral interview test. You have already taken the written test and you are now being called for the interview test – the final part of the formal examination.

You may think that it is not possible to prepare for an interview test and that there are no procedures to follow during an interview. Our purpose is to point out some things you can do in advance that will help you and some good rules to follow and pitfalls to avoid while you are being interviewed.

What is an interview supposed to test?

The written examination is designed to test the technical knowledge and competence of the candidate; the oral is designed to evaluate intangible qualities, not readily measured otherwise, and to establish a list showing the relative fitness of each candidate – as measured against his competitors – for the position sought. Scoring is not on the basis of "right" and "wrong," but on a sliding scale of values ranging from "not passable" to "outstanding." As a matter of fact, it is possible to achieve a relatively low score without a single "incorrect" answer because of evident weakness in the qualities being measured.

Occasionally, an examination may consist entirely of an oral test – either an individual or a group oral. In such cases, information is sought concerning the technical knowledges and abilities of the candidate, since there has been no written examination for this purpose. More commonly, however, an oral test is used to supplement a written examination.

Who conducts interviews?

The composition of oral boards varies among different jurisdictions. In nearly all, a representative of the personnel department serves as chairman. One of the members of the board may be a representative of the department in which the candidate would work. In some cases, "outside experts" are used, and, frequently, a businessman or some other representative of the general public is asked to serve. Labor and management or other special groups may be represented. The aim is to secure the services of experts in the appropriate field.

However the board is composed, it is a good idea (and not at all improper or unethical) to ascertain in advance of the interview who the members are and what groups they represent. When you are introduced to them, you will have some idea of their backgrounds and interests, and at least you will not stutter and stammer over their names.

What should be done before the interview?

While knowledge about the board members is useful and takes some of the surprise element out of the interview, there is other preparation which is more substantive. It *is* possible to prepare for an oral interview – in several ways:

1) Keep a copy of your application and review it carefully before the interview

This may be the only document before the oral board, and the starting point of the interview. Know what education and experience you have listed there, and the sequence and dates of all of it. Sometimes the board will ask you to review the highlights of your experience for them; you should not have to hem and haw doing it.

2) Study the class specification and the examination announcement

Usually, the oral board has one or both of these to guide them. The qualities, characteristics or knowledges required by the position sought are stated in these documents. They offer valuable clues as to the nature of the oral interview. For example, if the job involves supervisory responsibilities, the announcement will usually indicate that knowledge of modern supervisory methods and the qualifications of the candidate as a supervisor will be tested. If so, you can expect such questions, frequently in the form of a hypothetical situation which you are expected to solve. NEVER go into an oral without knowledge of the duties and responsibilities of the job you seek.

3) Think through each qualification required

Try to visualize the kind of questions you would ask if you were a board member. How well could you answer them? Try especially to appraise your own knowledge and background in each area, *measured against the job sought*, and identify any areas in which you are weak. Be critical and realistic – do not flatter yourself.

4) Do some general reading in areas in which you feel you may be weak

For example, if the job involves supervision and your past experience has NOT, some general reading in supervisory methods and practices, particularly in the field of human relations, might be useful. Do NOT study agency procedures or detailed manuals. The oral board will be testing your understanding and capacity, not your memory.

5) Get a good night's sleep and watch your general health and mental attitude

You will want a clear head at the interview. Take care of a cold or any other minor ailment, and of course, no hangovers.

What should be done on the day of the interview?

Now comes the day of the interview itself. Give yourself plenty of time to get there. Plan to arrive somewhat ahead of the scheduled time, particularly if your appointment is in the fore part of the day. If a previous candidate fails to appear, the board might be ready for you a bit early. By early afternoon an oral board is almost invariably behind schedule if there are many candidates, and you may have to wait. Take along a book or magazine to read, or your application to review, but leave any extraneous material in the waiting room when you go in for your interview. In any event, relax and compose yourself.

The matter of dress is important. The board is forming impressions about you – from your experience, your manners, your attitude, and your appearance. Give your personal appearance careful attention. Dress your best, but not your flashiest. Choose conservative, appropriate clothing, and be sure it is immaculate. This is a business interview, and your appearance should indicate that you regard it as such. Besides, being well groomed and properly dressed will help boost your confidence.

Sooner or later, someone will call your name and escort you into the interview room. *This is it.* From here on you are on your own. It is too late for any more preparation. But remember, you asked for this opportunity to prove your fitness, and you are here because your request was granted.

What happens when you go in?

The usual sequence of events will be as follows: The clerk (who is often the board stenographer) will introduce you to the chairman of the oral board, who will introduce you to the other members of the board. Acknowledge the introductions before you sit down. Do not be surprised if you find a microphone facing you or a stenotypist sitting by. Oral interviews are usually recorded in the event of an appeal or other review.

Usually the chairman of the board will open the interview by reviewing the highlights of your education and work experience from your application – primarily for the benefit of the other members of the board, as well as to get the material into the record. Do not interrupt or comment unless there is an error or significant misinterpretation; if that is the case, do not hesitate. But do not quibble about insignificant matters. Also, he will usually ask you some question about your education, experience or your present job – partly to get you to start talking and to establish the interviewing "rapport." He may start the actual questioning, or turn it over to one of the other members. Frequently, each member undertakes the questioning on a particular area, one in which he is perhaps most competent, so you can expect each member to participate in the examination. Because time is limited, you may also expect some rather abrupt switches in the direction the questioning takes, so do not be upset by it. Normally, a board member will not pursue a single line of questioning unless he discovers a particular strength or weakness.

After each member has participated, the chairman will usually ask whether any member has any further questions, then will ask you if you have anything you wish to add. Unless you are expecting this question, it may floor you. Worse, it may start you off on an extended, extemporaneous speech. The board is not usually seeking more information. The question is principally to offer you a last opportunity to present further qualifications or to indicate that you have nothing to add. So, if you feel that a significant qualification or characteristic has been overlooked, it is proper to point it out in a sentence or so. Do not compliment the board on the thoroughness of their examination – they have been sketchy, and you know it. If you wish, merely say, "No thank you, I have nothing further to add." This is a point where you can "talk yourself out" of a good impression or fail to present an important bit of information. Remember, *you close the interview yourself.*

The chairman will then say, "That is all, Mr. _____, thank you." Do not be startled; the interview is over, and quicker than you think. Thank him, gather your belongings and take your leave. Save your sigh of relief for the other side of the door.

How to put your best foot forward

Throughout this entire process, you may feel that the board individually and collectively is trying to pierce your defenses, seek out your hidden weaknesses and embarrass and confuse you. Actually, this is not true. They are obliged to make an appraisal of your qualifications for the job you are seeking, and they want to see you in your best light. Remember, they must interview all candidates and a non-cooperative candidate may become a failure in spite of their best efforts to bring out his qualifications. Here are 15 suggestions that will help you:

1) Be natural – Keep your attitude confident, not cocky

If you are not confident that you can do the job, do not expect the board to be. Do not apologize for your weaknesses, try to bring out your strong points. The board is interested in a positive, not negative, presentation. Cockiness will antagonize any board member and make him wonder if you are covering up a weakness by a false show of strength.

2) Get comfortable, but don't lounge or sprawl

Sit erectly but not stiffly. A careless posture may lead the board to conclude that you are careless in other things, or at least that you are not impressed by the importance of the occasion. Either conclusion is natural, even if incorrect. Do not fuss with your clothing, a pencil or an ashtray. Your hands may occasionally be useful to emphasize a point; do not let them become a point of distraction.

3) Do not wisecrack or make small talk

This is a serious situation, and your attitude should show that you consider it as such. Further, the time of the board is limited – they do not want to waste it, and neither should you.

4) Do not exaggerate your experience or abilities

In the first place, from information in the application or other interviews and sources, the board may know more about you than you think. Secondly, you probably will not get away with it. An experienced board is rather adept at spotting such a situation, so do not take the chance.

5) If you know a board member, do not make a point of it, yet do not hide it

Certainly you are not fooling him, and probably not the other members of the board. Do not try to take advantage of your acquaintanceship – it will probably do you little good.

6) Do not dominate the interview

Let the board do that. They will give you the clues – do not assume that you have to do all the talking. Realize that the board has a number of questions to ask you, and do not try to take up all the interview time by showing off your extensive knowledge of the answer to the first one.

7) Be attentive

You only have 20 minutes or so, and you should keep your attention at its sharpest throughout. When a member is addressing a problem or question to you, give him your undivided attention. Address your reply principally to him, but do not exclude the other board members.

8) Do not interrupt

A board member may be stating a problem for you to analyze. He will ask you a question when the time comes. Let him state the problem, and wait for the question.

9) Make sure you understand the question

Do not try to answer until you are sure what the question is. If it is not clear, restate it in your own words or ask the board member to clarify it for you. However, do not haggle about minor elements.

10) Reply promptly but not hastily

A common entry on oral board rating sheets is "candidate responded readily," or "candidate hesitated in replies." Respond as promptly and quickly as you can, but do not jump to a hasty, ill-considered answer.

11) Do not be peremptory in your answers

A brief answer is proper – but do not fire your answer back. That is a losing game from your point of view. The board member can probably ask questions much faster than you can answer them.

12) Do not try to create the answer you think the board member wants

He is interested in what kind of mind you have and how it works – not in playing games. Furthermore, he can usually spot this practice and will actually grade you down on it.

13) Do not switch sides in your reply merely to agree with a board member

Frequently, a member will take a contrary position merely to draw you out and to see if you are willing and able to defend your point of view. Do not start a debate, yet do not surrender a good position. If a position is worth taking, it is worth defending.

14) Do not be afraid to admit an error in judgment if you are shown to be wrong

The board knows that you are forced to reply without any opportunity for careful consideration. Your answer may be demonstrably wrong. If so, admit it and get on with the interview.

15) Do not dwell at length on your present job

The opening question may relate to your present assignment. Answer the question but do not go into an extended discussion. You are being examined for a *new* job, not your present one. As a matter of fact, try to phrase ALL your answers in terms of the job for which you are being examined.

Basis of Rating

Probably you will forget most of these "do's" and "don'ts" when you walk into the oral interview room. Even remembering them all will not ensure you a passing grade. Perhaps you did not have the qualifications in the first place. But remembering them will help you to put your best foot forward, without treading on the toes of the board members.

Rumor and popular opinion to the contrary notwithstanding, an oral board wants you to make the best appearance possible. They know you are under pressure – but they also want to see how you respond to it as a guide to what your reaction would be under the pressures of the job you seek. They will be influenced by the degree of poise you display, the personal traits you show and the manner in which you respond.

ABOUT THIS BOOK

This book contains tests divided into Examination Sections. Go through each test, answering every question in the margin. We have also attached a sample answer sheet at the back of the book that can be removed and used. At the end of each test look at the answer key and check your answers. On the ones you got wrong, look at the right answer choice and learn. Do not fill in the answers first. Do not memorize the questions and answers, but understand the answer and principles involved. On your test, the questions will likely be different from the samples. Questions are changed and new ones added. If you understand these past questions you should have success with any changes that arise. Tests may consist of several types of questions. We have additional books on each subject should more study be advisable or necessary for you. Finally, the more you study, the better prepared you will be. This book is intended to be the last thing you study before you walk into the examination room. Prior study of relevant texts is also recommended. NLC publishes some of these in our Fundamental Series. Knowledge and good sense are important factors in passing your exam. Good luck also helps. So now study this Passbook, absorb the material contained within and take that knowledge into the examination. Then do your best to pass that exam.

———

EXAMINATION SECTION

EXAMINATION SECTION
TEST 1

DIRECTIONS: Each question or incomplete statement is followed by several suggested answers or completions. Select the one that BEST answers the question or completes the statement. *PRINT THE LETTER OF THE CORRECT ANSWER IN THE SPACE AT THE RIGHT.*

1. When a signal report is referred to as *five nine plus 10 db,*   1.____

    A.   its bandwidth is 10 decibels above linearity
    B.   its relative signal strength reading is 10 decibels greater than strength 9
    C.   its signal strength has increased by a factor of 90
    D.   it should be repeated at a frequency 10 kHz higher

2. *Chirp* is a(n)   2.____

    A.   overload in a receiver's audio circuit whenever CW is received
    B.   slight change in a transmitter's frequency each time it is keyed
    C.   gradual change in transmitter frequency as the circuit warms up
    D.   high-pitched tone received with a CW signal

3. A vertical antenna sends out MOST of its radio energy   3.____

    A.   in two opposite directions
    B.   high into the air
    C.   equally in all horizontal directions
    D.   in one direction

4. For correct station identification when using a radiotelephone, FCC rules suggest using   4.____
    _____ as an aid.

    A.   a phonetic alphabet
    B.   unique words of the operator's choice
    C.   Q signals
    D.   a speech compressor

5. A COMMON result of an operator speaking too loudly into a hand-held FM transceiver is   5.____

    A.   interference to other stations operating near the operator's frequency
    B.   digital interference to computer equipment
    C.   atmospheric interference in the air around the antenna
    D.   interference to stations operating on a higher frequency band

6. When using a repeater to transmit a two-way radio signal, the operator should pause   6.____
    briefly between transmissions to

    A.   dial up the repeater's autopatch
    B.   listen for anyone wanting to break in
    C.   prepare for recording possible third-party communications
    D.   check the standing-wave ratio of the repeater

7. The USUAL input/output frequency separation for repeaters in the 2-meter band is   7.____

    A. 1 MHz   B. 5 MHz   C. 1.5 MHz   D. 600 kHz

8. What is the PROPER way to ask someone's location when using a repeater?   8.____

    A. What is your QTH?   B. What is your 20?
    C. Where are you?   D. Where's the break?

9. If an ammeter reads 4 amperes, the current flow, in milliamperes, is   9.____

    A. .004   B. 4,000,000   C. 4000   D. .0004

10. The purpose of repeater operation is to   10.____

    A. cut power costs by linking with another high-power system
    B. help mobile and low-power stations extend their ranges
    C. transmit signals for observing propagation and reception
    D. make calls within a range of 50 miles

11. For two-way systems situated in and around an urban area, what block of frequencies   11.____
are allocated for use by police, fire, and private industries? _____ MHz.

    A. 30   B. 40   C. 470-512   D. 900

12. What causes the MAXIMUM usable frequency to vary?   12.____

    A. The amount of ultraviolet radiation from the sun
    B. Windspeed in the upper atmosphere
    C. The temperature of the ionosphere
    D. The weather just below the ionosphere

13. A transmission line that has no change in voltage or current along its full length has a   13.____
standing-wave ratio of

    A. less than 1   B. greater than 1
    C. 1:1   D. 2:1

14. When a signal is referred to as *full quieting,* it   14.____

    A. is not strong enough to be received
    B. is being received, but no audio is being heard
    C. contains no extraneous sound
    D. is strong enough to overcome all receiver noise

15. During transmission, the antenna of a hand-held transceiver should be held pointing   15.____

    A. toward the ground
    B. away from the operator's head and away from others
    C. toward the station the operator means to contact
    D. away from the station the operator means to contact

16. A _____ system is MOST at risk of receiving a barrage of calls from different sources at   16.____
the same time.

    A. duplex   B. simplex   C. repeater   D. remote

17. The device that measures standing wave ratio should be connected between the   17.____

    A. transmitter and power supply
    B. ground and transmitter
    C. feed line and antenna
    D. receiver and transmitter

18. Electrical energy at a frequency of 7120 Hz is in the _____ frequency range.   18.____

    A. hyper   B. audio
    C. super-high   D. radio

19. The type of system in which the transmitter and receiver are at a different location from   19.____
the microphone and loudspeaker is the _____ system.

    A. remote   B. repeater   C. simplex   D. duplex

20. In the radio transmission of speech, the amplification added to a signal to prevent degra-   20.____
dation of consonant sounds is referred to as

    A. preemphasis   B. deemphasis
    C. loading   D. squelch

21. The bandwidth over which a receiver is capable of receiving signals is referred to as its   21.____

    A. monitor band   B. sideband
    C. skip zone   D. acceptance band

22. The output of a transceiver should NEVER be connected to a(n)   22.____

    A. antenna switch   B. receiver
    C. SWR meter   D. antenna

23. Which band may NOT be used by earth stations for satellite communications?   23.____

    A. 10 meters   B. 6 meters
    C. 2 meters   D. 70 centimeters

24. What is the term for the kind of interference created by sharp bursts of radio frequency   24.____
voltage?

    A. Chirp   B. Oscillation
    C. Impulse noise   D. Fluctuation noise

25. In repeater operations, a courtesy tone   25.____

    A. indicates a waiting message
    B. activates a receiver in case of severe weather
    C. identifies the repeater
    D. indicates that the transmission has been completed

KEY (CORRECT ANSWERS)

1.	B		11.	A
2.	B		12.	A
3.	C		13.	C
4.	A		14.	D
5.	A		15.	B
6.	B		16.	B
7.	D		17.	C
8.	C		18.	D
9.	C		19.	A
10.	B		20.	A

21.	D
22.	B
23.	B
24.	C
25.	D

TEST 2

DIRECTIONS: Each question or incomplete statement is followed by several suggested answers or completions. Select the one that BEST answers the question or completes the statement. *PRINT THE LETTER OF THE CORRECT ANSWER IN THE SPACE AT THE RIGHT.*

1. Maximum usable frequency means the _____ frequency signal that _____.   1._____

    A. highest; is most absorbed by the ionosphere
    B. lowest; is most absorbed by the ionosphere
    C. lowest; will reach its intended destination
    D. highest; will reach its intended destination

2. As its wavelength gets LONGER, a signal's frequency   2._____

    A. lengthens   B. shortens
    C. stays the same   D. disappears

3. The term for voice emissions that are radio-transmitted is   3._____

    A. RTTY   B. CW   C. data   D. phone

4. A _____ is used to inject a frequency calibration signal into a receiver.   4._____

    A. calibrated voltmeter   B. calibrated wavemeter
    C. crystal calibrator   D. calibrated oscilloscope

5. The basic unit of electric current is the   5._____

    A. volt   B. ampere   C. watt   D. ohm

6. An amateur radiotelephone station operated as a mobile station is identified by   6._____

    A. transmitting the word *mobile* after the call sign
    B. at the end of every ten minutes, transmitting the call sign followed by the word *mobile*
    C. after the call sign, transmitting the word *mobile,* followed by the call sign area in which the station is operating
    D. transmitting the area of operation after the call sign

7. Which type of repeater operation should be DISCOURAGED during commuter rush hours?   7._____

    A. Traffic information networks
    B. Low-power stations
    C. Mobile stations
    D. Third-party networks

8. The MOST effective way of checking the accuracy of a receiver's tuning dial would be to tune to   8._____

    A. one of the frequencies of station WWV or WWVH
    B. a popular amateur network frequency
    C. the frequency of a shortwave broadcasting station
    D. an amateur station and ask what frequency the operator is using

9. A(n) _____ produces a stable, low-level signal that can be set to a desired frequency.   9.____

    A. oscilloscope   B. reflectometer
    C. signal generator   D. wavemeter

10. What is the PROPER distress call to use when operating continuous-wave?   10.____

    A. MAYDAY   B. HELP   C. QRZ   D. SOS

11. What device should be connected to a transmitter's output when an operator is making   11.____
transmitter adjustments?

    A. Dummy antenna   B. Reflectometer
    C. Receiver   D. Multimeter

12. The BEST way to minimize on-air interference during a lengthy transmitter test proce-   12.____
dure is by

    A. using a resonant antenna that requires no loading-up
    B. using a dummy load
    C. using a non-resonant antenna
    D. choosing an unoccupied frequency

13. At what point in an operator's station is the transceiver power measured?   13.____

    A. At the power supply terminals
    B. At the antenna terminals
    C. On the antenna
    D. At the final amplifier input terminals

14. A(n) _____ meter is used to measure relative signal strength in a receiver.   14.____

    A. RST   B. signal deviation
    C. S   D. SSB

15. When a signal is referred to as *five seven,* it is   15.____

    A. perfectly readable, but weak
    B. readable with considerable difficulty
    C. perfectly readable and moderately strong
    D. readable with a nearly pure tone

16. What is the result of overdeviation in an FM transmitter?   16.____

    A. Increased transmitter power
    B. Out-of-channel emissions
    C. Increased transmitter range
    D. Poor carrier suppression

17. For safety, the BEST thing to do with transmitting antennas is   17.____

    A. use vertical polarization
    B. use horizontal polarization
    C. mount them close to the ground
    D. mount them where nobody can come near them

18. _____ may be caused by a multi-band antenna connected to a poorly-tuned antenna.   18._____

    A. Auroral distortion   B. Parasitic excitation
    C. Harmonic radiation   D. Intermodulation

19. Using a final amplifier capable of providing a 100 W output to a transmission line that pro-   19._____
vides a 10-decibel loss, the antenna will receive _____ W of power.

    A. 1   B. 10   C. 90   D. 100

20. For two-way systems situated in and around an urban area, what block of frequencies   20._____
are allocated for use by land mobile services? _____ MHz.

    A. 30   B. 40   C. 470-512   D. 900

21. What type of messages are sent into or out of a disaster area and concern the immediate   21._____
safety of human life? _____ traffic.

    A. Emergency   B. Tactical
    C. Formal message   D. Health and welfare

22. 50 hertz means 50   22._____

    A. meters per second   B. cycles per meter
    C. cycles per second   D. cycles per minute

23. A common result of operating an FM transmitter with the microphone gain set too high is   23._____

    A. atmospheric interference in the air around the antenna
    B. digital interference to computer equipment
    C. interference to other stations operating near the operator's frequency
    D. interference to stations operating on a higher frequency band

24. Which is the SIMPLEST type of system for which simultaneous transmission and recep-   24._____
tion are possible?

    A. Remote   B. Repeater   C. Duplex   D. Simplex

25. *Splatter interference* is caused by   25._____

    A. overmodulation of a transmitter
    B. keying a transmitter too quickly
    C. routing of a transmitter's output signals back to its input circuit
    D. a transmitting antenna of the wrong length

KEY (CORRECT ANSWERS)

1.	D	11.	A
2.	B	12.	B
3.	D	13.	B
4.	C	14.	C
5.	B	15.	C
6.	C	16.	B
7.	D	17.	D
8.	A	18.	C
9.	C	19.	B
10.	D	20.	D

21.	A
22.	C
23.	C
24.	B
25.	A

———

EXAMINATION SECTION
TEST 1

DIRECTIONS: Each question or incomplete statement is followed by several suggested answers or completions. Select the one that BEST answers the question or completes the statement. *PRINT THE LETTER OF THE CORRECT ANSWER IN THE SPACE AT THE RIGHT.*

1. The term for the place at which the control operator function is performed is the   1.____

    A. operating desk   B. control point
    C. station   D. manual control location

2. Before transmitting on any frequency, an operator should   2.____

    A. listen to make sure your signal will be heard
    B. make sure the standing-wave ratio on the antenna feed line is high enough
    C. listen to make sure others are not using the frequency
    D. check the antenna for resonance at the selected frequency

3. The _____ sideband is COMMONLY used for 10-meter phone operation.   3.____

    A. lower   B. upper
    C. amplitude-compandored   D. double

4. Which type of system does NOT permit the transmission and reception of any signals to take place at the same time?   4.____

    A. Repeater   B. Simplex   C. Remote   D. Duplex

5. Radio emissions are considered *wideband* if their deviation amounts are greater than a MINIMUM of _____ kHz.   5.____

    A. 10   B. 1   C. 15   D. 5

6. When a signal report is referred to as *three three,*   6.____

    A. its contact is serial number thirty-three
    B. it is unreadable and very weak
    C. it is readable with considerable difficulty
    D. its station is located at thirty-three degrees latitude

7. Generally, the type of communications that are capable of the GREATEST range are _____ band.   7.____

    A. low   B. high   C. aviation   D. side

8. For two-way systems situated in and around an urban area, what block of frequencies are allocated for use by mobile telephone services operated by common carriers? _____ MHz.   8.____

    A. 30   B. 40   C. 470-512   D. 900

9. The basic unit of electrical power is the   9.____

    A. ohm   B. ampere   C. volt   D. watt

10. In the radio transmission of speech, the amplification used at the receiver to maintain the natural balance of high and low speech frequencies is referred to as   10.__

    A. preemphasis   B. deemphasis
    C. loading   D. squelch

11. An antenna that is mounted horizontally would be MOST suitable for the reception of _____ polarized _____.   11.__

    A. horizontally; voltages   B. vertically; waves
    C. vertically; voltages   D. horizontally; waves

12. What is the PROPER distress call to use when operating a radiotelephone?   12.__

    A. MAYDAY   B. HELP   C. EMERGENCY   D. SOS

13. A two-way FM transmitter should be adjusted for a deviation that will produce a bandwidth _____ AM transmitter.   13.__

    A. less than that produced by an equivalently modulated
    B. greater than that produced by an equivalently modulated
    C. equal to that produced by an equivalently modulated
    D. that will not be capable of interacting with an

14. The term for the transmission of signals OUTSIDE the intended band is   14.__

    A. spurious emissions   B. off-frequency emissions
    C. side tones   D. chirping

15. Which of the following is TRUE of FM radio systems?   15.__

    A. The frequency is constant and the amplitude is varied.
    B. The amplitude is constant and the frequency is varied.
    C. The frequency and the amplitude are varied.
    D. Neither the frequency nor the amplitude is modulated.

16. During daytime hours, the BEST band for communications over a distance of 200 miles is the _____-m band.   16.__

    A. 160   B. 80   C. 40   D. 6

17. A transmission that disturbs other communications is called   17.__

    A. transponder signals   B. unidentified transmissions
    C. harmful interference   D. interrupted CW

18. A buzzing or hum in the signal of a high-frequency transmitter is USUALLY caused by   18.__

    A. an antenna of the wrong length
    B. a bad filter capacitor in the power supply
    C. energy from another transmitter
    D. a badly-designed power output circuit

19. If an operator's signal is extremely strong and perfectly readable, what adjustment should   19.____
    be made to the transmitter?

    A. Turn on the speech processor
    B. Turn down the power output
    C. Reduce the frequency
    D. Reduce the standing-wave ratio

20. What is generally considered to be the reliable range for UHF communications?   20.____
    _____ km.

    A. 20   B. 40   C. 60   D. 80

21. If a transmitter is operated WITHOUT the cover in place, it may   21.____

    A. transmit a weak signal
    B. transmit a chirping signal
    C. transmit onto unintended bands
    D. interfere with other transmitters operating on the same frequency

22. In transmitters used to convey speech, the deviation for the given amplitude   22.____

    A. increases as the modulation signal increases
    B. decreases as the modulation signal increases
    C. remains roughly half of the modulation signal
    D. is the same regardless of the frequency of the modulation signal

23. The purpose of a limiter in an FM receiver is to limit the   23.____

    A. audio output
    B. amplitude of the intermediate frequency signal fed to the detector
    C. gain of the radio frequency amplifier
    D. amplitude of the detected output signal

24. The FASTEST code speed a repeater may use for automatic identification is _____   24.____
    words per minute.

    A. 10   B. 20
    C. 40   D. no limit

25. The purpose of a squelch control is to   25.____

    A. set the sensitivity of the squelch circuit
    B. squelch all undesired noise signals
    C. set the limit of the noise amplitude
    D. squelch interference signals

KEY (CORRECT ANSWERS)

1.	B		11.	D
2.	C		12.	A
3.	B		13.	C
4.	B		14.	A
5.	D		15.	B
6.	C		16.	C
7.	A		17.	C
8.	B		18.	B
9.	D		19.	B
10.	B		20.	B

21.	C
22.	D
23.	B
24.	B
25.	A

———

TEST 2

DIRECTIONS: Each question or incomplete statement is followed by several suggested answers or completions. Select the one that BEST answers the question or completes the statement. *PRINT THE LETTER OF THE CORRECT ANSWER IN THE SPACE AT THE RIGHT.*

1. The basic unit of electrical resistance is the

    A. watt   B. ampere   C. volt   D. ohm

1._____

2. An autopatch is a device that

    A. automatically selects the strongest signal to be repeated
    B. allows repeater users to make telephone calls from their stations
    C. locks other repeaters out of important, confidential communications
    D. connects a mobile station to the next repeater if it moves out of range

2._____

3. Which of the following is NOT an advantage gained by using a crystal in radio equipment?
Increased

    A. power generation   B. frequency stability
    C. overtone generation   D. frequency accuracy

3._____

4. The purpose of a key-operated on/off switch in the main power line of a station is to

    A. keep the power company from shutting down power during an emergency
    B. protect against failure of the main fuses
    C. turn off the station in the event of an emergency
    D. keep unauthorized persons from using the station

4._____

5. For two-way systems situated in and around an urban area, what block of frequencies are allocated for use by citizen two-way users?
_____ MHz.

    A. 30   B. 40   C. 470-512   D. 900

5._____

6. A reactance tube is used to develop a(n) _____ signal.

    A. drift-free AM   B. FM
    C. SSB   D. TTY

6._____

7. Messages concerning a person's well-being that are sent into or out of a disaster area are _____ traffic messages.

    A. routine   B. tactical
    C. formal message   D. health and welfare

7._____

8. A(n) _____ is used to measure standing wave ratio.

    A. SWR meter   B. current bridge
    C. ammeter   D. ohmmeter

8._____

9. What is the USUAL remedy for an FM hand-held transceiver that is over-deviating?   9._

    A. Talk more loudly into the microphone
    B. Change to a higher power level
    C. Talk farther from the microphone
    D. Allow the transceiver to cool

10. *Backwave radiation* is radiation   10._

    A. from the rear of the antenna
    B. leaking from a CW antenna
    C. from a CW transmitter with the key open
    D. from a phone transmitter during silent periods

11. The input impedance of a grounded-grid amplifer is   11._

    A. low   B. moderate   C. high   D. very high

12. If a dial which reads 4.525 MHz were marked in kilohertz, it would read _____ kHz.   12._

    A. 4,525,000   B. 4525   C. .004525   D. 45.25

13. A _____ system uses a total of three transmission frequencies.   13._

    A. simplex   B. duplex   C. repeater   D. remote

14. The basic unit of frequency is the   14._

    A. hertz   B. ohm
    C. ampere   D. wave ratio

15. What type of feedback is required for an oscillator?   15._

    A. Split-phase   B. In-phase
    C. Grid-leak   D. Degenerative

16. Cross-band operation of a repeater station is   16._

    A. permitted, but requires a special state license
    B. permitted under the regular repeater station license
    C. permitted if the repeater receives signals in both bands
    D. not permitted under any circumstances

17. If an unlicensed third party is allowed to use your station, what must you do at your center of operations?   17._

    A. Monitor and supervise the third party's participation when communication occurs at below 30 MHz.
    B. Continuously monitor and supervise the third party's participation.
    C. Key the transmitter and make the station identification.
    D. Report the third party to the FCC.

18. Receiver overload is caused by   18._____

    A. too much voltage from the power supply
    B. interference from a poorly-adjusted volume control
    C. too much current from the power supply
    D. interference from the signals of a nearby transmitter

19. Equal but opposite signals are required for operating a _____ amplifier.   19._____

    A. parallel   B. push-pull   C. class C   D. series

20. The MAIN purpose of shielding a transmitter is to   20._____

    A. prevent unwanted radio-frequency radiation
    B. keep electronic parts warmer and more stable
    C. give low-pass air filter a solid support
    D. help the sound quality

21. In an FM signal, whether modulated or unmodulated, the   21._____

    A. carrier frequency amplitude is fixed
    B. modulating frequency varies
    C. carrier frequency varies
    D. modulating frequency is fixed

22. For voice operation, the microphone is connected to the   22._____

    A. antenna switch   B. transceiver
    C. power supply   D. antenna

23. Harmonic radiation is unwanted signals   23._____

    A. that are combined with a 60-Hz hum
    B. caused by vibrations from a nearby transmitter
    C. at frequencies which are multiples of an operator's chosen frequency
    D. which cause skip propagation

24. The LOWEST frequency of electrical energy that is usually known as radio frequency is   24._____
_____ Hz.

    A. 20   B. 2,000   C. 20,000   D. 200,000

25. What is the term for the kind of interference created by a continuous broad band of   25._____
numerous unrelated radio frequency pulses?

    A. Chirp   B. Oscillation
    C. Impulse noise   D. Fluctuation noise

KEY (CORRECT ANSWERS)

1.	D		11.	A
2.	B		12.	B
3.	A		13.	B
4.	D		14.	A
5.	C		15.	B
6.	B		16.	D
7.	D		17.	B
8.	A		18.	D
9.	C		19.	B
10.	C		20.	A

21.	C
22.	B
23.	C
24.	C
25.	D

———

EXAMINATION SECTION
TEST 1

DIRECTIONS: Each question or incomplete statement is followed by several suggested answers or completions. Select the one that BEST answers the question or completes the statement. *PRINT THE LETTER OF THE CORRECT ANSWER IN THE SPACE AT THE RIGHT.*

1. The transmission of signals by electromagnetic waves is referred to as   1.____

   A. biotelemetry   B. radio
   C. noise   D. all of the above

2. The transmission of physiologic data, such as an ECG, from the patient to a   2.____
   distant point of reception is called

   A. biotelemetry   B. simplex
   C. landline   D. none of the above

3. The assembly of a transmitter, receiver, and antenna connection at a fixed   3.____
   location creates a

   A. transceiver   B. radio
   C. biotelemetry   D. base station

4. The portion of the radio frequency spectrum between 30 and 150 mhz is called   4.____

   A. very high frequency (VHF)   B. ultrahigh frequency (UHF)
   C. very low frequency (VLF)   D. all of the above

5. A _____ is a miniature transmitter that picks up a radio signal and rebroad-   5.____
   casts it, thus extending the range of a radiocommunication system.

   A. transceiver   B. repeater   C. simplex   D. duplex

6. The portion of the radio frequency spectrum falling between 300 and 3,000   6.____
   mhz is called

   A. ultrahigh frequency (UHF)   B. very high frequency (VHF)
   C. very low frequency (VLF)   D. none of the above

7. One cycle per second equals one _____ in units of frequency.   7.____

   A. hertz   B. kilohertz   C. megahertz   D. gigahertz

8. The sources of noise in ECG telemetry include   8.____

   A. loose ECG electrodes
   B. muscle tremors
   C. sources of 60-cycle alternating current such as transformers, power lines,
      and electric equipment
   D. all of the above

9. The method of radio communications called _____ utilizes a single frequency that enables either transmission or reception of either voice or an ECG signal, but is incapable of simultaneous transmission and reception.

   A. duplex
   B. simplex
   C. multiplex
   D. none of the above

9.____

10. A terminal that receives transmissions of telemetry and voice from the field and transmits messages back through the base is referred to as a

   A. transceiver
   B. remote control
   C. remote console
   D. ten-code

10.____

11. The role of dispatcher includes

   A. reception of requests for help
   B. arrangements for getting the appropriate people and equipment to a situation which requires them
   C. deciding upon and dispatching of the appropriate emergency vehicles
   D. all of the above

11.____

12. A dispatcher should NOT

   A. maintain records
   B. scope a problem by requesting additional information from a caller
   C. direct public safety personnel
   D. receive notification of emergencies and call for assistance from both individual citizens and public safety units

12.____

13. The professional society of public safety communicators has developed a standard set of ten codes, the MOST common of which is 10-

   A. 1
   B. 4
   C. 12
   D. 18

13.____

14. What is the meaning of 10-33?

   A. Help me quick
   B. Arrived at scene
   C. Reply to message
   D. Disregard

14.____

15. One of the MAIN purposes of ten-codes is to

   A. shorten air time
   B. complicate the message
   C. increase the likelihood of misunderstanding
   D. none of the above

15.____

Questions 16-20.

DIRECTIONS: In Questions 16 through 20, match each translation of a commonly used ten-code with its appropriate code, listed in Column I.

<u>COLUMN I</u>

16.	What is your location?	A. 10-1	16._____
17.	Urgent.	B. 10-9	17._____
18.	Signal weak.	C. 10-18	18._____
19.	Arrived at the scene.	D. 10-20	19._____
20.	Please repeat.	E. 10-23	20._____

_____

KEY (CORRECT ANSWERS)

1.	B		11.	D
2.	A		12.	C
3.	D		13.	B
4.	A		14.	A
5.	B		15.	A
6.	D		16.	D
7.	A		17.	C
8.	D		18.	A
9.	B		19.	E
10.	C		20.	B

_____

TEST 2

DIRECTIONS: Each question or incomplete statement is followed by several suggested answers or completions. Select the one that BEST answers the question or completes the statement. *PRINT THE LETTER OF THE CORRECT ANSWER IN THE SPACE AT THE RIGHT.*

1. FCC rules prohibit

   A. deceptive or unnecessary messages
   B. profanity
   C. dissemination or use of confidential information transmitted over the radio
   D. all of the above

   1.____

2. Penalties for violations of FCC rules and regulations range from

   A. prison to death
   B. $20,000 to $100,000
   C. $100 to $10,000 and up to one year in prison
   D. up to 10 years in prison

   2.____

3. Which of the following is NOT true about base stations?

   A. The terrain and location do not affect the function.
   B. A good high-gain antenna improves transmission and reception efficiency.
   C. Multiple frequency capability is available at the base station.
   D. Antenna should be as close as possible to the base station transmitter/receiver.

   3.____

4. Radio frequencies are designated by cycles per second. 1,000,000 cycles per second equals one

   A. kilohertz   B. megahertz   C. gigahertz   D. hertz

   4.____

5. The Federal Communications Commission (FCC) is the agency of the United States government responsible for

   A. licensing and frequency allocation
   B. establishing technical standards for radio equipment
   C. establishing and enforcing rules and regulations for the operation of radio equipment
   D. all of the above

   5.____

6. Information relayed to the physician should include all of the following EXCEPT

   A. patient's age, sex, and chief complaint
   B. pertinent history of present illness
   C. detailed family history
   D. pertinent physical findings

   6.____

7. True statements regarding UHF band may include all of the following EXCEPT: 7._____

    A. It has better penetration in the dense metropolitan area
    B. Reception is usually quiet inside the building
    C. It has a longer range than VHF band
    D. Most medical communications occur around 450 to 470 mhz

8. Which of the following statements is NOT true regarding VHF band?   8._____

    A. Low band frequency may have ranges up to 2000 miles, but are unpredictable.
    B. VHF band may cause *skip interference,* with patchy losses in communication.
    C. High band frequency is wholly free of skip interference.
    D. High band frequencies for emergency medical purposes are in the 300 to 3000 mhz range.

9. 1000 cycles per second is equal to one   9._____

    A. hertz   B. kilohertz   C. megahertz   D. gigahertz

10. _____ achieves simultaneous transmission of voice and ECG signals over a single radio frequency.   10._____

    A. Duplex   B. Multiplex
    C. Channel   D. None of the above

11. Radio equipment used for both VHF and UHF band is   11._____

    A. frequency modulated
    B. amplitude modulated
    C. double amplitude modulated
    D. all of the above

12. ECG telemetry over UHF frequencies is confined to _____ of a 12 lead ECG.   12._____

    A. 1   B. 2   C. 6   D. 12

13. All of the following further clarity and conciseness EXCEPT   13._____

    A. understandable rate of speaking
    B. knowing what you want to transmit after transmission
    C. clear presentation of numbers, names, and dates
    D. using phrases and words which are easy to copy

14. The LEAST preferred of the following words is   14._____

    A. check   B. desire   C. want   D. advise if

15. All of the following are techniques useful during a call EXCEPT   15._____

    A. answering promptly
    B. identifying yourself and your department
    C. speaking directly into the mouthpiece
    D. none of the above

Questions 16-20.

DIRECTIONS: In Questions 16 through 20, match each definition with the term it describes, listed in Column I.

COLUMN I
A. Frequency
B. Noise
C. Patch
D. Duplex
E. Transceiver

16. A radio transmitter and receiver housed in a single unit; a two-way radio   16._____

17. The number of cycles per second of a radio signal, inversely related to the wavelength.   17._____

18. Interference in radio signals.   18._____

19. A radio system employing more than one frequency to permit simultaneous transmission and reception.   19._____

20. Connection between a telephone line and a radio communication system, enabling a caller to get *on the air* by special telephone.   20._____

_____

KEY (CORRECT ANSWERS)

1.	D	11.	A
2.	C	12.	A
3.	A	13.	B
4.	B	14.	C
5.	D	15.	D
6.	C	16.	E
7.	C	17.	A
8.	D	18.	B
9.	B	19.	D
10.	B	20.	C

EXAMINATION SECTION
TEST 1

DIRECTIONS: Each question or incomplete statement is followed by several suggested answers or completions. Select the one that BEST answers the question or completes the statement. *PRINT THE LETTER OF THE CORRECT ANSWER IN THE SPACE AT THE RIGHT.*

1. You answer a phone complaint from a person concerning an improper labeling practice in a shop in his neighborhood. Upon listening to the complaint, you get the impression that the person is exaggerating and may be too excited to view the matter clearly.
Of the following, your BEST course would be to

    A. tell the man that you can understand his anger but think it is not a really serious problem
    B. suggest to the man that he file a complaint with the Department of Consumer Affairs
    C. tell the man to stay away from the shop and have his friends do the same
    D. take down the information that the man offers so that he will see that the Police Department is concerned

1.＿＿＿

2. Suppose that late at night you receive a call on 911.
The caller turns out to be an elderly man who is not able to get out much, and who is calling you not because he needs help but because he wants to talk with someone.
The BEST way to handle such a situation is to

    A. explain to him that the number is for emergencies and his call may prevent others from getting the help they need
    B. talk to him if not many calls are coming in but excuse yourself and cut him off if you are busy
    C. cut him off immediately when you find out he does not need help because this will be the most effective way of discouraging him
    D. suggest that he call train or bus information as the clerks there are often not busy at night

2.＿＿＿

3. While you are on duty, you receive a call from a person whose name you recognize to be that of a person who calls frequently about matters of no importance. The caller requests your name and your supervisor's name so that she can report you for being impolite to her.
You should

    A. ask her when and how you were impolite to her
    B. tell her that she should not call about such minor matters
    C. make a report about her complaint for your superior
    D. give her the information that she requests

3.＿＿＿

4. Of the following, the MOST important reason for requiring each employee of the Police Department to be responsible for good public relations is that

    A. the Police Department has better morale when employees join in an effort to improve public relations
    B. the public judges the Department according to impressions received at every level in the Department

4.＿＿＿

C. most employees will not behave well toward the public unless required to do so
D. employees who improve public relations will receive commendations from superiors

5. Assume that you are in the Bureau of Public Relations. You receive a telephone call from a citizen who asks if a study has been made of the advisability of combining the city's police and fire departments. Assume that you have no information on the subject.
Of the following, your BEST course would be to

    A. tell the caller that undoubtedly the subject has been studied, but that you do not have the information available
    B. suggest to the caller that he telephone the Fire Department's Community Relations section for further information
    C. explain to the caller that the functions of the two departments are distinct and that combining them would be inefficient
    D. take the caller's number in order to call back, and then find information or referrals to give him

5.__

6. Suppose that Police Department officials have discouraged representatives of the press from contacting police administrative aides (except aides in the Public Relations Bureau) for information.
Of the following, the BEST reason for such a policy would be to

    A. assure proper control over information released to the press by the Department
    B. increase the value of official press releases of the Department
    C. make press representatives realize that the Department is not seeking publicity
    D. reduce the chance of crimes being committed in imitation of those reported in the press

6.__

7. People who phone the Police Department often use excited, emotional, and sometimes angry speech.
The BEST policy for you to take when speaking to this type of caller is to

    A. tell the person directly that he must speak in a more civil way
    B. tell the caller to call back when he is in a better mood
    C. give the person time to settle down, by doing most of the talking yourself
    D. speak calmly yourself to help the caller to gradually become more relaxed

7.__

8. On a particularly busy evening, the police administrative aide assigned to the telephones had answered a tremendous number of inquiries and complaints by irate citizens.
His patience was exhausted when he received a call from a citizen who reported, *Officer, a bird just flew into my bedroom. What should I do?* In a release of tension, the aide responded, *Keep it for seven days; and if no one claims it, it is yours.*
This response by the aide would usually be considered

    A. *advisable,* because the person should see how unusual his question was
    B. *advisable,* because he avoided offering police services that were unavailable
    C. *not advisable,* because such a remark might be regarded as insulting rather than humorous
    D. *not advisable,* because the person might not want a bird for a pet

8.__

9. While temporarily assigned to switchboard duty, you receive a call from a man who says   9.____
   his uncle in Pittsburgh has just called him and threatened to commit suicide. The man is
   convinced his uncle intends to carry out his threat.
   Of the following, you should

   A. advise the man to have neighbors of the uncle check to see if the uncle is all right
   B. politely inform the man that such out-of-town incidents are beyond the authority of
      the local precinct
   C. take the uncle's name, address, and telephone number and immediately contact
      police authorities in Pittsburgh
   D. get the man's name, address, and telephone number so that you can determine
      whether the call is a hoax

10. Assume that in the course of your assigned duties, you have just taken a necessary   10.____
    action which you feel has angered a citizen. After he has gone, you suddenly realize that
    the incident might result in an unjustified complaint. The MOST advisable action for you
    to take now would be to

    A. contact the person and apologize to him
    B. make complete notes on the incident and on any witnesses who might be helpful
    C. ask your superior what you might expect in case of such a complaint, without giv-
       ing any hint of the actual occurrence
    D. accept the situation as one of the hazards of your job

11. Your job may bring you in contact with people from the community who are confronted   11.____
    with emergencies, and are experiencing feelings of tension, anxiety, or even hostility. It is
    good to keep in mind what attitude is most helpful to people who, in such situations, need
    information and help. Suppose a person approaches you under circumstances like
    these.
    Which of the following would be BEST to do?

    A. Present similar examples of your own problems to make the person feel that his
       problems are not unusual.
    B. Recognize the person's feelings, present information on available services, and
       make suggestions as to proper procedures.
    C. Expect that some of the information is exaggerated and encourage the person to
       let some time pass before seeking further help.
    D. Have the person wait while you try to make arrangements for his problem to be
       solved.

12. Suppose that while on duty you receive a call from the owner of a gas station which is   12.____
    located within the precinct. The owner is annoyed with a certain rule made by the Police
    Department which concerns the operation of such stations. You agree with him.
    Of the following, the BEST action for you to take is to

    A. make a report on the call and suggest to the owner that he write a letter to the
       Department about the rule
    B. tell the owner that there is little that can be done since such rules are departmental
       policy
    C. tell the owner that you agree with his complaint and that you will write a memo of
       his call
    D. establish good relations with the owner by suggesting how to word a letter that will
       get action from the Department

13. Suppose that you are working at the switchboard when a call comes in late at night from a woman who reports that her neighbors are having a very noisy party. She gives you her first name, surname, and address, and you ask whether her title is *Miss* or *Mrs.* She replies that her title is irrelevant to her complaint, and wants to know why you ask.
Of the following possible ways of handling this, which is BEST?

    A. Insist that the title is necessary for identification purposes.
    B. Tell her that it is merely to find out what her marital status is.
    C. Agree that the information is not necessary and ask her how she wants to be referred to.
    D. Find out why she shows such a peculiar reaction to a request for harmless information.

14. While covering an assignment on the switchboard, you receive a call from a young girl who tells you of rumored plans for a gang fight in her neighborhood.
You should

    A. take down the information so that a patrol squad can investigate the area and possibly keep the fight from starting
    B. discourage the girl from becoming alarmed by reminding her that it is only a rumor
    C. realize that this is a teenager looking for attention, humor her, and dismiss the matter
    D. take down the information but tell the girl that you need concrete information, and not just rumors, to take any action on her call

15. The one of the following which would MOST likely lead to friction among police administrative aides in a unit would be for the supervisor in charge of the unit to

    A. defend the actions of the aides he supervises when discussing them with his own supervisor
    B. get his men to work together as a team in completing the work of the unit
    C. praise each of the aides he supervises *in confidence* as the best aide in the unit
    D. consider the point of view of the aides he supervises when assigning unpleasant tasks

16. Suppose that a police administrative aide who had been transferred to your office from another unit in your Department because of difficulties with his supervisor has been placed under your supervision.
The BEST course of action for you to take FIRST is to

    A. analyze the aide's past grievance to determine if the transfer was the best settlement of the problem
    B. advise him of the difficulties his former supervisor had with other employees and encourage him not to feel bad about the transfer
    C. warn him that you will not tolerate any nonsense and that he will be watched carefully while assigned to your unit
    D. instruct him in the duties he will be performing in your unit and make him feel *wanted* in his new position

17. In which of the following circumstances would it be MOST appropriate for you to use an   17.____
impersonal style of writing rather than a personal style, which relies on the use of personal pronouns and other personal references?
When writing a memorandum to

   A. give your opinion to an associate on the advisability of holding a weekly staff meeting
   B. furnish your superior with data justifying a proposed outlay of funds for new equipment
   C. give your version of an incident which resulted in a complaint by a citizen about your behavior
   D. support your request for a transfer to another division

18. A newly appointed supervisor should learn as much as possible about the backgrounds   18.____
of his subordinates. The statement is generally CORRECT because

   A. effective handling of subordinates is based upon knowledge of their individual differences
   B. knowing their backgrounds assures they will be treated objectively, equally, and without favor
   C. some subordinates perform more efficiently under one supervisor than under another
   D. subordinates have confidence in a supervisor who knows all about them

19. You have found it necessary, for valid reasons, to criticize the work of one of the female   19.____
police administrative aides. She later comes to your desk and accuses you of criticizing her work because she is a woman.
The BEST way for you to deal with this employee is to

   A. ask her to apologize, since you would never allow yourself to be guilty of his kind of discrimination
   B. discuss her complaint with her, explaining again and at greater length the reason for your criticism
   C. assure her you wish to be fair, and ask her to submit a written report to you on her complaint
   D. apologize for hurting her feelings and promise that she will be left alone in the future

20. The following steps are recognized steps in teaching an employee a new skill: 20.____
   I. Demonstrate how to do the work
   II. Let the learner do the work himself
   III. Explain the nature and purpose of the work
   IV. Correct poor procedures by suggestion and demonstration
The CORRECT order for these steps is:

   A. III, II, IV, I   B. II, I, III, IV
   C. III, I, II, IV   D. I, III, II, IV

21. Suppose you have arranged an interview with a subordinate to try to help him overcome   21.___
a serious shortcoming in his technical work. While you do not intend to talk to him about
his attitude, you have noticed that he seems to be suspicious and resentful of people in
authority. You need a record of the points covered in the discussion since further interviews are likely to be necessary.
Your BEST course would be to

   A. write a checklist of points you wish to discuss and carefully check the points off as
       the interview progresses
   B. know exactly how you wish to proceed, and then make written notes during the
       interview of your subordinate's comments
   C. frankly tell your subordinate that you are recording the talk on tape but place the
       recorder where it will not hinder discussion
   D. keep in mind what you wish to accomplish and make notes on the interview imme-
       diately after it is over

22. A police administrative aide has explained a complicated procedure to several subordi-   22.___
nates. He has been talking clearly, allowing time for information to sink in. He has also
encouraged questions. Yet, he still questions his subordinates after his explanation, with
the obvious objective of finding out whether they completely understand the procedure.
Under these circumstances, the action of the police administrative aide, in asking
questions about the procedure, is

   A. *not advisable,* because subordinates who do not now know the procedure which
       has been explained so carefully can read and study it
   B. *not advisable,* because he endangers his relationship with his subordinates by
       insulting their intelligence
   C. *advisable,* because subordinates basically resent instructions and seldom give
       their full attention in a group situation
   D. *advisable,* because the answers to his questions help him to determine whether he
       has gained his objective

23. The most competent of the police administrative aides is a pleasant, intelligent young   23.___
woman who breaks the rules of the Department by occasionally making long personal
telephone calls during working hours. You have not talked to her up until now about this
fault. However, the calls are beginning to increase, and you decide to deal directly with
the problem.
The BEST way to approach the subject with her would be to

   A. review with her the history of her infractions of the rules
   B. point out that her conduct is not fair to the other workers
   C. tell her that her personal calls are excessive and discuss it with her
   D. warn her quietly that you intend to apply penalties if necessary

24. Assume that you are supervising eight male police administrative aides who do similar   24.___
clerical work. A group of four of them work on each side of a row of files which can be
moved without much trouble. You notice that in each group there is a clique of three
aides, leaving one member isolated. The two isolated members are relative newcomers
to the unit though they have been there a few months.
Your BEST course in such a case would be to

A. ignore the situation because to concern yourself with informal social arrangements of your subordinates would distract you from more important matters
B. ask each of the cliques to invite the isolated member in their working group to lunch with them from time to time
C. tell each group that you cannot allow cliques to form as it is bad for the morale of the unit
D. find an excuse to move the file cabinets to the side of the room and then move the desks of the two isolated members close together

25. Suppose that your supervisor, who has recently been promoted and transferred to your division, asks you to review a certain procedure with a view to its possible revision. You know that several years ago a sergeant made a lengthy and intensive report based on a similar review.
    Which of the following would it be BEST for you to do FIRST?

    A. Ask your supervisor if he is aware of the previous report.
    B. Read the sergeant's report before you begin work to see what bearing it has on your assignment.
    C. Begin work on the review without reading his report so that you will have a fresh point of view.
    D. Ask the sergeant to assist you in your review.

26. Using form letters in business correspondence is LEAST effective when

    A. answering letters on a frequently recurring subject
    B. giving the same information to many addressees
    C. the recipient is only interested in the routing information contained in the form letter
    D. a reply must be keyed to the individual requirements of the intended reader

27. From the viewpoint of an office administrator, the BEST of the following reasons for distributing the incoming mail before the beginning of the regular work day is that

    A. distribution can be handled quickly and most efficiently at that time
    B. distribution later in the day may be distracting to or interfere with other employees
    C. the employees who distribute the mail can then perform other tasks during the rest of the day
    D. office activities for the day based on the mail may then be started promptly

28. Suppose you have had difficulty locating a document in the files because you could not decide where it should have been filed. You learn that other people in the office have had the same problem. You know that the document will be needed from time to time in the future.
    Your BEST course, when refiling the document, would be to

    A. make a written note of where you found it so that you will find it more easily the next time
    B. reclassify it and file it in the file where you first looked for it
    C. file it where you found it and put cross-reference sheets in the other likely files
    D. make a mental association to help you find it the next time and put it back where you found it

29. Suppose that your supervisor is attending a series of meetings of police captains in Philadelphia and will not be back until next Wednesday. He has left no instructions with you as to how you should handle telephone calls for him.
In most instances, your BEST course would be to say,

    A. He isn't here just now
    B. He is out of town and won't be back until next Wednesday
    C. He won't be in today
    D. He is in Philadelphia attending a meeting of police captains

29._

30. The one of the following which is USUALLY an important *by-product* of the preparation of a procedure manual is that

    A. information uncovered in the process of preparation may lead to improvement of procedures
    B. workers refer to the manual instead of bothering their supervisors for information
    C. supervisors use the manual for training stenographers
    D. employees have equal access to information needed to do their jobs

30._

31. You have been asked to organize a clerical job and supervise police administrative aides who will do the actual work. The job consists of removing, from several boxes of data processing cards which are arranged in alphabetical order, the cards of those whose names appear on certain lists. The person removing the card then notes a date on the card. Assume that the work will be done accurately whatever system is used.
Which of the following statements describes both the MOST efficient method and the BEST reasons for using that method?
Have

    A. two aides work together, one calling names and the other extracting cards, and dating them, because the average production of any two aides working together should be higher, under these circumstances, than that of any two aides working alone
    B. each aide work alone, because it is easier to check spelling when reading the names than when listening to them
    C. two aides work together, one calling names and the other extracting cards and dating them, because social interaction tends to make work go faster
    D. each aide work alone, because the average production of any two aides, each working alone, should be higher, under these circumstances, than that of any two aides working together

31._

32. The term *work flow,* when used in connection with office management or the activities in an office, generally means the

    A. rate of speed at which work flows through a single section of an office
    B. use of charts in the analysis of various office functions
    C. number of individual work units which can be produced by the average employee
    D. step-by-step physical routing of work through its various procedures

32._

Questions 33-40.

DIRECTIONS:

Name of Offense	V A N D S B R U G H
Code Letter	c o m p l e x i t y
File Number	1 2 3 4 5 6 7 8 9 0

Assume that each of the above capital letters is the first letter of the name of an offense, that the small letter directly beneath each capital letter is the code letter for the offense, and that the number directly beneath each code letter is the file number for the offense.

In each of Questions 33 through 40, the code letters and file numbers should correspond to the capital letters.
If there is an error only in Column 2, mark your answer A.
If there is an error only in Column 3, mark your answer B.
If there is an error in both Column 2 and Column 3, mark your answer C.
If both Columns 2 and 3 are correct, mark your answer D.

Sample Questions:

COLUMN 1	COLUMN 2	COLUMN 3
BNARGHSVVU	emoxtylcci	6357905118

The code letters in Column 2 are correct, but the first 5 in Column 3 should be 2. Therefore, the answer is B.

	COLUMN 1	COLUMN 2	COLUMN 3	
				32.____
33.	HGDSBNBSVR	ytplxmelcx	0945736517	33.____
34.	SDGUUNHVAH	lptiimycoy	5498830120	34.____
35.	BRSNAAVUDU	exlmooctpi	6753221848	35.____
36.	VSRUDNADUS	cleipmopil	1568432485	36.____
37.	NDSHVRBUAG	mplycxeiot	3450175829	37.____
38.	GHUSNVBRDA	tyilmcexpo	9085316742	38.____
39.	DBSHVURANG	pesycixomt	4650187239	39.____
40.	RHNNASBDGU	xymnolepti	7033256398	40.____

KEY (CORRECT ANSWERS)

1.	B	11.	B	21.	D	31.	D
2.	A	12.	A	22.	D	32.	D
3.	D	13.	C	23.	C	33.	C
4.	B	14.	A	24.	D	34.	D
5.	D	15.	C	25.	A	35.	A
6.	A	16.	D	26.	D	36.	C
7.	D	17.	B	27.	D	37.	B
8.	C	18.	A	28.	C	38.	D
9.	C	19.	B	29.	B	39.	A
10.	B	20.	C	30.	A	40.	C

EXAMINATION SECTION
TEST 1

DIRECTIONS: Each question or incomplete statement is followed by several suggested answers or completions. Select the one that BEST answers the question or completes the statement. *PRINT THE LETTER OF THE CORRECT ANSWER IN TEE SPACE AT THE RIGHT.*

1. Police Communications Technicians must connect the caller to Transit Police when an incident occurs on a subway train or in the subway station.
   Which one of the following calls should be reported to Transit Police?

    A. The newsstand outside the entrance to the 86th Street subway was just robbed, and the suspects fled down the street.
    B. Soon after James Pike left the Columbus Circle subway station, his chain was snatched on the street corner.
    C. While traveling to work on the *D* line subway train, John Smith was mugged.
    D. A noisy group of school children have just come out of the Times Square subway station and are now annoying passersby on the street.

1._____

Question 2.

DIRECTIONS: Question 2 is to be answered SOLELY on the basis of the following information.
    When a Police Communications Technician is notified by patrol cars that they are in a vehicular pursuit, the dispatcher should obtain the following in the order given:
        I. Location of pursuit
        II. Type of vehicle, color of vehicle, and direction of travel
        III. Nature of offense
        IV. License plate number and state
        V. Number of occupant(s) in vehicle
        VI. Identity of the patrol car in pursuit

2. Police Communications Dispatcher Johnson is working the 26th Division when an unknown patrol car announces via car radio that he is in pursuit of a white 1986 Cadillac traveling north on Vanbrunt Street from Ainsley Place. Dispatcher Johnson then asks the pursuing patrol car, *What is the car wanted for?* The Officer replies, *The car is wanted for a hit and run.*
   What information should Dispatcher Johnson obtain NEXT?

    A. The number of occupant(s) in the vehicle
    B. Location of pursuit
    C. License plate number and state
    D. Identity of the patrol car in pursuit

2._____

Question 3.

DIRECTIONS: Question 3 is to be answered SOLELY on the basis of the following information.
Robbery - involves the unlawful taking of property from a person by force or attempted use of immediate force.

Robbery in Progress - crime is occurring at the time the call came into 911, 5 minutes in the past or when suspects are still in the area.

3. Which of the following situations would be considered a ROBBERY IN PROGRESS?   3.___

   A. Female calls 911 stating that she has just arrived home and found her apartment has been robbed.
   B. Male calls 911 stating that he just discovered that someone picked his pocket.
   C. Female calls 911 stating that she saw a man grab an elderly woman's purse.
   D. Child calls 911 stating that some man is beating up his mother and is trying to take her purse.

4. On June 20, 2007 at 6:30 P.M., Police Communications Technician White receives a call   4.___
   from an anonymous complainant stating the following facts:
   Incident: Male with a gun sitting in a blue car
   Location of Incident: In front of 185 Hall St.
   Description of Suspect: Male, Black, bald, approximately 25 years old, dressed in red
   Dispatcher White needs to be accurate and clear when transferring above information to the police dispatcher. Which one of the following expresses the above information MOST clearly and accurately?

   A. On June 20, 2007 at 6:30 P.M., a call was received stating that a bald man, dressed in red, was in front of 185 Hall St. A black male, approximately 25 years old, is sitting in a blue car holding a gun.
   B. A call was received on June 20, 2007. at 6:30 P.M. stating that a bald black male, approximately 25 years old, who is dressed in red, is armed with a gun sitting in a blue car in front of 185 Hall St.
   C. A call was received on June 20, 2007 at 6:30 P.M. Sitting in a blue car in front of 185 Hall St. is a Black male, approximately 25 years old. Dressed in red with a bald head, a man is armed with a gun.
   D. A call was received stating that in front of 185 Hall St., a bald male, approximately 25 years old, dressed in red, is sitting in a blue car. A Black male is armed with a gun at 6:30 P.M. on June 20, 2007.

5. Police Communications Technician Dozier receives a call from a female who has just wit-   5.___
   nessed the following:
   Incident: White female police officer being assaulted
   Location of Incident: Surf Avenue and West 30th Street, in front of a candy store
   Description of Suspectp;   Hispanic female wearing a green dress, possibly armed with a gun
   Dispatcher Dozier is about to relay the information to the dispatcher.
   Which one of the following expresses the above information MOST clearly and accurately?

   A. A call was received from a female on Surf Avenue and West 30th Street stating that a white female police officer is being assaulted by a Hispanic female wearing a green dress. She is possibly armed with a gun in front of a candy store.
   B. In front of a candy store at Surf Avenue and West 30th Street, a call was received from a female stating that a white female police officer is being assaulted by a Hispanic female wearing a green dress. She is possibly armed with a gun.

C. A call was received from a female stating that at the corner of Surf Avenue and West 30th Street in front of a candy store, there is a white female police officer being assaulted. The suspect is a Hispanic female wearing a green dress, who is possibly armed with a gun.

D. A call was received from a female stating that at the corner of West 30th Street and Surf Avenue, there is a white female police officer in front of a candy store being assaulted. She is wearing a green dress. The Hispanic female is possibly armed with a gun.

Questions 6-8.

DIRECTIONS: Questions 6 through 8 are to be answered SOLELY on the basis of the following passage.

At 10:35 A.M., Police Communications Technician Ross receives a second call from Mrs. Smith who is very upset because she has been waiting for the police and an ambulance since her first call, one hour ago. Mrs. Smith was mugged, and in resisting the attack, her nose was broken. The location of the incident is the uptown side of the subway station for the IND #2 train located at Jay Street and Borough Hall. Operator Ross advises Mrs. Smith to hold on and that she will check the status of her complaint. Operator Ross calls the Emergency Medical Service (EMS) and connects Mrs. Smith to the EMS operator. The EMS operator informs Mrs. Smith that an ambulance is coming from a far distance away and will be at the location at approximately 11:03 A.M. Operator Ross then calls the Transit Authority Police Department (TAPD). The TAPD received Mrs. Smith's first call at 9:37 A.M., and police arrived at location at 9:46 M. However, the police arrived at the downtown side of the subway station for the IND #3 train. TAPD informs Operator Ross that a police car will arrive at the correct location as soon as possible.

6. What is the CLOSEST approximate time that Mrs. Smith made her first call for help? 6.____
   _____ A.M.

   A. 9:35   B. 9:46   C. 10:35   D. 11:03 .

7. The ambulance was delayed because 7.____

   A. the ambulance responded to the downtown side of the subway station for the IND #2 train
   B. EMS never received Mrs. Smith's request for an ambulance
   C. a broken nose is not a priority request for an ambulance
   D. the ambulance was coming from a far distance

8. There was a delay in TAPD response to the crime scene because TAPD 8.____

   A. was coming from a far distance
   B. responded on the uptown side of the subway station for the IND #2 train
   C. was waiting for the -Police Department to respond first
   D. responded on the downtown side of the subway station for the IND #3 train

9. Extreme care must be taken when assigning solo cars (one police officer in a vehicle) to   9.___
incidents. If anything in the job indicates that the job may be a potentially violent situation, a solo car should not be assigned.
In which one of the following incidents should a Police Communications Technician
assign a solo car?
A

   A. disorderly male carrying a knife
   B. house that was broken into two days ago
   C. suspiciously occupied auto
   D. group of rowdy teenagers throwing beer bottles at passersbys

Question 10.

DIRECTIONS: Question 10 is to be answered SOLELY on the basis of the following informa-
               tion.
On the Police Communications Technician's screen, the following incidents appear which
were called in at the same time:
     I. Caller states that she is looking out her 10th floor window and sees a man
        sleeping on the street in front of her home at Crescent Street and 4th Avenue.
     II. Caller states that he was driving down the block of Crescent Street between
        3rd and 4th Avenues and just witnessed a man being beaten and mugged. The
        caller thinks that the victim is unconscious.
     III. Caller states there is a car accident at Crescent Street and 3rd Avenue, and
        one of the passengers suffered a broken arm.

10. Which of the above should the operator MOST likely consider as the same incident?   10.___

   A. I and II   B. II and III
   C. I and III   D. I, II, and III

11. Police Communications Operator Raymond receives a call regarding a rape and obtains   11.___
the following information:
Time of Rape: 10:35 P.M.
Place of Rape: Sam's Laundromat, 200 Melrose Avenue
Victim: Joan McGraw
Crime: Rape
Suspect: Male, Hispanic, carrying a gun
Operator Raymond is about to enter the incident into the computer.
Which one of the following expresses the above information MOST clearly and accu-
rately?

   A. At 10:35 P.M., Joan McGraw was raped in Sam's Laundromat, located at 200 Mel-
      rose Avenue, by a Hispanic male carrying a gun.
   B. A Hispanic male was carrying a gun at 10:35 P.M. Joan McGraw was raped in
      Sam's Laundromat located at 200 Melrose Avenue.
   C. Carrying a gun, Joan McGraw was raped by a Hispanic male. This occurred in
      Sam's Laundromat located at 200 Melrose Avenue at 10:35 P.M.
   D. At 10:35 P.M., Joan McGraw was raped by a Hispanic male carrying a gun. Sam's
      Laundromat is located at 200 Melrose Avenue.

12. Police Communications Dispatcher Gold receives a call concerning a disorderly male in   12.____
a local drug store. He obtains the following information:

Place of Occurrence: Rapid-Serve Drug Store
Complainant: George Meyer
Crime: Threatening gestures and abusive language
Suspect: Male, white
Action Taken: The suspect was removed from premises by the police.

Dispatcher Gold is about to enter the incident into the computer.
Which one of the following expresses the above information MOST clearly and accurately?

    A. George Meyer called the police because a white male was removed from the Rapid-Serve Drug Store. He was making threatening gestures and using abusive language.

    B. George Meyer called the police and was removed from the Rapid-Serve Drug Store. A white male was making threatening gestures and using abusive language.

    C. At the Rapid-Serve Drug Store, a white male was making threatening gestures and using abusive language. George Meyer called the police and removed the suspect from the drug store.

    D. George Meyer called the police because a white male was making threatening gestures and using abusive language in the Rapid-Serve Drug Store. The suspect was removed from the drug store by the police.

Question 13.

DIRECTIONS: Question 13 is to be answered SOLELY on the basis of the following information.

When dispatching an incident involving a suspicious package, a Police Communications Technician should do the following in the order given:

    I.   Assign a patrol car and Patrol Sergeant.
    II.   Enter into the computer additional information received from assigned cars.
    III.   Notify appropriate Emergency Assistance.
    IV.   Notify the Bomb Squad.
    V.   Notify the Duty Captain.

13. Police Communications Technician Berlin receives a call involving a suspicious package   13.____
located on the corner of Gates Avenue and Blake Street. Dispatcher Berlin promptly assigns a patrol car and a Patrol Sergeant to the incident. Upon arrival, the Sergeant determines that there is a ticking sound coming from the box. The Sergeant immediately advises Dispatcher Berlin of the situation and tells Dispatcher Berlin to call the Fire Department and have them respond.
What should Dispatcher Berlin to NEXT?

    A. Call the Fire Department.
    B. Notify the Bomb Squad.
    C. Enter additional information received from assigned cars into the computer.
    D. Notify the Duty Captain.

Questions 14-16.

DIRECTIONS: Questions 14 through 16 are to be answered SOLELY on the basis of the following passage.

Police Communications Technician Robbins receives a call at 5:15 P.M. from Mr. Adams reporting he witnessed a shooting in front of 230 Eagle Road. Mr. Adams, who lives at 234 Eagle Road, states he overheard two white males arguing with a Black man. He describes one white male as having blonde hair and wearing a black jacket with blue jeans, and the other white male as having brown hair and wearing a white jacket and blue jeans.

Mr. Adams recognized the Black man as John Rivers, the son of Mrs. Mary Rivers, who lives at 232 Eagle Road. At 5:10 P.M., the blonde male took a gun, shot John in the stomach, and dragged his body into the alleyway. The two males ran into the backyard of 240 Eagle Road and headed west on Randall Boulevard. Dispatcher Robbins connects Mr. Adams to the Emergency Medical Service. The Ambulance Receiving Operator processes the call at 5:25 P.M. and advises Mr. Adams that the next available ambulance will be sent.

14.   Who was the eyewitness to the shooting?   14._____

A.   Dispatcher Robbins   B.   Mr. Adams
C.   Mrs. Rivers   D.   John Rivers

15.   In front of what address was John Rivers shot?   15._____
_____ Eagle Road.

A.   230   B.   232   C.   234   D.   240

16.   What is the description of the male who fired the gun? A male wearing a _____ jacket   16._____
and blue jeans.

A.   white blonde-haired; white
B.   white brown-haired; black
C.   white blonde-haired; black
D.   Black brown-haired; white

17.   A Police Communications Technician can have several calls for police response on their   17._____
computer screen at one time. A dispatcher may have to determine which of the calls is
the most serious and assign that one to the police first.
Which one of the following situations should a dispatcher assign to the police FIRST?

A.   A robbery which occurred two hours ago, and the suspects have fled the scene
B.   A suspicious man offering a child candy to get the child into his van at the time of
the call
C.   A woman returns to her car and finds her left fender dented
D.   A group of youths playing cards in the hallway

18.   The following information was obtained by Police Communications Technician Fried   18._____
regarding a call of an auto accident with injuries:
Date of Accident: March 7, 2007
Place of Accident: 50 West 96th Street
Time of Accident: 3:15 P.M.
Drivers: Susan Green and Nancy White

Injured: Nancy White
Action Taken: Emergency Medical Services (EMS) Operator 600 was notified
Dispatcher Fried is about to enter the above information into the computer.
Which one of the following expresses the above information MOST clearly and accurately?

- A. At 50 West 96th Street, Susan Green and Nancy White had an auto accident resulting in an injury to Nancy White. EMS Operator 600 was notifed to send an ambulance at 3:15 P.M. on March 7, 2007.
- B. EMS Operator 600 was notified to send an ambulance to 50 West 96th Street due to an auto accident between Nancy White and Susan Green, who was injured on March 7, 2007 at 3:15 P.M.
- C. Susan Green and Nancy White were involved in an auto accident at 50 West 96th Street on March 7, 2007. At 3:15 P.M., EMS Operator 600 was notified to send an ambulance for Nancy White.
- D. On March 7, 2007 at 3:15 P.M., Susan Green and Nancy White were involved in an auto accident at 50 West 96th Street. EMS Operator 600 was notified to send an ambulance for Nancy White who was injured in the accident.

Questions 19-20.

DIRECTIONS: Questions 19 and 20 are to be answered SOLELY on the basis of the following information.

At the beginning of their tours, Police Communications Technicians need to call the precinct to find out what patrol cars are covering which sections of the precinct and which special assignment cars are being used. Special assignment cars are used instead of regular patrol cars when certain situations arise. Special assignment cars should be assigned before a patrol car when a call comes in that is related to the car's special assignment, regardless of what section the incident is occurring in. Otherwise, a regular patrol car should be assigned.

Police Communications Technician Tanner is assigned to the 83rd Precinct. He calls the precinct and determines the following patrol cars and special assignment cars are being used:

Patrol cars are assigned as follows:
     Patrol Car 83A - Covers Sections A, B, C
     Patrol Car 83D - Covers Sections D, E, F
     Patrol Car 83G - Covers Sections G, H, I

Special assignment cars are assigned as follows:
     83SP1 - Burglary Car
     83SP2 - Religious Establishment
     83SP8 - Anti-Crime (plainclothes officers)

19. Dispatcher Tanner receives a call located in the 83rd Precinct in *E* Section. Which car should be assigned?   19.____

     A. 83D   B. 83A   C. 83SP8   D. 83SP2

20. Dispatcher Tanner receives a call concerning a burglary in *B* Section. Which is the CORRECT car to be assigned?   20.____

     A. 83A   B. 83G   C. 83SP1   D. 83SP2

KEY (CORRECT ANSWERS)

1.	C		11.	A
2.	C		12.	D
3.	D		13.	C
4.	B		14.	B
5.	C		15.	A
6.	A		16.	C
7.	D		17.	B
8.	D		18.	D
9.	B		19.	A
10.	A		20.	C

TEST 2

DIRECTIONS: Each question or incomplete statement is followed by several suggested answers or completions. Select the one that BEST answers the question or completes the statement. *PRINT THE LETTER OF THE CORRECT ANSWER IN THE SPACE AT THE RIGHT.*

1.   Police Communications Technician Daniel receives a call stating the following: 1._____
Date and Time of Call: June 21, 2007 at 12:30 P.M.
Incident: Shots being fired
Location: The roof of a building, located between Moore Street and Bushwick Avenue, exact address unknown
Suspect: Male
Complainant: Mr. Bernard
Comments: Mr. Bernard will be wearing a brown coat and will direct officers to location of the incident.

Dispatcher Daniel is about to enter the information into the computer.
Which one of the following expresses the above information MOST clearly and accurately?
On June 21, 2007,

A.   at 12:30 P.M., Dispatcher Daniel receives a call from a complainant stating that a male is on a roof of a building with an unknown address firing a gun, and he is wearing a brown coat. The complainant, Mr. Bernard, will be in front of the building to direct the police to the exact location of the incident.

B.   a male is firing a gun from a roof, stated complainant Mr. Bernard to Dispatcher Daniel. This is at Moore Street and Bushwick Avenue. At 12:30 P.M., the caller will be at the location to direct the police to the building where the male is firing the gun. He is wearing a brown coat.

C.   at 12:30 P.M., Dispatcher Daniel receives a call from a complainant, Mr. Bernard, who states that at a building with an unknown address, located between Moore Street and Bushwick Avenue, a male is firing a gun from a roof. Mr. Bernard will be at the location wearing a brown coat to direct the police to the exact building.

D.   Dispatcher Daniel receives a call from a complainant, Mr. Bernard, who is calling from a building with an unknown address. He informs Dispatcher Daniel that a male is firing a gun from a roof of a building between Moore Street and Bushwick Avenue. At 12:30 P.M., Mr. Bernard will be wearing a brown coat to direct the police to the incident.

Questions 2-4.

DIRECTIONS: Questions 2 through 4 are to be answered SOLELY on the basis of the following passage.

Mrs. Arroyo returns from work one evening to find her door open and loud noise coming from her apartment. She peeks through the crack of the door and sees a white male moving rapidly through her apartment wearing blue jeans and a pink T-shirt. She runs to the nearest public telephone and dials 911. Police Communications Technician Ms. Lopez takes the call. Mrs. Arroyo informs Operator Lopez that there is a strange man in her apartment. The operator asks the caller for her address, apartment number, name, and telephone number, and then puts Mrs. Arroyo on hold. Operator Lopez enters the address in the computer and, realizing it is a high priority call, tries to notify the Radio Dispatcher directly by depressing the *hotline* button.

The Radio Dispatcher does not respond, and Operator Lopez realizes the *hotline* button is not working. The operator then continues to enter the rest of the information into the computer and notifies the caller that the police will respond. Operator Lopez then walks into the dispatcher's room to make sure the dispatcher received the information entered into the computer, and then notifies the supervisor of her malfunctioning equipment.

2. The operator notified her supervisor because

    A. the suspect was still in the apartment
    B. the *hotline* button was not working
    C. she could not enter the address in the computer
    D. it was a high priority call

2.____

3. What was the FIRST action the operator took after putting the complainant on hold?

    A. Entered the caller's telephone number and name in the computer.
    B. Walked into the dispatcher's room.
    C. Entered the caller's address into the computer.
    D. Tried to notify the Radio Dispatcher by depressing the *hotline* button.

3.____

4. Operator Lopez depressed the *hotline* button

    A. to check if the *hotline* button was working properly
    B. because it was a high priority call
    C. to make sure the dispatcher received the information entered into the computer
    D. because the computer was not working properly

4.____

Question 5.

DIRECTIONS: Question 5 is to be answered SOLELY on the basis of the following information.

    A Police Communications Technician occasionally receives calls from persons making threats against public officials, visiting dignitaries, or members of the Police Department. When this occurs, the Dispatcher should do the following in the order given:

    I. Obtain details of the threat
        (A) Who is being threatened and how
        (B) When it is going to happen
    II. Attempt to determine the sex and ethnicity of the caller
    III. Try to obtain the identity, address, and telephone number of the caller
    IV. Notify the supervisor

5. Police Communications Operator Frye receives a call and obtains from the caller that he is going to shoot the mayor on Election Day. Operator Frye determine the caller to be a male with a heavy Hispanic accent. Operator Frye asks the male for his name, address, and phone number. The caller does not respond and hangs up.
What should Operator Frye do NEXT?

    A. Obtain details of the threats.
    B. Determine the sex and ethnicity of the caller.
    C. Obtain the identity, address, and phone number of the caller.
    D. Notify the supervisor.

5.____

Question 6.

DIRECTIONS: Question 6 is to be answered SOLELY on the basis of the following information.

A Police Communications Technician will call back complainants only under the following conditions:

1.   Dispatcher needs clarification of information previously received from the complainant and/or
2.   To notify the complainant that police need to gain entry to the location of the incident.

6.   In which one of the following situations should a Police Communications Technician call back the complainant?   6.____

   A.   While responding to an assigned incident, Patrol Car 79A gets a flat tire. Patrol Car 79A radios the dispatcher and advises the dispatcher to call the complainant and notify the complainant that there will be a delay in police response.
   B.   Patrol Car 83B is assigned to an incident that occurred approximately 30 minutes ago. Patrol Car 83B advises the dispatcher that he is coming from a far distance and the dispatcher should call the complainant to find out which is the best way to get to the incident location.
   C.   Patrol Car 66B is on the scene of an incident and is having a problem gaining entry into the building. Patrol Car 66B asks the dispatcher to call the complainant and ask him to meet the police officers from the patrol car outside the building.
   D.   Patrol Car 90B is assigned to a burglary that occurred in the complainant's private home. It is raining heavily outside, so Patrol Car 90B asks the dispatcher to call and request the complainant to meet the police by the patrol car.

7.   Police Communications Dispatcher Blake receives a call reporting a bank robbery and obtains the following information: 7.____

Time of Robbery: 11:30 A.M.
Place of Robbery: Fidelity Bank
Crime: Bank Robbery
Suspect: Male, white, wearing blue jeans, blue jacket, carrying a brown bag
Witness: Susan Lane of 731 Madison Avenue

Dispatcher Blake is about to inform his supervisor of the facts concerning the bank robbery.

Which one of the following expresses the above information MOST clearly and accurately?

   A.   At 11:30 A.M., the Fidelity Bank was robbed. Susan Lane lives at 731 Madison Avenue. The witness saw a white male wearing blue jeans, a blue jacket, and carrying a brown bag.
   B.   Susan Lane of 731 Madison Avenue witnessed the robbery of Fidelity Bank at 11:30 A.M. The suspect is a white male and was wearing blue jeans, a blue jacket, and carrying a brown bag.
   C.   Wearing blue jeans, a blue jacket, and carrying a brown bag, Susan Lane of 731 Madison Avenue saw a white male robbing the Fidelity Bank. The robbery was witnessed at 11:30 A.M.

D. At 11:30 A.M., Susan Lane of 731 Madison Avenue witnessed the robbery of the Fidelity Bank. A white male wore blue jeans, a blue jacket, and carried a brown bag.

8. Police Communications Technician Levine receives an incident for dispatch containing the following information:

Incident: A female being beaten
Location: In front of 385 Wall Street
Victim: White female
Suspect: White, male, wearing a grey shirt, possibly concealing a gun underneath his shirt

Dispatcher Levine is about to relay this information to the patrol car.
Which one of the following expresses the above information MOST clearly and accurately?

A. A white female is being beaten by a white male wearing a grey shirt, who is possibly concealing a gun underneath his shirt. This is occurring in front of 385 Wall Street.
B. A white male is beating a white female wearing a grey shirt. He is possibly concealing a gun underneath his shirt in front of 385 Wall Street.
C. A female is being beaten in front of 385 Wall Street. A white male is possibly concealing a gun underneath his shirt. She is white, and the suspect is wearing a grey shirt.
D. In front of 385 Wall Street, a white female is being beaten by a suspect, possibly concealing a gun underneath his shirt. A white male is wearing a grey shirt.

Questions 9-11.

DIRECTIONS: Questions 9 through 11 are to be answered SOLELY on the basis of the following passage.

Police Communications Technician John Clove receives a call from a Social Worker, Mrs. Norma Harris of Presbyterian Hospital, who states there is a 16-year-old teenager on the other line, speaking to Dr. Samuel Johnson, a psychologist at the hospital. The teenager is threatening suicide and claims that she is an out-patient, but refuses to give her name, address, or telephone number. She further states that the teenager took 100 pills of valium and is experiencing dizziness, numbness of the lips, and heart palpitations. The teenager tells Dr. Johnson that she wants to die because her boyfriend left her because she is pregnant.

Dr. Johnson is keeping her on the line persuading her to give her name, telephone number, and address. The Social Worker asks the dispatcher to trace the call. The dispatcher puts the caller on hold and informs his supervisor, Mrs. Ross, of the incident. The supervisor contacts Telephone Technician Mr. Ralph Taylor. Mr. Taylor contacts the telephone company and speaks to Supervisor Wallace, asking him to trace the call between Dr. Johnson and the teenager. After approximately 10 minutes, the dispatcher gets back to the Social Worker and informs her that the call is being traced.

9. Why did the Social Worker call Dispatcher Clove?

A. A teenager is threatening suicide.
B. Mrs. Ross took 100 pills of valium.

C. Dr. Johnson felt dizzy, numbness of the lips, and heart palpitations.

D. An unmarried teenager is pregnant.

10. Who did Mr. Clove notify FIRST? 10.____

    A. Mrs. Norma Harris   B. Dr. Samuel Johnson

    C. Mr. Wallace   D. Mrs. Ross

11. The conversation between which two individuals is being traced? 11.____

    A. Mrs. Norma Harris and the 16-year-old teenager

    B. The Telephone Technician and Telephone Company Supervisor

    C. Dr. Johnson and the 16-year-old teenager

    D. The dispatcher and the Hospital Social Worker

Question 12.

DIRECTIONS: Question 12 is to be answered SOLELY on the basis of the following information.

On the Police Communications Technician's screen, the following incidents appear which were called in at the same time by three different callers:

    I. A fight is occurring at 265 Hall Street between Myrtle and Willoughby Ave. The fight started in Apartment 3C, and the two men are now fighting in the street.

    II. A fight took place between a security guard and a suspected shoplifter in a store at Hall St. and Willoughby Ave. The security guard is holding the suspect in the security office.

    III. A fight is occurring between two white males on the street near the corner of Hall Street and Myrtle Ave. One of the males has a baseball bat.

12. Which of the above should a Police Communications Technician MOST likely consider as the same incident? 12.____

    A. I and II   B. II and III

    C. I and III   D. I, II, and III

Questions 13-15.

DIRECTIONS: Questions 13 through 15 are to be answered SOLELY on the basis of the following passage.

Police Communications Technician Flood receives a call from Mr. Michael Watkins, Program Director for *Meals on Wheels,* a program that delivers food to elderly people who cannot leave their home. Mr. Watkins states he received a call from Rochelle Berger, whose elderly aunt, Estelle Sims, is a client of his. Rochelle Berger informed Mr. Watkins that she has just received a call from her aunt's neighbor, Sally Bowles, who told her that her aunt has not eaten in several days and is in need of medical attention.

After questioning Mr. Watkins, Dispatcher Flood is informed that Estelle Sims lives at 300 79th Street in Apartment 6K, and her telephone number is 686-4527; Sally Bowles lives in Apartment 6H, and her telephone number is 678-2456. Mr. Watkins further advises that if there is difficulty getting into Estelle Sims' apartment, to ring Sally Bowies' bell and she will let you in. Mr. Watkins gives his phone number as 776-0451, and Rochelle Berger's phone number is 291-7287. Dispatcher Flood advises Mr. Watkins that the appropriate medical assistance will be sent.

13. Who did Sally Bowles notify that her neighbor needed medical attention?   13.__

    A. Dispatcher Flood   B. Michael Watkins
    C. Rochelle Berger   D. Estelle Sims

14. If the responding medical personnel are unable to get into Apartment 6K, they should   14.__
speak to

    A. Rochelle Berger   B. Sally Bowles
    C. Dispatcher Flood   D. Michael Watkins

15. Whose telephone number is 686-4527?   15.__

    A. Michael Watkins   B. Estelle Sims
    C. Sally Bowles   D. Rochelle Berger

16. Police Communications Technicians often receive calls regarding incidents where a   16.__
response from the Fire Department may be necessary.
In which one of the following situations would a request from the dispatcher for the Fire
Department to respond be MOST critical?
A(n)

    A. fire hydrant has been opened by children on a hot August afternoon
    B. abandoned auto is parked in front of a fire hydrant
    C. neighbor's cat has climbed up a tree and is stuck
    D. excited woman smells smoke coming from the floor below

Question 17.

DIRECTIONS: Question 17 is to be answered SOLELY on the basis of the following information.

When a patrol car confirms that a murder has taken place, the Police Communications
Technician should notify the following people in the order given:
     I. Patrol Sergeant
    II. Dispatching Supervisor
    III. Operations Unit
    IV. Crime Scene Unit
    V. Precinct Detective Unit
    VI. Duty Captain

17. Police Communications Technician Rodger assigns a patrol car to investigate a man who   17.__
was shot and killed. The patrol car arrives on the scene and confirms that a murder has
taken place. The Patrol Sergeant hears what has happened on his police radio and
informs Dispatcher Rodger that he is going to respond to the scene. The Dispatching
Supervisor walks over to Dispatcher Rodger and is informed of the situation.
Who should Dispatcher Rodger notify NEXT?

    A. Operations Unit   B. Patrol Sergeant
    C. Precinct Detective Unit   D. Crime Scene Unit

18. Police Communications Technician Peterson receives a call from a woman inside the   18.____
subway station reporting that her purse has just been snatched. Dispatcher Peterson
obtained the following information relating to the crime:

Place of Occurrence: E. 42nd Street and Times Square
Time of Occurrence: 5:00 P.M.
Crime: Purse Snatched
Victim: Thelma Johnson

Description of Suspect: Black, female, brown hair, blue jeans, red T-shirt
Dispatcher Peterson is about to relay the information to the Transit Authority Police
Dispatcher.

Which one of the following expresses the above information MOST clearly and accurately?

    A.   At 5:00 P.M., a brown-haired Black woman snatched a purse inside the subway
station at E. 42nd Street and Times Square belonging to Thelma Johnson. She
was wearing blue jeans and a red T-shirt.
    B.   A purse was snatched from Thelma Johnson by a woman with brown hair in the
subway station at 5:00 P.M. A Black female was wearing blue jeans and a red T-
shirt at E. 42nd Street and Times Square.
    C.   At 5:00 P.M., Thelma Johnson's purse was snatched inside the subway station at
E. 42nd Street and Times Square. The suspect is a Black female with brown hair
who is wearing blue jeans and a red T-shirt.
    D.   Thelma Johnson reported at 5:00 P.M. her purse was snatched. In the subway sta-
tion at E. 42nd Street and Times Square, a Black female with brown hair was wearing blue jeans and a red T-shirt.

19. Police Communications Technician Hopkins receives a call of an assault and obtains the   19.____
following information concerning the incident:

Place of Occurrence: Times Square
Time of Occurrence: 3:15 A.M.
Victim: Peter Polk
Victim's Address: 50 E. 60 Street
Suspect: Male, Hispanic, 5'6", 140 lbs., dressed in black
Injury: Broken nose
Action Taken: Victim transported to St. Luke's Hospital

Dispatcher Hopkins is about to enter the job into the computer system.

Which one of the following expresses the above information MOST clearly and accurately?

    A.   At 3:15 A.M., Peter Polk was assaulted in Times Square by a Hispanic male, 5'6",
140 lbs., dressed in black, suffering a broken nose. Mr. Polk lives at 50 E. 69 Street
and was transported to St. Luke's Hospital.
    B.   At 3:15 A.M., Peter Polk was assaulted in Times Square by a Hispanic male, 5'6",
140 lbs., dressed in black, who lives at 50 E. 69 Street. Mr. Polk suffered a broken
nose and was transported to St. Luke's Hospital.
    C.   Peter Polk, who lives at 50 E. 69 Street, was assaulted at 3:15 A.M. in Times
Square by a Hispanic male, 5'6", 140 lbs., dressed in black. Mr. Polk suffered a
broken nose and was transported to St. Luke's Hospital.
    D.   Living at 50 E. 69 Street, Mr. Polk suffered a broken nose and was transported to
St. Luke's Hospital. At 3:15 A.M., Mr. Polk was assaulted by a Hispanic male, 5'6",
140 lbs., who was dressed in black.

20. A Police Communications Technician is required to determine which situations called in   20.__
to 911 require police assistance and which calls require non-emergency assistance.
Which one of the following calls should a dispatcher MOST likely refer to non-emergency assistance?

    A. Mr. Moss threatens the owner of Deluxe Deli with bodily harm for giving him incor-
rect change of twenty dollars.
    B. The manager refuses to take back Mrs. Thompson's defective toaster because she
doesn't have a receipt. Mrs. Thompson leaves the store.
    C. Mrs. Frank is having a violent argument with the manager of Donna's Dress Shop
because he is refusing to exchange a dress she recently purchased.
    D. The manager of Metro Supermarket refuses to take back a stale loaf of bread, so
the consumer punches him in the face.

_____

KEY (CORRECT ANSWERS)

1.	C	11.	C
2.	B	12.	C
3.	C	13.	C
4.	B	14.	B
5.	D	15.	B
6.	C	16.	D
7.	B	17.	A
8.	A	18.	C
9.	A	19.	C
10.	D	20.	B

_____

EXAMINATION SECTION
TEST 1

DIRECTIONS: Each question or incomplete statement is followed by several suggested answers or completions. Select the one that BEST answers the question or completes the statement. *PRINT THE LETTER OF THE CORRECT ANSWER IN THE SPACE AT THE RIGHT.*

1. Police Communications Technicians Clay and Robinson are told by their supervisor that they would have to share the computer terminal on Position 77 in the overflow because the terminal at Position 78 has been removed for repair. Dispatcher Clay signs into the terminal using her tax number, 505873. A few minutes later, Dispatcher Robinson tries to sign in with her tax number, 555873, and her attempt is rejected.
    As her supervisor, you should instruct Dispatcher Robinson that the PROPER format to use is _____/555873/to (ENTER)

    A. BSIA   B. BSIP   C. BSIO   D. BSIB

1.____

2. On January 2, 2009, Police Communications Dispatcher Quinones receives a call on 911 from a Mrs. Turnbaum. She states that she and her husband were fighting, and her husband struck her across the face. Dispatcher Quinones asks Mrs. Turnbaum if she is injured and whether her husband is still there. Mrs. Turnbaum replies in the negative to both questions. Dispatcher Quinones asks you, the supervisor, how to handle this call.
    You should direct Dispatcher Quinones to

    A. enter a 10-24Q1
    B. enter a 10-52D1
    C. refer the caller to Family Court
    D. refer the caller to her local precinct

2.____

3. Police Communications Operator Lucas, assigned to 911 in Brooklyn, receives a call from a Mrs. Spano, who lives at 1205 Elm Avenue in the 70th Precinct. She states that she called twice before to report that her apartment was burglarized. She says that no police have shown up yet. Dispatcher Lucas does an Incident Query of the location. He finds that the job was previously entered in 911 and then displays it on his screen. He sees that 70SP10 is assigned to the job. Dispatcher Lucas then notifies you that he has received a third call on this incident.
    As the supervisor, you should instruct Dispatcher Lucas to enter the job as additional information indicating that the caller was referred to the precinct, that the supervisor was notified, and then have Dispatcher Lucas

    A. route the job R
    B. route the job Z
    C. route the job D
    D. enter the job with no routing

3.____

4. Police Communications Technician Sands receives a call from an ABC Alarm Company operator stating that they have an alarm of a hold-up or burglary in progress at Met's Jewelry Store at 1259 Broadway in Manhattan. The operator then states that a phone call she made to the Met's Jewelry Store was answered by someone who did not properly identify himself. Dispatcher Sands is unsure of what action to take and asks Supervising Police Communications Technician Rain for assistance.

4.____

Supervisor Rain should instruct Dispatcher Sands to enter the job as a

    A. 10-11C4 code with all pertinent information
    B. 10-10P1 for prowler on the premises
    C. 10-31C code with all pertinent information
    D. 10-68Q2 to meet alarm company personnel to check the premises

5. While you are working as a Supervising Dispatcher, one of your operators receives a call   5.__
from a grocery store manager who states that he was held up *five minutes in the past* by
two male Hispanics who took all the cash from his register and fled in a green auto that
headed south on Broadway. Your operator quickly inputs a 10-30C and hotlines the job
to the dispatcher concerned.
As the supervisor, you should instruct the operator to change the code to a

    A. 10-20C   B. 10-20Q1   C. 10-30Q1   D. 10-30Q2

6. As the Supervising Police Communications Technician, you ask Police Communications   6.__
Technician Glass to prepare a list of screenable jobs that have been entered into 911 in
the borough of Brooklyn in the last half hour.
The following is a list of jobs that Dispatcher Glass has before her:
A(n)

    1. auto accident involving property damage
    2. dead horse in the street
    3. tree down on the sidewalk
    4. unoccupied auto that might be stolen
    5. female who has found a wallet
    6. request to assist a female in serving a summons

Dispatcher Glass is not sure which of the above jobs is screenable.
Which of these incidents should you have Dispatcher Glass include in the screenable
list?

    A. 1, 2, 4, and 5, but not 3 and 6
    B. 1, 3, 4, and 6, but not 2 and 5
    C. 1, 3, 5, and 6, but not 2 and 4
    D. 2, 3, 4, and 6, but not 1 and 5

7. Police Communications Dispatcher Howard, assigned to Position 38 on Brooklyn Dis-   7.__
patch, receives a call from a Mr. Green, Chief of Security for the Starlight Security Company. Mr. Green states that one of his uniformed guards is holding five males on a
charge of shoplifting. He asks that a unit respond at once since their holding cell can
accommodate only two persons.
As the Supervising Dispatcher assigned to Brooklyn, you should instruct Dispatcher
Howard to input the job as follows:

    A. IE/68Q1/SECURITY HOLDING 5*
    B. IE/32Q1/SECURITY HOLDING 5*
    C. IE/12U1/SECURITY HOLDING 5*
    D. IE/68Q1/1085* NO EMERGENCY, SECURITY HOLDING 5

8. Police Communications Operator Street, assigned to Brooklyn Dispatching, receives a   8.__
call on 911 from a male stating that his apartment is being flooded by a leak that is com
ing from the vacant apartment above him. He insists that the police come to his home to
correct the condition. Dispatcher Street asks you, the supervisor, how to handle this call.

You should instruct Dispatcher Street to

    A.   refer the caller to his local precinct
    B.   enter a 10-65S
    C.   enter a 10-68Q1
    D.   refer the caller to his superintendent

9.   A male who does not wish to reveal his name calls a dispatcher to report that his landlord   9._____
at 16 Hollywood River Drive, Apartment 1H, appears to be selling drugs and guns. He
tells the dispatcher that this usually occurs every night after 9 P.M. The dispatcher inputs
the job into Sprint as a Code 10-Y3.
Upon reviewing this job, you, as the supervisor, should

    A.   ensure that a patrol car is sent
    B.   call the Narcotics Unit and Precinct Detective Unit by landline and have them dis-
        patch units
    C.   tell the operator to route the job to Citywide and the Organized Crime Control
        Bureau
    D.   tell the operator to change the code to a 10-69S defer to be referred to the Orga-
        nized Crime Control Bureau

10.   Police Communications Tech. Proctor receives a call on 911 from PAA Gamble of the   10._____
71st Precinct in Brooklyn. PAA Gamble is the telephone switchboard operator for the stationhouse. She states that she just received a call from an unknown male who stated that
at 250 Fenimore Street, Apartment 3E, there is a male named Jack Daniels who is selling cocaine. The caller stated that when a buyer stands at the door and whistles, Daniels
opens it and the deal is made. Dispatcher Proctor asks PAA Gamble to hold on. She
summons you, the supervisor, for assistance on how to handle this call.
You should instruct Dispatcher Proctor to

    A.   enter a 10-69S defer for the Organized Crime Control Bureau
    B.   enter a 10-10Y3 man selling drugs
    C.   advise PAA Gamble to call her Precinct Detective Unit directly
    D.   advise PAA Gamble to call the Organized Crime Control Bureau directly

Questions 11-16.

DIRECTIONS: Questions 11 through 16 are to be answered SOLELY on the basis of the fol-
                lowing information.
       Supervising Police Communications Technician Noel is assigned to monitor Police Com-
munications Technician Casey on dispatching. The following calls were received and handled
by Dispatcher Casey during the monitoring period:

Call 1.   Operator 512 from the AZU Alarm Company called to report a burglary alarm for the
roof and rear door at the Zero Savings Bank at 1 Park Row in Manhattan. Dispatcher Casey
asked the caller to hold on, hotlined the job as an 11B4, and then returned to Operator 512. Dispatcher Casey was advised that the alarm company was responding, and that AZU Alarm Company's phone number is 999-8888. Dispatcher Casey entered the job as follows:
    IQ/7/1 PARK ROW (ENTER)
    IE/11B4/ZERO SAVINGS BANK* BURGLARY ALARM FOR REAR DOOR - AZU
      ALARM CO. - RESPONDING - OPR. 512 - CB9998888 - HOTLINED -
      OPR. 52-5 (ENTER)

IF/OPR. 512/9998888 (ENTER)

Call 2.   Nurse Manning from New York Hospital, located at East 68th Street and York Avenue in Manhattan, called to report an aided case in the emergency room. Mrs. Carmen, who came for emergency treatment after being beaten by her neighbor during a dispute, wanted to see the police to file a report. Dispatcher Casey asked for the phone number in the hospital emergency room. The phone number was given as 999-8989, and Dispatcher Casey told the nurse that the police would respond as soon as possible. Dispatcher Casey entered the job as follows:
        IQ/7/NY HOSPITAL MD (ENTER)
        IE/68Q1/AIDED CASE* SFC CARMEN IN THE EMERGENCY ROOM - REGARDING
            A PAST ASSAULT THAT OCCURRED AT HER RESIDENCE - OPR. 52-5=P2
            (ENTER)
        IF/MANNING/9998989 (ENTER)

Call 3.   Security Guard Joseph called to report an explosion and fire in the lobby of the Empire State Building in Manhattan. Dispatcher Casey immediately connected the caller with the Fire Department. After giving the necessary information to Fire Department Operator 32, the caller stated that there were at least three people injured at the location. Dispatcher Casey connected the caller to Ambulance Receiving Operator 117, exchanged information, hotlined the job, and notified Supervisor Noel of the incident. Dispatcher Casey entered the job as follows:
        IQ/7/EMPIRE STATE BUILDING UNK (ENTER)
        IE/33/EXPLOSION AND FIRE* IN THE LOBBY - SECURITY GUARD JOSEPH
            STATES THAT AT LEAST THREE PEOPLE HAVE BEEN INJURED - FD 32
            NTFD - RO 117 NTFD - HOTLINED - SPCT NOEL NTFD - OPR. 52-5=P9
            (ENTER)
        IF/JOSEPH/ (ENTER)

Call 4.   Ms. Topps called 911 to report that two teenagers were drag racing in an empty parking lot. Ms. Topps told Dispatcher Casey that it was a dangerous condition and she wanted the police to respond. Dispatcher Casey told the caller that this was not a 911 emergency and referred Ms. Topps to the local precinct. Ms. Topps said she had the phone number and hung up.

Call 5.   Mr. Janzen called to report that his shoe store, located at Hyland Boulevard and Robinson Avenue in Staten Island, was just robbed about six minutes in the past. Mr. Janzen said he was robbed by two males, white, both dressed in blue; they each had a gun. He did not see which way they ran and could give no further description. Dispatcher Casey asked the caller for his phone number. Mr. Janzen gave 777-9999, and Dispatcher Casey told him that the police would respond as soon as possible. Dispatcher Casey entered the job as follows:
        IQ/4/HYLAND BLVD - ROBINSON AVE (ENTER)
        IE/20Q1/SHOE STORE* SMC JANZEN - STATES SIX MINUTES IN PAST STORE
            WAS HELD UP BY TWO MALES - DRESSED IN BLUE - UNKNOWN DIRECTION
            OF FLIGHT - OPR. 52-5 (ENTER)
        IF/JANZEN/7779999 (ENTER)

Call 6.   Mr. Peters called 911 to report that, in the parking lot of Jacobi Hospital in the Bronx, an auto's horn has been blasting for the past ten minutes. The owner of the car was unable to shut off the horn. Dispatcher Casey told the caller that this was not a 911 emergency, and he could call the 43rd Precinct at 822-5611.

Call 7.   Mrs. Arnold called 911 and stated that she called 15 minutes ago to request that the police respond to a dispute on the street in front of 2011 Broadway. She stated that the police had not responded yet, and now one of the males has been stabbed. Dispatcher Casey found that a 10-52D2 was entered in the system at the location, and a patrol car had been dispatched. Dispatcher Casey hotlined the new information to the dispatcher and then connected the caller to Emergency Medical Service Operator 320. The caller could give no descriptions. Dispatcher Casey notified Supervisor Noel of the incident and entered the information as follows:

    II/34K2* ANOTHER CALL - CALLER STATES ONE OF THE MALES HAS BEEN
       STABBED - RO 320 NTFD - NO DESCRIPTIONS AVAILABLE - SPCT NOEL
       NTFD - HOTLINED _ OPR. 52-5=DNSP3A:SA320-HOSP-HOSQ (ENTER)

Call 8.   Dispatcher Casey received a job via 911 from Telephone Switchboard Operator PAA Thomas of the 90th Precinct, advising of an anonymous call reporting gas fumes at 193 Grand Street, Brooklyn, on the 4th floor. Dispatcher Casey connected the caller to the Fire Department and entered the job as follows:

    IQ/6/193 GRAND ST (ENTER)
    IE/65S/GAS FUMES* FD 161 NTFD - AUTH 90 TS PAA THOMAS -
       RECEIVED FROM ANON CALLER - OPR. 52-5 (ENTER)
    IF/PAA THOMAS/6834219 (ENTER)

The following questions are based on the monitoring of Dispatcher Casey by Supervisor Noel.

11.   Supervisor Noel should identify errors in coding for which of the following calls?   11._____

    A. 1, 2, 7   B. 1, 3, 8   C. 2, 3, 5   D. 2, 5, 8

12.   For which of the following calls were there errors or omissions in routing?   12._____

    A. 1, 3, 5   B. 1, 3, 7   C. 1, 5, 7   D. 3, 5, 7

13.   Which of the following calls were handled properly according to 911 screening procedures?   13._____

    A. 1, 4, 6   B. 1, 4, 8   C. 1, 6, 8   D. 4, 6, 8

14.   During which of the following calls did Dispatcher Casey fail to enter pertinent data given   14._____
by the caller?

    A. 1, 5, 8   B. 1, 3, 7   C. 2, 3, 5   D. 2, 7, 8

15.   During which of the following calls did Dispatcher Casey fail to follow established hotline   15._____
procedure?

    A. 3   B. 5   C. 7   D. 8

16.   For which one of the following calls did Dispatcher Casey fail to walk the job into the dispatcher as required by procedure?   16._____

    A. 1   B. 3   C. 5   D. 7

17.   On June 6, the Sprint System suddenly ceases operation. You, as the supervisor,   17._____
immediately assign Police Communications Dispatcher Black as the scanner for the borough of the Bronx.
As a scanner, the FIRST task that Dispatcher Black should do is

A. check the address file for the incident location
B. deliver slips to the radio dispatchers and other necessary locations
C. return rejected slips to operators for completion or correction
D. walk behind operators and pick up completed slips

18. Police Communications Operator Lincoln, assigned to Brooklyn Dispatching, receives a call from a Mrs. Gomez who states that she and her husband just had a violent argument. She also states that her husband was discharged from a psychiatric hospital last week and is threatening to kill himself. Mrs. Gomez further states that her husband stormed out of the house five minutes ago, and at this time she is unsure of his present location. She wants the police and an ambulance to come to her house to find her husband and take him back to the hospital. Dispatcher Lincoln is unsure of how to handle this call, and he asks you, his supervisor, for assistance.
You should direct him to

    18.____

A. refer the caller to her local precinct
B. tell the caller to call 911 as soon as her husband returns
C. enter a job as a 10-54E1
D. enter a job as a 10-68Q1

19. Police Communications Dispatcher Baker, assigned to overflow Position 85, receives a call from Police Officer Marin of the 63rd Precinct. Officer Marin advises Dispatcher Baker that the precinct has just received another call regarding an alarm at 1183 Avenue He further states that he called in the alarm about an hour ago and has not yet heard the job go over the air. Dispatcher Baker enters an incident query message into Sprint and sees that a job was entered but was not dispatched because the location, 1183 Avenue H, has been designated as *chronic*. Dispatcher Baker tells Officer Marin that a car will not be sent because it is a chronic location. You, as the supervisor, overhear Dispatcher Baker's final remark to Officer Marin.
You should instruct her to

    19.____

A. input a new job as a 10-11
B. input a new job as a 10-68
C. refer the job back to the precinct
D. refer Officer Marin to the FATN section

20. Police Communications Operator Milbrook calls you, her supervisor, to ask for assistance in handling a caller who is reporting a flooding condition. You advise Dispatcher Milbrook that you would not order a job input unless *possible aggravating circumstances* existed.
Which one of the following is NOT an example of a *possible aggravating circumstance?*

    20.____

A. Water pressure emergency
B. Local flooding caused by a broken hydrant
C. Flooding the ground floor of a residence
D. Flooding of an intersection

21. Police Communications Technician Healy receives a call via 911 from a female who resides at a housing project located at 2340 Nostrand Avenue, Apartment 6E. The caller is angry about what she states is a dangerous condition. She reports that there is garbage strewn all over the exit steps and that someone may fall. Dispatcher Healy is not sure what to do in this situation and asks you, the supervisor, for assistance.
You should instruct Dispatcher Healy to

    A. input a 10-10Y3 *dangerous condition*
    B. input a 10-68Q1
    C. take the information and refer it to the Housing Authority Police Department
    D. refer the caller to the Environmental Protection Agency

21.____

22. Police Communications Technician Zenith tells you, the overflow supervisor, that he received a call from an hysterical male who said he was traveling southbound on the Clearview Expressway in Queens. He said he was driving to the hospital with his pregnant wife, who is in labor, but his car broke down on the highway. The caller didn't know the name of the nearest exit, but he saw a mile marker listing the numbers 2076 on the bottom and 295I on the top of the marker. Dispatcher Zenith could not get the location into the system and asks you how he should enter this information.
You should instruct him to use which one of the following formats?
IQ/5/

    A. 295I RTE S 2076   B. RTE S 295I
    C. RTE 2076I 295S   D. 2076 295I RTE S

22.____

23. On January 9, all operators are given a memo detailing a planned visit by President Bush to Manhattan during your tour of duty. At approximately 0930 hours this date, Police Communications Technician Jones, an operator assigned to the borough of Queens, receives a call from Captain Barnes of the 113th Precinct. He requests information regarding the planned time that the Presidential motorcade will pass through his precinct as indicated in the memo. Recalling the memo, Operator Jones provides him with the information requested. Operator Jones then informs you, his supervisor, that he was able to provide Captain Barnes with the requested information. As his supervisor, you should instruct Operator Jones that the CORRECT procedure is to

    A. tell the caller that you cannot provide him with the information requested
    B. input a 10-69S DEFER-INFO ONLY* - TIME NOTING PLANNED VISIT
    C. notify the supervisor who will interview the caller providing necessary details of the memo
    D. input a 10-69S DEFER - INFO ONLY* = P9N

23.____

24. Police Communications Technician Roberts receives a call from Mr. Rich requesting a Med-Evac Helicopter for an emergency transport of blood from New York Hospital in Manhattan to Smithtown Hospital in Long Island. Dispatcher Roberts is unfamiliar with the procedure for Med-Evac and requests assistance.
As a supervisor, you should direct Dispatcher Roberts to

    A. enter a 10Y3 and hotline to Citywide for the dispatching of a helicopter
    B. connect the caller to the Emergency Medical Service and enter a 10Y3 with routing for Citywide and Notifications

24.____

C. tell the caller that Med-Evac can only be requested by a member of the service
D. tell the caller to speak to the Emergency Medical Service via their direct phone number to request Med-Evac

25. Police Communications Technician Grow, an operator, receives a call from Transit Police Officer Brown. Officer Brown states that there is an elderly female who is having difficulty breathing at the token booth at the West 50th Street Station on the IND line. Officer Brown tells Operator Grow that the transit officer on the scene wants an ambulance. However, Officer Brown cannot stay on the telephone to speak with the Emergency Medical Service because he must respond to another emergency. Operator Grow attempts to enter the location and receives an error message.
Operator Grow asked for the supervisor's assistance and was instructed according to procedures to use which one of the following formats? IQ/7/_____ and process the job as a _____.

A. W 50 ST TRAN (ENTER); 10-55
B. 50 ST IND TRAN (ENTER); 10-54S1
C. IND W 50 ST TRAN (ENTER); 10-54S1
D. IND 50 ST TRAN (ENTER); 10-55

25.__

———

KEY (CORRECT ANSWERS)

1. D		11. C	
2. D		12. B	
3. B		13. B	
4. A		14. A	
5. A		15. A	
6. B		16. D	
7. C		17. A	
8. D		18. D	
9. D		19. A	
10. C		20. B	

21. D
22. D
23. A
24. D
25. B

———

TEST 2

DIRECTIONS: Each question or incomplete statement is followed by several suggested answers or completions. Select the one that BEST answers the question or completes the Statement. *PRINT THE LETTER OF THE CORRECT ANSWER IN THE SPACE AT THE RIGHT.*

Questions 1-5.

DIRECTIONS: Questions 1 through 5 are to be answered on the basis of the following information.

Call #1
0305 Hours

OPERATOR	Police Operator 712, where is the emergency?
CALLER	I'm Mrs. Piermont and I need the police.
OPERATOR	Where do you need the police?
CALLER	I live at 1436 Broadway, Apartment 3B, and I'm having an argument with my husband.
OPERATOR	May I have your phone number?
CALLER	It's 3933939. Send the police now.
OPERATOR	The police will be there as soon as possible.

-- caller hangs up --

The operator entered the job as follows:

IQ/7/1436 BROADWAY (ENTER)
IE/52D1/APT 3D* SFC PIERMONT - STATES SHE IS HAVING A
 DISPUTE WITH HER HUSBAND - OPR. 712-2 (ENTER)
IF/PIERMONT/3933939 (ENTER)

Call #2
0315 Hours

OPERATOR	Police Operator 010, where is the emergency?
CALLER	Hello, my name is Mrs. Conway. I live at 1436 Broadway in Apartment 4B on the 4th floor. There's a fight going on in the apartment below. I hear a woman screaming. The voice sounds like that nice Mrs. Piermont with the two kids. Would you please send someone over to see what's going on?
OPERATOR	That's 1436 Broadway, Apartment 4B as in *Boy*.
CALLER	Yes.
OPERATOR	What's your telephone number?
CALLER	It's 3934646.
OPERATOR	O.K. Madam, the police will be there as soon as possible.
CALLER	Thank you.

-- caller hangs up --

The operator queries the system, finds the previous entry, and sees that no patrol car has been dispatched. She then proceeds to enter an additional information message as follows:

IQ/7/1436 BROADWAY (ENTER)
IA* ANOTHER CALL - DISPUTE IN APARTMENT BELOW 4B.
 FEMALE STATES SHE HEARS SCREAMING - OPR. 010-12 (ENTER)
IF/CONWAY/3934646 (ENTER)

Call #3
0327 Hours

OPERATOR	Police Operator 219, where is the emergency?
CALLER	Help me! My mommy has been stabbed!
OPERATOR	How old are you?
CALLER	What?
OPERATOR	I said, how old are you?
CALLER	I'm nine.
OPERATOR	Put someone else on the phone!
CALLER	Just my sister and I are here.
OPERATOR	How old is your sister.
CALLER	She's six years old.
OPERATOR	Okay, what is the address?
CALLER	1436 Broadway, on the third floor.
OPERATOR	We have the job already. That's between 37th and 38th Streets, right?
CALLER	No. I live near Eastern Parkway.
OPERATOR	You live in Brooklyn?
CALLER	Yes!
OPERATOR	Is your name Piermont?
CALLER	Yes!
OPERATOR	The police will be there as soon as possible.

The operator entered the job as follows:
IC/6/1436 BROADWAY* ANOTHER CALL RECEIVED - CHILD CALLER STATES MOTHER HAS BEEN STABBED - ON THE THIRD FLOOR -NO FURTHER INFORMATION OPR. 219-85 (ENTER)

Call #4
0332 Hours

OPERATOR	Police Operator 956, where is the emergency?
CALLER	I called before. I told you there was a violent argument downstairs. The woman has been stabbed; there's blood all over the place.
OPERATOR	Calm down lady! What's your address?
CALLER	1436 Broadway, Apartment 4B; but the woman stabbed is in Apartment 3B.
OPERATOR	Is that 3*B* as in *Boy* or 3*D* as in *David?*
CALLER	Hurry up! I gave you all this information before. The apartment is 3B as in *Boy.*
OPERATOR	OK Ma'am. I see the job in the system. The police are on the way. What is your name and phone number?
CALLER	Please hurry! She could be dying. My name is Conway, and my phone number is 393-4646.
OPERATOR	Alright! Hold on for the Emergency Medical Service.
	At this point, the operator attempts to notify the Ambulance Receiving Operator. After six rings, they fail to answer. The operator subsequently tells the caller that she will process the call and that the police will be there as soon as possible. The operator then enters the message as follows:
	II/34K1* APT. 3B - ANOTHER CALL - CALLER STATES FEMALE STABBED - APARTMENT CORRECTION - UNABLE TO NOTIFY ARO. CALL BACK NUMBER - 393-4646 SPCT BRUCCI NOTIFIED OPR. 956-43 = NP3DAS:HOSP-HOSQ

Supervising Police Communications Technician Brucci now has the task of reinstructing the operator or operators concerned on any or all of the four jobs entered into 911. On these calls, the various operators neglected to follow several procedures or guidelines established by the Police Department.

1. During which of the following calls did the operator fail to verify the address?   1.____

   A. 1, 2, 3   B. 1, 2, 4   C. 1, 3, 4   D. 2, 3, 4

2. During which of the following calls did the operator fail to enter the name and callback   2.____
   correctly?

   A. 2   B. 3   C. 1, 2   D. 2, 4

3. During which of the following calls did the operator fail to properly handle the callback?   3.____

   A. 2   B. 3   C. 2, 3   D. 3, 4

4. Which of the following calls were NOT properly routed?   4.____

   A. 2, 3   B. 1, 3   C. 2, 4   D. 3, 4

5. For which of the following calls was the operator required to walk the job into the dis-   5.____
   patcher?

   A. 2   B. 4   C. 1, 3   D. 2, 4

6. Upon being notified of a report received by Police Communications Technician Gray   6.____
   regarding an AWOL (absent without leave) member of the armed forces, the supervisor
   should instruct the 911 operator to take which of the following actions?
   1. Refer the caller to the Military Police of the branch of the service concerned.
   2. Input a Sprint job with full details so that the first available patrol car can be sent.
   3. Refer the caller to the local precinct.
   4. Input a 69 Defer with full details and route for the Operations Unit.
   The CORRECT answer is:

   A. 1 or 4   B. 2 or 3   C. 1 or 2   D. 3 or 4

7. While on duty as an operator in the borough of Manhattan, Police Communications Tech-   7.____
   nician Brown receives a call from a concerned citizen regarding a patrol car double-
   parked in front of an abandoned building. The caller states that two police officers are
   apparently transferring property from the trunk of a car into their patrol car. The caller
   also states that the officers' behavior is somewhat suspicious. While processing this call,
   Operator Brown calls for your assistance.
   As the supervisor, your FIRST task is to

   A. instruct the operator to input a 10-69 defer, detailing the incident
   B. obtain details from Operator Brown and report the complaint in writing
   C. interview the caller to obtain details of the incident
   D. instruct the operator to tell the caller to contact the Civilian Complaint Review
       Board

8. Police Communications Technician Jones, an operator, receives a call from a merchant describing a series of incidents in which a male, who identifies himself as a police officer, routinely collects money from merchants for what he describes as a local police fund to help support a neighborhood youth basketball team. Operator Jones does not know how to handle this call, so he asks you, the supervisor, for assistance.
As the supervisor, you should instruct Operator Jones

    A.   to enter a 10-68 to obtain further details
    B.   to tell the merchant to call his local precinct
    C.   that you will interview the caller and advise the patrol supervisor over landline to investigate
    D.   that you will interview the caller and notify the Internal Affairs Division

8.___

9. On May 12, a memo is issued and distributed to all operators concerning reoccurring incidents of youths spraypainting graffiti on subway cars. The memo essentially restates the procedure that should be followed in such cases. Police Communications Technician Benson, a newly assigned operator, receives a call regarding youths in the subway with spray cans vandalizing a station. Operator Benson asks you, the supervisor, what she should do regarding this call.
You should instruct Operator Benson that her FIRST action should be to

    A.   connect the caller to the Transit Authority Police Department via the add-on button
    B.   input a 10-39 incident code into Sprint, hotlining the incident
    C.   input a 10-50G2 incident code into Sprint, hotlining the incident
    D.   give the caller the Transit Authority Police Department's telephone number

9.___

10. Police Communications Technician Garber, a Manhattan operator, receives a call from a civil service employee who works in the emergency room at Elmhurst General Hospital. The caller states that while he was on duty a couple of hours ago, two police officers brought in a female in labor. As the nurses were preparing the female for the delivery room, the hospital clerk approached one of the officers and asked for identification of the female. The officer who was holding the female's coat and purse opened the purse to seek identification. He took out a wallet, which contained the female's drivers license. As the hospital clerk turned to leave, the caller saw the police officer take a large amount of money from the female's wallet. He gave several of the bills to the clerk and put the remainder of the money inside his holster. The caller does not wish to speak to a 911 supervisor, for fear of losing his job, but he feels it is his duty as a good citizen to report the incident. Operator Garber does not know how to handle this call and asks you, the Manhattan supervisor, for assistance.
You should instruct Operator Garber to

    A.   send a sergeant to Elmhurst General
    B.   give the caller the telephone number of the Civilian Complaint Review Board
    C.   insist that the caller speak to you, the supervisor
    D.   give the caller the special corruption number

10.___

11. Police Communications Dispatcher Reiner receives a call from a Mr. Nathan, who states that an ambulance had been sent to his friend's home but a problem arose. When the Emergency Medical Service crew arrived and learned that Mr. Nathan's friend was an AIDS patient, they refused to take him to the hospital. The ambulance crew told Mr. Nathan that they were not required to transport AIDS patients, but they would do so if they were given $25 each. Mr. Nathan refused to pay, and the ambulance crew left. Dis

11.___

patcher Reiner is unsure of the proper procedure to follow and asks you for assistance. As the supervisor, you should speak with Mr. Nathan and

    A. ensure that another ambulance is sent and then refer him to the Civilian Complaint Review Board

    B. connect him to the Emergency Medical Service Supervisor to handle the complaint regarding the ambulance crew

    C. ensure that another ambulance is sent, and then report the details to the Internal Affairs Division

    D. ensure that another ambulance is sent, and also send a patrol car to take the details of the incident

Questions 12-15.

DIRECTIONS: Questions 12 through 15 are to be answered SOLELY on the basis of the following information.

As a Supervising Dispatcher, you are required to review tapes of 10-13's and other serious jobs received by Operator 010, who was assigned to Position 58 from 1600 hours to 2000 hours on May 17.

Tape for Job #1 is as follows:

OPERATOR	Police Operator 010, where is the emergency?
CALLER	This is Police Officer Doyle from Transit. I need some help here. I was down on the southbound platform in the station on Parsons Boulevard and Hillside Avenue. There is a man on the tracks trying to catch a dog who fell from the platform. I jumped down to assist, but the dog's leg is stuck between the rails.
OPERATOR	Do you know the booth number, sir?
CALLER	Yes; 1 am at Booth 217, my badge number is 6006, and I am in uniform. I have already notified the Station Master to shut off the power, and the shut-off has been confirmed. I need the Police Department's Emergency Service Unit.
OPERATOR	Okay, we will get help there. (HOTLINE) In the 117 Precinct, A Sector, I have a 10-13 at Parsons Boulevard and Hillside Avenue. Officer going down on the subway tracks.
DISPATCHER	I got it. Put the job in, please.

> Entry for Job #1 is as follows:
> IQ/5/PARSONS BLVD - HILLSIDE AVE (ENTER)
> IE/13U1/P.O. ON TRACKS* P.O. ON TRACKS WITH A DOG -
> REQUEST ASSISTANCE - HOTLINED - OPR. 010-58 (ENTER)
> IF/DOYLE/ (ENTER)

Tape for Job #2 is as follows:

OPERATOR	Police Operator 010, where is the emergency?
CALLER	Hello, police. This is Mrs. McLina. My husband is having chest pains. He is a retired police Captain. I am at 5700 Broadway, Apartment 3F - 3rd Floor. My telephone number is 094-0606.
OPERATOR	Is he unconscious, madam?
CALLER	No, but he's clutching his chest.
OPERATOR	Does he have a cardiac history?

CALLER	Not that I know of.
OPERATOR	Well, loosen his clothing, begin cardiopulmonary resuscitation, and I will get a car rolling. Hold on - do not hang up. (HOTLINE) I have a 10-13, in the 27th Precinct, A Sector, 5700 Broadway. It is a retired cop having a heart attack.
DISPATCHER	Okay, put the job in.
OPERATOR	Madam, I am now connecting you to the ambulance service. CALLER I can't stay on the telephone any longer. I have to go to my husband.
	- caller hangs up -

Entry for Job #2 is as follows;
IQ/7/5700 BROADWAY (ENTER)
IE/13X1/HEART ATTACK* MC MCLINA - RETIRED CAPTAIN - APT 3F - 3FL
- HOTLINED - CALLER HUNG UP - UNABLE TO REACH RO - SUPERVI-
SOR ON ANOTHER LINE - OPR. 010-58 (ENTER)
IF/MCLINA/0940606 (ENTER)

Tape for Job #3 is as follows:

OPERATOR	Police Operator 010, where is the emergency?
CALLER	This is Police Officer Lonzo. I am off duty. I've just witnessed a break-in at 142-09 164th Street. It's a private house. I am calling from the phone booth on the corner in front of A1's Grocery Store. I am going after them.
OPERATOR	Wait a minute. Don't hang up. (HOTLINE) I have a 31 in progress in the 117th Precinct, B Sector, 142-09 164th Street. It was called in by an off-duty police officer who is going after them.
DISPATCHER	Okay, please enter the job.
OPERATOR	Police Officer, what are you wearing, and do you have any description on the perpetrators?
CALLER	I am wearing a...listen, they've spotted me.... They're firing shots at me.... I've been shot.... (phone disconnects).

Entry for Job #3 is as follows:
IQ/5/142-09 164 ST (ENTER)
IE/31R/OFF DUTY* P.O. STATED HE WAS GOING AFTER PERPETRATORS
- THEN HE SAID HE HAD BEEN SHOT - UNABLE TO REACH RO - HOT-
LINED - SUPV VALLEY NTFD OPR. 010-58=SWNP9 AS:HOSP-HOSQ
(ENTER)
IF/P.O. LONZO/(ENTER)

Tape for Job #4 is as follows:

OPERATOR	Police Operator 010, where is the emergency?
CALLER	This is Police Officer Thomas. I am a uniformed officer on duty. My partner and I are here at Hillside Avenue and 161st Street. We are being assaulted with bottles and rocks by a large crowd of people. Get us some help fast.
	- caller hangs up -
OPERATOR	(HOTLINE) In the 117th Precinct, G Sector, I have a 10-13 at Hillside Avenue and 161st Street. Two police officers are being assaulted by a large crowd with rocks and bottles.
DISPATCHER	That's Hillside and 161, in uniform?
OPERATOR	Yes.

DISPATCHER   Enter the job, please.

> Entry for Job #4 is as follows:
> IQ/5/HILLSIDE AVE - 161 ST (ENTER)
> IE/13U2/P.O. ASSAULTED* TWO OFFICERS UNDER ASSAULT WITH BOT-
> TLES AND ROCKS BY A LARGE CROWD - NFI - CALLER HUNG UP - HOT-
> LINED - SUPV VALLEY NTFD - OPR. 010-58 (ENTER)
> IF/THOMAS/(ENTER)

After listening to the tapes and reviewing the entries, you notice that the operator made several errors.

12. Which of the following jobs were coded improperly?   12.____

   A. 1, 2, 3   B. 1, 2, 4   C. 1, 3, 4   D. 2, 3, 4

13. For which of the following jobs did the operator fail to notify a supervisor or fail to include   13.____
   appropriate routing?

   A. 1, 2   B. 1, 4   C. 2, 3   D. 2, 4

14. For which of the following jobs was information excluded in the entry that should be con-   14.____
   sidered extremely important in processing the call?

   A. 1, 2   B. 1, 3   C. 2, 4   D. 3, 4

15. On which one of the following jobs did the operator fail to follow the proper ambulance   15.____
   procedure?

   A. 1   B. 2   C. 3   D. 4

16. Police Communications Technician Borne receives a call from a Mrs. Hiller, who states   16.____
   that her landlord threw her out of the apartment that she has been renting for the past
   year. The landlord told her it was because she had not paid rent for the past three
   months. The landlord, who did not present an Eviction Notice to Mrs. Hiller, put a new
   lock on the door, and she then called 911. Dispatcher Borne is not familiar with the procedure covering evictions and asked Supervising Dispatcher Washington, her supervisor,
   for assistance.
   Supervising Dispatcher Washington should direct the operator to

   A. refer the caller to Landlord-Tenant Court
   B. enter the job as a 39Q1
   C. refer the caller to her local precinct
   D. refer the caller to the Department of Building Complaints

17. Police Communications Technician James, an experienced operator, is aware of the   17.____
   department's Solo Unit Procedure, where one-officer units are assigned to respond to 38
   different code signals. He asks you, his supervisor, which of the following code signals
   are considered appropriate for one officer to handle.
   1. 10-24Q1
   2. 10-68Q1
   3. 10-11Q4
   4. 10-59T
   The CORRECT answer is:

   A. 1, 2   B. 1, 4   C. 2, 3   D. 3, 4

18. Supervising Dispatcher Carlson is instructing one of her new operators in the procedure to follow for screening jobs received from a Housing Authority Police Service Area. All of the following jobs are appropriate for 911 entry EXCEPT a

    A. request to see a complainant on found property
    B. request for a patrol car to respond for a bank deposit escort
    C. request for police response to a stuck occupied elevator
    D. report of youths throwing firecrackers into apartment windows

18.__

19. Police Communications Dispatcher Proper does not understand the procedure set forth in the 911 Guide regarding public morals incidents. Supervising Dispatcher Gibson gives a copy of the procedure to Dispatcher Proper and instructs her in detail in the handling of particular public morals incidents.
Based on 911 procedures, in which one of the following cases did the Dispatcher handle the incident PROPERLY? A caller stated that

    A. the Star Lite Bar on West 165th Street and Seventh Avenue is selling liquor to a minor seated at the bar - Dispatcher entered the job for a patrol car to be dispatched
    B. in a vacant apartment on the 1st floor at 706 West 46th Street two male whites are selling drugs to people lined up in the hall - Dispatcher entered a defer job for Organized Crime Control Bureau
    C. there is illegal gambling taking place in a private club at 922 West 12th Street in Manhattan - Dispatcher entered a job for a patrol car to be dispatched
    D. there is a female on the corner of West 57th Street and Thirteenth Avenue soliciting for prostitution, and she is there every day from 4:00 P.M. to 8:00 P.M. - Dispatcher entered a defer job for the Organized Crime Control Bureau

19.__

20. Police Communications Technician Rossi reports to you, her supervisor, that she is sure that another dispatcher is using drugs. She believes that the drugs are kept in his locker, although she has never actually seen the drugs.
As a supervisor, what is the FIRST action you should take?

    A. Request the name of the dispatcher and conduct a preliminary investigation.
    B. Tell Dispatcher Rossi to observe the dispatcher; and if she sees any drugs, she should report the incident to the Internal Affairs Division.
    C. Report the incident to the Internal Affairs Division.
    D. Request Dispatcher Rossi to prepare a written report and submit it to you as soon as possible.

20.__

21. As a newly appointed supervisor, you are assigned to the borough of Brooklyn to supervise dispatchers. Prior to the start of your tour, you are advised by the Platoon Commander to begin a Back-up Slip Operation at approximately 0830 hours. During your tour, you assign one dispatcher runner along with one scanner.
During a Back-up Slip Operation, it is the responsibility of the scanner to

    A. check the address file for the incident location
    B. assist the supervisor with slip operation recovery procedures
    C. deliver intact slips to radio dispatchers
    D. return rejected slips to operators for completion or correction

21.__

22. The 911 operator's information area is located at the bottom left side of the screen where symbols indicate whether or not a job can be entered into the system. Police Communications Technician Wellwater is prepared to enter a 911 job. However, instead of the correct symbols being visible, only the symbol X appears on the screen.
As the supervisor, you should instruct Dispatcher Wellwater to try to correct this condition by FIRST depressing the _____ button.

    A. enter   B. shift   C. display   D. reset

22.____

23. Supervising Dispatcher Simpson is called by Police Communications Technician Eli to ask her direction regarding a caller he is holding on the line. Dispatcher Eli tells Supervising Dispatcher Simpson that the call is from a male who is a resident of Ohio and wants to report his wife missing in New York. He states that his wife has been staying at the New York Hilton for the past two weeks so she could visit her sick mother at Roosevelt Hospital. He has called the hotel, and the clerk told him that his wife had not been seen, nor has she picked up her key in the past 24 hours, but her luggage is still in the room. The caller also states that his wife is in good physical and mental health.
Supervising Dispatcher Simpson should direct Dispatcher Eli to tell the caller

    A. to call the Ohio police to make the report
    B. that we will send a patrol car to investigate
    C. that we have no jurisdiction over his wife because she is in good physical and mental health
    D. that we will not take a report because the circumstances do not indicate involuntary disappearance

23.____

24. On a Monday morning, about 0835 hours, Police Communications Technician Franklin receives a call from a young female who is very upset. She states that a Transit Authority Police Officer had taken her wallet containing her student subway pass and refused to give it back. She states that she had just put out a cigarette and was about to enter through the gate after showing the token clerk her subway pass. She was then stopped by a Transit Authority Police Officer, who informed her that he was going to write up a violation for smoking in the subway. She also states that he was very abusive, took her wallet out of her hand, and refused to return it. Dispatcher Franklin notifies you, the supervisor, about the caller on the line.
You should direct Dispatcher Franklin

    A. to refer the caller to Transit Authority Police Headquarters
    B. that you will take the call and refer it to the Civilian Complaint Review Board
    C. that you will take the call and refer it to the Internal Affairs Division
    D. to have the caller report the incident to her school authorities

24.____

25. Police Communications Technician Blakely receives a second call on a 10-13 at 5 Berkeley Place in Brooklyn. He is given a description of the perpetrator involved, enters this information into the system, and then notifies you, the supervisor, of the second call.
Upon reviewing this call, you should tell Operator Blakely that he should have

    A. notified you first before entering the second call into the system
    B. entered the information, hotlined the information to the dispatcher, routed D, and then notified you
    C. hotlined the information to the dispatcher, notified you, and then entered the information
    D. hotlined the information to the dispatcher, entered it into the system, routed D, and then notified you

25.____

KEY (CORRECT ANSWERS)

1.	B		11.	C
2.	A		12.	A
3.	C		13.	A
4.	A		14.	B
5.	B		15.	B
6.	A		16.	B
7.	C		17.	A
8.	D		18.	B
9.	A		19.	A
10.	D		20.	C

21.	A
22.	D
23.	B
24.	C
25.	D

EXAMINATION SECTION
TEST 1

DIRECTIONS: Each question or incomplete statement is followed by several suggested answers or completions. Select the one that BEST answers the question or completes the statement. *PRINT THE LETTER OF THE CORRECT ANSWER IN THE SPACE AT THE RIGHT.*

1. A newly assigned operator tells you, his supervisor, that he thinks something is wrong with Emergency Reporting System Box Number 2515. He states that for the last minute, the box has been coming in with a series of tapping sounds, two followed by three. After you listen and hear the tapping yourself, you should direct the operator to

    1.____

    A. move to the next Emergency Reporting System box and input a job so that a patrol car can be dispatched to check the condition of the first box
    B. call the Fire Department and request a test on the line
    C. input a job at the Emergency Reporting System box location as a priority run
    D. call the Fire Department and advise them that the Emergency Reporting System box is out of order

2. Police Communications Technician Cheppo, assigned to Richmond Dispatching, during the eight to four tour, receives a call from a Mr. Victor of 245 Robinson Avenue. Mr. Victor states that he is a victim of wife abuse. He tells Dispatcher Cheppo that he is a disabled veteran and his wife constantly abuses him, both physically and emotionally. Mr. Victor insists that he needs help, but he does not want the police to come to his home. His wife is not there now, but he states that she has threatened to beat him up when she returns. Dispatcher Cheppo is familiar with the Victim Services Agency referral program, but she is uncertain as to how to process the call.
You, as her immediate supervisor, should instruct her to

    2.____

    A. ask Mr. Victor to hold on, and then dial transfer to 6580
    B. input a job as a 10-68
    C. input a job as a 10-52, dispute, then dial transfer to 6420
    D. ask Mr. Victor to call 911 when his wife returns home

3. Police Communications Technician Nigil receives a call from a male who states that his blind 36-year-old brother is missing. His brother was supposed to report to the New York Guild for the Blind two hours ago, but has not arrived there. The caller states that his brother also disappeared last month, and the police found him sitting in Central Park feeding the birds. Operator Nigil asks the caller to hold on while he seeks assistance from the supervisor. He asks you, the supervisor, what action he should take.
You should direct him to

    3.____

    A. tell the caller that since his brother is not a minor, he must wait a while longer, but he should call back if his brother does not show up
    B. refer the caller directly to the Missing Persons Squad
    C. refer the caller to his local precinct and inform them of the situation
    D. enter a job indicating that a patrol car will be sent to the caller's location to take a report

4. Police Communications Technician Phillips, while working on 911, receives a call concerning an off-duty police officer who is having an argument with his wife. The caller states that the argument sounds violent, and the police officer has a gun. Dispatcher Phillips asks if the caller can see exactly what is going on. The caller reports that he is unable to see anything. Dispatcher Phillips, who does not know the proper code to input, brings this call to your attention.
   As the Supervising Dispatcher, you should instruct Dispatcher Phillips to enter which one of the following codes?

    A. 10-13Z1   B. 10-52F1   C. 10-13X1   D. 10-69S

4.____

5. Police Communications Technician Wilder approaches you, the Supervising Dispatcher, and asks you to listen to his last call. You replay the tape and hear the following situation. The caller, a Mr. Monroe, claims that he saw two police officers enter a bar at West 146th Street and 7th Avenue. He followed the officers inside to see what was going on. Once inside the bar, Mr. Monroe saw three males who were sitting at the bar drop several plastic packets to the floor. The packets appeared to contain drugs. Mr. Monroe claims that one of the police officers picked up the packets and stuffed them into his pocket. At that point, both of the officers looked around the bar as if they were searching for someone. They remained in the bar for about five minutes and then returned to their patrol car, license plate number 1269. Mr. Monroe gave his address and telephone number to Dispatcher Wilder and asked if there was anything else he wanted to know. Dispatcher Wilder stated, *No, but thank you for calling. I will relay this information to my supervisor at once.* You, as the supervisor, look at his screen and see that Dispatcher Wilder has entered an *IA* message on a previous job involving *a man with a gun* inside the same bar. A notation was made that he had *hotlined* the information. In this situation, the action taken by Dispatcher Wilder should be considered

5.____

    A. *correct;* chiefly because he immediately hotlined the information and notified the supervisor of a serious incident
    B. *incorrect;* chiefly because he should have given the caller the telephone number of the Internal Affairs Division
    C. *correct;* chiefly because he obtained all of the pertinent information
    D. *incorrect;* chiefly because he should have tried to hold the caller on the line in order to notify a supervisor

Questions 6-8.

DIRECTIONS: Questions 6 through 8 are to be answered SOLELY on the basis of the following information.

    Police Communications Technician Maurice receives a call over Position 25 from Sgt. Jacobs requesting that the power be shut off on the northbound IND, A, and CC subway line at the Broadway-Nassau Station. The Sergeant states that there is a man down under a train. Dispatcher Maurice tells the Sergeant that it is not in his jurisdiction to order that power be shut off. Sgt. Jacobs then asks to speak to a supervisor, and Dispatcher Maurice calls you to the line.

6. As the supervisor, you should tell Dispatcher Maurice that the FIRST action he should take is to

6.____

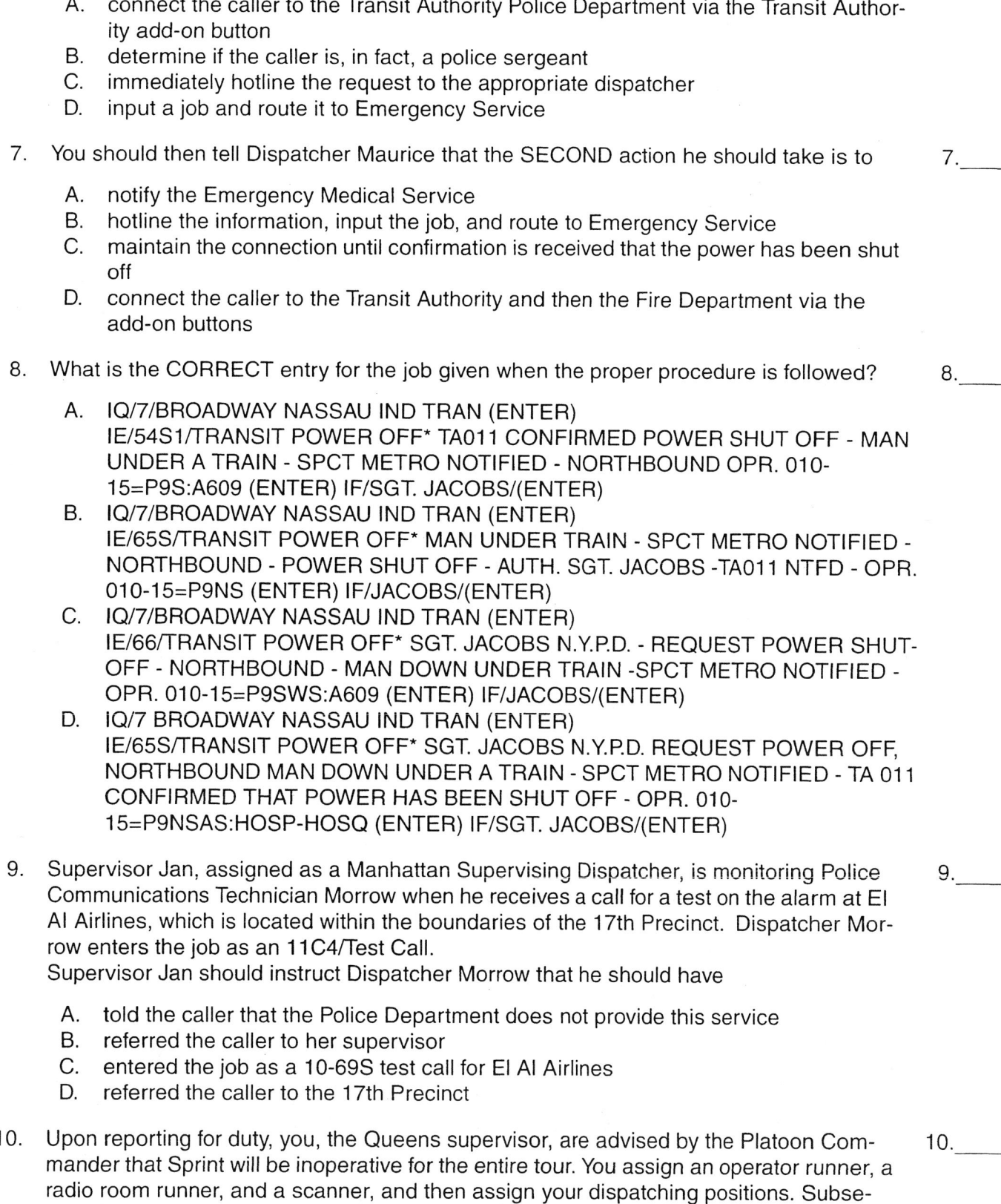

    A.   connect the caller to the Transit Authority Police Department via the Transit Author-
ity add-on button

    B.   determine if the caller is, in fact, a police sergeant

    C.   immediately hotline the request to the appropriate dispatcher

    D.   input a job and route it to Emergency Service

7.   You should then tell Dispatcher Maurice that the SECOND action he should take is to   7._____

    A.   notify the Emergency Medical Service

    B.   hotline the information, input the job, and route to Emergency Service

    C.   maintain the connection until confirmation is received that the power has been shut
off

    D.   connect the caller to the Transit Authority and then the Fire Department via the
add-on buttons

8.   What is the CORRECT entry for the job given when the proper procedure is followed?   8._____

    A.   IQ/7/BROADWAY NASSAU IND TRAN (ENTER)
IE/54S1/TRANSIT POWER OFF* TA011 CONFIRMED POWER SHUT OFF - MAN
UNDER A TRAIN - SPCT METRO NOTIFIED - NORTHBOUND OPR. 010-
15=P9S:A609 (ENTER) IF/SGT. JACOBS/(ENTER)

    B.   IQ/7/BROADWAY NASSAU IND TRAN (ENTER)
IE/65S/TRANSIT POWER OFF* MAN UNDER TRAIN - SPCT METRO NOTIFIED -
NORTHBOUND - POWER SHUT OFF - AUTH. SGT. JACOBS -TA011 NTFD - OPR.
010-15=P9NS (ENTER) IF/JACOBS/(ENTER)

    C.   IQ/7/BROADWAY NASSAU IND TRAN (ENTER)
IE/66/TRANSIT POWER OFF* SGT. JACOBS N.Y.P.D. - REQUEST POWER SHUT-
OFF - NORTHBOUND - MAN DOWN UNDER TRAIN -SPCT METRO NOTIFIED -
OPR. 010-15=P9SWS:A609 (ENTER) IF/JACOBS/(ENTER)

    D.   IQ/7 BROADWAY NASSAU IND TRAN (ENTER)
IE/65S/TRANSIT POWER OFF* SGT. JACOBS N.Y.P.D. REQUEST POWER OFF,
NORTHBOUND MAN DOWN UNDER A TRAIN - SPCT METRO NOTIFIED - TA 011
CONFIRMED THAT POWER HAS BEEN SHUT OFF - OPR. 010-
15=P9NSAS:HOSP-HOSQ (ENTER) IF/SGT. JACOBS/(ENTER)

9.   Supervisor Jan, assigned as a Manhattan Supervising Dispatcher, is monitoring Police   9._____
Communications Technician Morrow when he receives a call for a test on the alarm at El
Al Airlines, which is located within the boundaries of the 17th Precinct. Dispatcher Mor-
row enters the job as an 11C4/Test Call.
Supervisor Jan should instruct Dispatcher Morrow that he should have

    A.   told the caller that the Police Department does not provide this service

    B.   referred the caller to her supervisor

    C.   entered the job as a 10-69S test call for El Al Airlines

    D.   referred the caller to the 17th Precinct

10. Upon reporting for duty, you, the Queens supervisor, are advised by the Platoon Com-   10._____
mander that Sprint will be inoperative for the entire tour. You assign an operator runner, a
radio room runner, and a scanner, and then assign your dispatching positions. Subsequently, you remind both the radio room runner and the scanner of the procedures
regarding slips involving ambulance calls. Of the following, you should emphasize to the
radio room runner that it is MOST important to ensure that the

A. dispatcher gets the second copy
B. operator has identified herself by number
C. operator has noted the time the call was received
D. liaison gets the second copy

Questions 11-15.

DIRECTIONS: Questions 11 through 15 are to be answered SOLELY on the basis of the following information.

You, as a supervising dispatcher, have been assigned to review several 10-13 tapes and job inputs that have come into the borough of Brooklyn from 0730 to 1530 hours.

Job #1. At 0807 hours, Police Communications Technician Sherman receives a call from an unknown male stating that there is an accident on the corner of Coney Island Avenue and Avenue J. He also states that there is a police car involved. It is not known if there are any injuries. Dispatcher Sherman advises the caller to hold on. He hotlines a 10-13 to the Radio Dispatcher. When he goes back to the caller, he finds that the caller has been disconnected. Dispatcher Sherman enters the job as follows:
    IQ/6/CONEY ISLAND AVE - J AVE (ENTER)
    IE/13U2/RMP COLLISION* MALE CALLER STATES UNKNOWN INJURIES
    INVOLVED - OPR. 689-36 = P9SWD (ENTER)
    IF/UNKNOWN MALE/(ENTER)
    IA* JOB HOTLINED - OPR 689-36 (ENTER)

Job #2. At 1135 hours, Police Communications Technician Sykes receives a call from a female who states that there is a police officer in uniform lying on the street at Campus Road and Nostrand Avenue. Dispatcher Sykes tells the female to hold on, and hotlines the call to the Radio Dispatcher as a 10-13. Dispatcher Sykes then goes back to the caller, who could provide no further information. He does, however, get the female's name and callback. He depresses the dial transfer button and phones the Emergency Medical Service. He gives them the information and enters the job. He then notifies his supervisor. Dispatcher Sykes enters the job as follows:
    IQ/6/CAMPUS RD - NOSTRAND AVE (ENTER)
    IE/13U2/OFFICER DOWN* FEMALE STATES AT THIS LOCATION -
    ARO 617 NOTIFIED - JOB HOTLINED - OPR. 312-46=AS:A617-
    HOSP-HOSQ (ENTER)
    IF/FLANNERY/6897213 (ENTER)
    IA*SPCT GUZMAN NOTIFIED (ENTER)

Job #3. Police Communications Technician Andrews receives a call at 1136 hours that there is a police officer in uniform who has been shot at Campus Road and Nostrand Avenue. Dispatcher Andrews queries the location. The caller states that he believes a man who ran into the Oklahoma Country Ribs Store did the shooting. Dispatcher Andrews asks the caller to hold on, and hotlines the information to the Radio Dispatcher. He then goes back to the caller. He sees that a call has already been entered into the system and dispatched. He asks the caller for his name and callback, but the male refuses. Dispatcher Andrews thanks the caller and enters the information as follows:

IA* UNKNOWN MALE CALLER STATES POLICE OFFICER SHOT AT
LOCATION - POSSIBLE PERPETRATOR RAN INTO THE OKLAHOMA
COUNTRY RIBS STORE - ANONYMOUS MALE CALLER - NO FURTHER
INFO. OPR 809-41=SDFAS:HOSP-HOSQ (ENTER)

Job #4. At 1450 hours, Police Communications Technician Fisher receives a call from a young
male stating that a man who appears to be a police officer is having trouble with another man at
the corner of Ashford Street and Hegeman Avenue. Dispatcher Fisher asks the caller if the
police officer is in uniform. The caller states that he is not. Dispatcher Fisher asks the caller for
his name and callback, but he refuses to answer and hangs up. Dispatcher Fisher then hotlines
a 10-13 to the Radio Dispatcher, enters the job, and notifies his supervisor. He enters the job as
follows:

IQ/6/ASHFORD ST - HEGEMAN AVE (ENTER)
IE/13X2/P.O. FIGHTING*WITH ANOTHER MALE AT THE CORNER - NO
FURTHER INFO - OPR. 248-33 (ENTER)
IF/MALE REFUSED/(ENTER)
IA* SPCT TEMPLE NOTIFIED - OPR. 248-33 (ENTER)

Job #5. At 1525 hours, Police Communications Technician Tyson receives a call from a male
identifying himself as Police Officer Shore from the 90th Precinct. He states that he is off duty
and just observed a male Hispanic breaking into a house at 1780 East 13th Street. He requests
assistance in apprehending the perpetrator. Dispatcher Tyson asks the officer what he is wearing and his race. She then hotlines the information, indicating that she has a 10-13, and gets a
full description of the perpetrator - a male Hispanic, 5 feet 6 inches to 5 feet 8 inches, wearing a
blue down jacket, green pants, and white sneakers. She is also told that the perpetrator entered
the house through the second floor rear window. The officer states that he will be in front of the
house. Dispatcher Tyson then enters the job and notifies her supervisor. The job is entered as
follows:

IQ/6/1780 E 13 ST (ENTER)
IE/13Z2/BURGLARY* SEE POLICE OFFICER IN FRONT OF LOCATION -
STATES MALE HISPANIC BREAKING INTO REAR WINDOW - WEARING
BLUE COAT - GREEN PANTS - SNEAKERS - MALE 5FT 6 TO 8 -
OPR. 836-43 (ENTER)
IF/P.O. SHORE/(ENTER)
IA* JOB HOTLINED - SPCT TOPPER NOTIFIED - OPR 836-43 (ENTER)

As the supervisor, you must now correct the errors made on each call received and
entered for the jobs described above.

11. Which of the following jobs are NOT 10-13's?   11.____

   A. 1, 4   B. 1, 5   C. 2, 3   D. 4, 5

12. For which of the following jobs did the operator fail to get a necessary description of the   12.____
   perpetrator?

   A. 2, 3   B. 2, 5   C. 3, 4   D. 4, 5

13. For which one of the following jobs did the operator fail to follow proper hotline proce-   13.____
   dure?

   A. 2   B. 3   C. 4   D. 5

14. For which one of the following jobs did the operator fail to walk in to the dispatcher, as required by procedure?

    A. 1   B. 2   C. 3   D. 4

14.____

15. For which of the following jobs did the operator unnecessarily route the entries?

    A. 1, 3   B. 1, 4   C. 2, 4   D. 3, 5

15.____

16. Police Communications Technician Kind, a newly appointed operator, receives a call at 0910 hours from a female who reports that she repeatedly receives obscene phone calls concerning her children. Operator Kind requests the location of the caller and inputs a 10-68 code to investigate the incident.
As a Supervising Dispatcher, you should reinstruct Operator Kind that she should have

    A. referred the caller to the New York Telephone Company during regular business hours
    B. changed the code to 10-29Q1 *Phone Threats*
    C. told the caller to contact her local precinct
    D. change the code to 10-50P1 *Phone Threats*

16.____

17. As a Supervising Dispatcher, while monitoring Police Communications Technician Jones, you notice that he has made several errors involving his processing of ambulance calls. You decide to take Dispatcher Jones aside to reinstruct him in the proper ambulance procedures.
You should instruct Dispatcher Jones to do all of the following EXCEPT

    A. input a 10-54 for an elderly sick called in by an aide at a nursing home
    B. connect the caller to the Emergency Medical Service when hospital personnel requests a bus to transfer a patient from one hospital to another
    C. release the call from the dispatching position when extended interviewing by the Ambulance Receiving Operator is necessary
    D. enter a 10-55 when the Ambulance Receiving Operator advises that a nurse will call the complainant back

17.____

18. Police Communications Technician Ramos receives a call on 911 from an English-speaking male with a distinct Spanish accent. Dispatcher Ramos, who speaks Spanish, asks the caller, *Do you speak Spanish?* The male replies, *Si!* Dispatcher Ramos tells the caller, *Un momento, por favor,* and transfers the call to a Spanish translator.
As a supervisor, you should advise Dispatcher Ramos that the procedure he followed was

    A. *correct,* primarily because he is not a translator
    B. *incorrect,* primarily because he should have processed the call since he speaks Spanish
    C. *correct,* primarily because the caller spoke with a Spanish accent
    D. *incorrect,* primarily because he did not question the male

18.____

Question 19.

DIRECTIONS: Question 19 is to be answered SOLELY on the basis of the following information and the chart which appears on the following page.

As a supervisor, you have assigned Police Communications Technician Newhardt to work ERS for the day. During the tour, he received the calls listed below:

1. Spanish Assist
2. Report of a fire at 366 East 66th Street, Apt. 9
3. Request for the 14th Precinct's address and telephone number
4. Request for an ambulance for an E.D.P. in front of 1717 Broadway
5. Fire Department test call
6. Series of tapping (2-3) from ERS box 2514

Near the end of the tour (1520 hours), you inspect his ERS log, and you notice that he has failed to complete certain information.

EMERGENCY REPORTING SYSTEM LOG

DATE _MARCH 21_   BOROUGH _MANHATTAN_

TOUR _0800 X 1600_   POSITION _Pos 10_

	A	B	C	D	E	F	G	H	I	J	K	L	M	N
	TIME	BOX#	CPR#	PRAM	INFO	TEST	NA	MISC	INPUT	JOB#	CODE SIGNAL	INCIDENT LOCATION	RMP ASSIGNED	FINAL DISPOSITION
1	1430	3691	001					✓				REFERRED TO SPANISH		
2	1436	4266	001								S2611	366 E. 66 ST.	23A	91
3	1439		001											
4	1445		001									1717 BROADWAY	34B	90Z
5		4444	001											
6	1449	2514	001					✓					26A	93C
7														
8														
9														
10														
11														
12														
13														
14														
15														
16	TOTALS											VERIFIED BY _____		

SUPERVISOR'S SIGNATURE

PD 112-140 (11-79) (Formerly Misc. 702m)

19. Which of the following series of letters and numbers represents information omitted in the log?   19.____

    A. A5, B4, J5, MI, G16, D16, I4, F16, E3, J6, K2, G7, M4, N6, B2, L1, M2, I1, I16
    B. A5, B4, E4, K9, J6, M6, L1, M2, B5, L3, I5, C6, B3, L6, M6, L5, G6, I16
    C. A5, B4, J5, K4, E3, G5, K6, I4, I2, K2, K6, D16, B2, LI, M2, I1, G6, I16
    D. A5, B3, B4, E3, F5, J4, K2, K4, J6, K6, L6, E16, F16, H16, I16, I16, I4, I2, D16, G16

20. Police Communications Technician Gibson, assigned to dispatching position 38 in Brooklyn, receives a call from a male who states that he sees an ambulance on the scene at 1822 Clarkson Avenue. He states that the ambulance crew appears to be having a heated argument with the family of an aided victim in front of the location. Dispatcher Gibson enters the job as 10-52D1.
As the supervising dispatcher, you should reinstruct Dispatcher Gibson to correct the code to

    A. 10-56S   B. 10-10Y3   C. 10-58S   D. 10-58D

20.____

21. The 27th Precinct calls 911 to report that Police Officer Arlen, who was assigned to Harbor High School as the security officer for the day, had picked up a youth for trespassing. The officer needs a patrol car to transport the youth to the stationhouse.
The operator turns to you, the supervisor, to ask what code he should use. You should instruct him to

    A. hotline and enter a 10-13
    B. have the police officer call the precinct to 10-1 a car
    C. hotline and enter a 10-39
    D. hotline and enter a 10-12

21.____

22. Mrs. James calls 911 demanding to speak to someone in charge. You, the supervisor, *jack-in* to your operator's position to find out what the problem is. Mrs. James tells you that she was driving along New York Boulevard when three police cars from the 117th Precinct raced past her and ran a red light. She further states that the police from the same precinct gave her a ticket last week for accidentally running a red light, and she feels something should be done to discipline the officers who drove through the red light. She asks, *What gives them the right to break the law and go unpunished? This type of corruption has to stop!*
As the supervisor, you should advise the caller that

    A. she should register her complaint with the Commanding Officer of the 117th Precinct
    B. she can call the Civilian Complaint Review Board to register her complaint
    C. the officers were probably on their way to an emergency
    D. you will send the Patrol Sergeant to take her complaint

22.____

23. Assume that the Spring system fails and all Bronx operators are told by Supervising Dispatcher Shelton that a Backup Slip Operation will be in effect. Police Communications Technician Jordan then receives a call over the Emergency Reporting System indicating a call from fire box 7215. A Mrs. Smith is on the line reporting a heavy smoke condition in her 3rd floor hallway at 6773 Daytona Drive. Operator Jordan disengages the call with Mrs. Smith and proceeds to connect to the Bronx fire operator.
Fire Operator 737 accepts the information and advises Operator Jordan that a unit will be sent, although there have been numerous unfounded alarms at this location in the past. Operator Jordan then gives the slip to Supervising Dispatcher Shelton, who is passing by her position.
The slip is shown below.

23.____

After checking the slip, Supervising Dispatcher Shelton should return it to Operator Jordan and tell her that she omitted the

- A. caller's name, routing, fire box number, time, precinct
- B. fire box number, caller's name, fire operator's number, time
- C. fire operator's number, fire box number, sector, date
- D. fire box number, precinct, intersection, time

24. As supervisor, you receive a notification from the 911 Platoon Commander that the Sprint Computer Operation will change over to a Backup Slip Operation at 0930 hours. Prior to the transition to slips, you assign two operators to serve as dispatching runners. Which one of the following is a responsibility of a dispatching runner?

- A. Enter precinct and sector covering location on slip and leave it for the radio room scanner.
- B. Check address file for incident location entered on slip.
- C. Walk behind operators and pick up completed slips.
- D. Collect slips from scanner with precinct and sector designations entered.

25. Police Communications Technician Greenwald receives a call from a male who states that he was involved in a car accident at West 204th Street and Broadway in Manhattan. He also states that he has exchanged information with the other driver, but he wants the police to respond because the bumpers of the cars are locked together and the cars cannot be moved. Dispatcher Greenwald is unsure of the procedure to follow and asks you, the supervising dispatcher, for assistance. You should direct Dispatcher Greenwald to

- A. report the accident to the Motor Vehicle Department
- B. tell the caller to contact the ABC Tow Company
- C. enter a job indicating that the cars are locked together
- D. refer the caller to the local precinct

KEY (CORRECT ANSWERS)

1.	C		11.	B
2.	A		12.	C
3.	D		13.	C
4.	B		14.	C
5.	D		15.	A
6.	A		16.	A
7.	C		17.	A
8.	D		18.	D
9.	B		19.	D
10.	D		20.	D

21.	D
22.	B
23.	B
24.	C
25.	C

———

TEST 2

DIRECTIONS: Each question or incomplete statement is followed by several suggested answers or completions. Select the one that BEST answers the question or completes the statement. *PRINT THE LETTER OF THE CORRECT ANSWER IN THE SPACE AT THE RIGHT.*

1. An hysterical female calls 911 to report that she and her husband are having an argument. She tells the operator that her husband is now storming out of the house with their child, and she is afraid that her husband will do the child bodily harm. The operator has the caller's name, address, apartment number, and telephone number. The operator turns to you, the supervising dispatcher, and asks how she should handle this call. You should instruct her to

    A.   input the job as a kidnapping
    B.   input the job as a family or custodial dispute
    C.   input the job as a possible abduction
    D.   refer the caller to Family Court

1.____

2. Police Communications Technician Curtis receives a call from Fire Dispatcher 249 requesting assistance at the scene of a residence fire on West 125th Street and Amsterdam Avenue. Dispatcher 249 states that they have a disorderly group harassing firemen, requests a signal red, and hangs up. Dispatcher Curtis, uncertain of the correct code to use, requests your assistance.
As the supervising dispatcher, you should instruct Dispatcher Curtis to enter

    A.   10-39C/CODE RED* HARASSING FIREMEN - SEND RMP -OPROO-5
    B.   10-59/CODE RED* HARASSING FIREMEN - SEND SUPERVISOR OPROO-5
    C.   10-50G2/CODE RED* HARASSING FIREMEN - OPROO-5=P9
    D.   10-59R/CODE RED* HARASSING FIREMEN - SEND RMPS AND SUPERVISOR OPROO-5=P9

2.____

3. At 0315 hours on April 1, Police Communications Technician Karter received a call on 911 of a 10-13 at the intersection of Avenue M and East 21st Street. Operator Karter entered a 10-13U2 at the above location. While reviewing the tape of the 10-13 with Operator Karter, you, the supervisor, find that the following statements made by the caller were omitted from the job:
    Statement 1. The officer said he was on the southwest corner.
    Statement 2. The officer gave his badge number.
    Statement 3. The officer gave his name, race, and rank.
    Statement 4. The officer stated that he was in trouble and requested two units as a
               back-up.
Which one of the above statements should be considered the MOST serious omission?
Statement

    A. 1   B. 2   C. 3   D. 4

3.____

4. On May 9, all operators are informed of a memo emphasizing the need to carefully screen calls not requiring an immediate response by 911. Police Communications Technician Jones, a newly assigned operator, receives a call from a female who reports that there is a large dead dog blocking a busy roadway. Operator Jones asks his supervisor what action he should take concerning this call.
As the supervisor, you should instruct Operator Jones to

    A. input a job as a 67S/DEAD DOG* BLOCKING INTERSECTION=N
    B. input a job as a 65S/DEAD DOG* BLOCKING INTERSECTION=N
    C. input a job as a 68S/DEAD DOG* REFER TO ASPCA=N
    D. refer the caller to the ASPCA

4.___

5. Police Communications Technician Ultra, assigned to Manhattan Dispatching, receives a call from a Mr. Ray, who states that there is a late model green Dodge station wagon with New Jersey license plates parked at the fire hydrant in front of his apartment building. Mr. Ray states that the vehicle has been parked there for two days. He demands that you send a patrol car at once since the automobile is illegally parked and could be stripped. Dispatcher Ultra, uncertain as to how to enter the job, requests your assistance.
As the supervising dispatcher, you should instruct her to

    A. input a job as a 22V2
    B. refer the caller to his local precinct
    C. input a job as a 10V2 unoccupied suspicious
    D. refer the caller to the Fire Department via the add-on button so they will be aware of the blocked fire hydrant

5.___

6. Police Communications Technician Whitney, a 911 operator, receives a call from a male, wishing to remain anonymous, who states that there are two police officers from the 29th Precinct drinking in an after-hours club. The caller states that the police officers have just completed their tour of duty at the precinct and are in the club in civilian clothes. The 911 operator is unsure of what procedure to follow and asks you what she should do. As the supervisor, you should tell Dispatcher Whitney

    A. that you will speak to the caller and then notify the Internal Affairs Division with the details
    B. to refer the caller to the Precinct Commanding Officer
    C. that you will obtain the details from the caller, notify the Duty Captain, and have the Patrol Sergeant respond
    D. to tell the caller that there is no violation since the officers are off-duty

6.___

7. While monitoring Police Communications Technician Reilly, you observe that he entered a job for a burglary in progress. During the conversation, the caller asked Dispatcher Reilly for his operator's number, his name, and his address. Dispatcher Reilly refused to give the information.
As a supervisor, you should instruct Dispatcher Reilly that he is required to give

    A. the information as requested
    B. his operator's number only
    C. his operator's number, name, and 1 Police Plaza as his address
    D. his operator's number and name

7.___

8. Police Officer Smith from the 5th Precinct calls 911 and states that he received a robot   8.____
alarm of a hold-up or burglary in progress at 732 West 126th Street. The location is a
bodega. No further information is given. The 911 operator is unsure of the correct code
and asks you, the supervisor, for instruction.
You should instruct the operator that the proper code is

    A. 11C4   B. 11C3   C. 11Q3   D. 11Q4

9. When Police Communications Technician Miles reports for duty at 0730 hours on Mon-   9.____
day, Supervising Dispatcher Bell notices that she is visibly upset. Supervising Dispatcher
Bell takes her aside and asks what the problem is and whether she can be of any assistance. Dispatcher Miles states that she went to a party Saturday night and saw Police
Officer Denim behaving in an irrational manner. She observed the officer swallow what
appeared to be a Quaalude, along with several glasses of wine. His behavior then
became noticeably irrational. Dispatcher Miles states that she is concerned about Officer
Denim because she had worked with him. She feels that the officer disgraced himself
even though he was off-duty. Dispatcher Miles then asks Supervising Dispatcher Bell
what she should do. Supervising Dispatcher Bell should tell Dispatcher Miles
to

    A. keep the incident to herself because Officer Denim was off-duty
    B. report the incident to the Civilian Complaint Review Board
    C. keep the incident to herself because there is no way to verify the story
    D. report the incident to her Integrity Officer

10. Police Communications Technician Rapelye receives a call from a male who states that   10.____
his uncle is having difficulty breathing. The caller also states that his uncle is experiencing chest pains and a neighbor is administering cardio-pulmonary resuscitation. Operator
Rapelye, after obtaining the address, callback, and apartment number, connects the
caller with Emergency Medical Service. The Ambulance Receiving Operator gets on the
line and obtains the necessary information. With the call completed, Operator Rapelye
must now enter a job but is unsure of what code to use.
As his supervisor, you should direct Operator Rapelye to enter the code as a

    A. 10-54C1   B. 10-54S1   C. 10-54C3   D. 10-54C3PO

11. Police Communications Technician Williams, assigned to dispatching position 39 in   11.____
Brooklyn, enters into the 911 terminal the following input: IQ/7/3000 BEDFORD AVE.
Sprint responds with the following:
    1. ID IQ
    2. Boro 7 *ERROR MSG*
    3. NO 3000
    4. SEL ST1 Bedford Ave
       0 Bedford St
Dispatcher Williams asks you, the supervisor, to assist in getting this address into the
system.
You should tell Dispatcher Williams to

    A. IQ the location again
    B. make a correction by entering E/L:2/6
    C. clarify the location with the caller
    D. make a correction by entering E/L:4/S:0

12. Police Communications Technician Parnell receives a call from Mrs. Barker, who states 12.___ that she received a call from a man who identified himself as Detective Sampson of the Midtown South Precinct Detective Unit. The man told Mrs. Barker that he was working on a case of employee theft from customer accounts at the New York Savings Bank. He asked Mrs. Barker to go with him to the bank to withdraw $3,000 from her own savings account so he could observe the suspected teller's actions. Mrs. Barker agreed to meet the man in one hour in front of the bank, but now she thinks that the man is trying to swindle her out of her money. Dispatcher Parnell, unsure of what action to take, asks her supervisor for instructions.
The supervisor should

   A. tell Dispatcher Parnell to advise Mrs. Barker to call the Midtown South Precinct to verify that a Detective Sampson is assigned to the precinct
   B. tell Dispatcher Parnell to enter the job as a 68Q1 see complainant for a con game and male impersonating a police officer
   C. take the information from the caller, enter it as 69S, and refer it to the Precinct Anti-Crime Officers by landline so they can stake out the bank
   D. take the information from the caller and report the incident to the Internal Affairs Division even though it is not clear that an officer is involved

13. A call is received by Police Communications Technician Roman from Mrs. Smith, who 13.___ states that two police officers responded to her house on a family dispute at 1200 Broadway. She says that one of the officers was very rude and verbally abused both her and her husband. Operator Roman refers the caller to the Internal Affairs Division and notifies her supervisor.
Her supervisor should tell Operator Roman that

   A. the caller should have been referred to the Precinct Commanding Officer
   B. the caller should have been interviewed by a supervisor and information forwarded to the Internal Affairs Division
   C. a job should have been entered for the Patrol Supervisor to respond
   D. the caller should have been referred to the Civilian Complaint Review Board directly or a report should have been taken by a supervisor

14. On March 9, a memo is distributed to all operators regarding the excessive num- 14.___ ber of jobs being input into 911 regarding flea market peddlers. The memo emphasizes the need to carefully screen all unnecessary calls to local precincts or appropriate agencies. No change in procedure is noted. At approximately 1030 hours, Police Communications Technician Greeny, an operator assigned to Brooklyn, receives a call from the owner of a jewelry store located at Fulton Street and Nostrand Avenue concerning a large crowd spilling into the street attempting to purchase items which peddlers are selling in front of his shop.
As a supervisor, you should tell Operator Greeny to

   A. input a 50G2
   B. input a 52D2
   C. refer the caller to the local precinct
   D. refer the caller to the Department of Consumer Affairs

15. While monitoring Police Communications Technician Newly, you hear a conversation involving Blockwatcher 79-1. At the end of the conversation, Dispatcher Newly requests the name, address, and phone number of the blockwatcher, but the blockwatcher refuses to give the information.
At the monitoring interview with Dispatcher Newly, you, the supervisor, should instruct her that

    A. a telephone number should be requested from a block-watcher but not a name and address
    B. blockwatchers are required to give only their assigned identification number but should give their address upon request
    C. blockwatchers should give an address and phone number in case more information is needed regarding their calls
    D. the blockwatcher should have identified herself as a member of the service since only information regarding the incident would have been requested

15._____

16. Police Dispatcher Breen asks you, a supervising dispatcher, to speak to a caller complaining about an unlicensed Las Vegas Night in the basement of a church at 600 West 20th Street. The caller states that gambling is going on now, and he is sure they do not have a license.
You should tell Dispatcher Breen to

    A. send a patrol car using 10Y3, unlicensed Las Vegas Night
    B. enter a 69S, to be referred to the Organized Crime Control Bureau
    C. enter a 69S, to be referred to the precinct for a supervisor to investigate
    D. refer the caller to the Department of Consumer Affairs for an unlicensed operation

16._____

17. Police Communications Technician Butler receives a call from Mr. Rhet, who states that a female at 300 56th Street, Apartment #3, in Brooklyn is an illegal alien. Mr. Rhet states that the female is now in front of the building, and he will meet the police to point her out. Dispatcher Butler asks the caller to hold on and asks you, the supervising dispatcher, for advice.
You should instruct the operator to

    A. refer the caller to the appropriate agency
    B. enter the information as a 69S, to be referred to the Organized Crime Control Bureau
    C. refer the caller to Precinct Detective Unit
    D. enter the information as a 68Q2 (see complainant)

17._____

18. Police Communications Technician Mark receives a recorded alarm of a medical emergency at 570 West 42nd Street in Apartment #5. No further information is given. Operator Mark is unfamiliar with the correct procedure and asks you for your assistance.
As the supervisor, you should direct the operator to enter the job as a(n)

    A. 11Q4   B. 56S   C. 11R4   D. 54Q1

18._____

19. During random monitoring of Police Communications Technicians, the supervising dispatcher stops to listen to a call answered by Dispatcher Belaire. An alarm company is telling Dispatcher Belaire that an alarm was called in 15 minutes ago. He is now placing another call for the same location. The supervisor hears the operator *IQ* the location. The roll out is as follows:

19._____

INCIDENT 19A   S5   PP60   T09   2345   D3   T9049

10-11   COMMERCIAL/BURGLARY
TV TRADERS PR4
3692 WASHINGTON AVENUE
WEST 194TH STREET - WEST 195TH STREET

*2345 G + G ALARM CO. OPR 1056 - OWNER NTFD - OPR500-9
*2347 PREVIOUS INCIDENT CODE 10-11C4 - CT BROWN

Dispatcher Belaire then tells the caller, *Sir, I will place another call for you and the police will be there as soon as possible.* She enters the *IA* message and routes the job Z and At the monitoring interview with Dispatcher Belaire, the supervisor should tell her that this job was handled

- A. *correctly* because you, the supervisor, should ascertain what caused the delay
- B. *incorrectly* because the job should have been entered again
- C. *correctly* because she routed the job Z and D
- D. *incorrectly* because she should have routed the second call *R*

20. Police Communications Technician Brent receives a call from a Mr. Renna reporting that his store was just robbed. Mr. Renna states that one of his customers was shot during the robbery by a white male dressed in blue. Operator Brent asks for the location and the phone number of the store. He then connects the caller to Ambulance Receiving Operator 666 and advises the operator that the incident occurred at West 42nd Street and Broadway at the Royal Shoe Store. After the Ambulance Receiving Operator finishes his questioning of the caller, the operator asks the caller to hold on and hotlines the job to the dispatcher. When Operator Brent returns to the line, the caller had hung up. Operator Brent enters the job as a 30C with the pertinent information and the following routing - AS:A666-HOSP-HOSQ.
Supervisor Jones, who had monitored this call, should provide reinstruction because Operator Brent failed to

- A. enter a direction of flight
- B. follow proper hotline procedure
- C. route the job properly
- D. enter a description of the perpetrator

21. A new memo is issued detailing the services provided by the Victim Services Agency. Supervising Police Communications Technician Rios instructs Police Communications Technician Alonzo in the details of the memo.
Which of the following services are provided by the Victim Services Agency?

- A. 1. Replacement of stolen documents
  2. Installation of window pins for senior citizens
  3. Court appearance notification
- B. 1. Replacement of lost or stolen Transit Reduced Fare Cards for the elderly
  2. On-the-job injury disability insurance
  3. Property release assistance
- C. 1. Crisis counseling
  2. Emergency money for crime victims
  3. Assistance with income tax relating to theft or casualty loss
- D. 1. Applying for State Crime Victims Compensation
  2. Fee payments for stolen checks which were stopped
  3. Emergency services for families of homicide victims

22. While you are working as a supervising dispatcher assigned to the borough of Queens, one of your operators receives a call on 911 from a Dr. Green. He asks for a patrol car to take him from his home at 125-13 Sutphin Boulevard in Queens to 1126 President Street, a high crime area in Brooklyn, to make an emergency visit to a sick patient. Dr. Green tells the operator that he also wants the patrol car to take him back to his home when the visit is completed. The operator, unsure of how to handle the call, requests your assistance.
    As the supervisor, you should instruct her to

    22._____

  A. tell Dr. Green that he must provide his own transportation when making house calls
  B. input a job at 1126 President Street as a 68Q2/MEET DOCTOR IFO*
  C. input a job at 125-13 Sutphin Boulevard as a 68Q1/ DOCTORS ESCORT*
  D. tell Dr. Green that the patrol car will transport him to the location, but it cannot wait for him to complete his visit

23. Police Communications Technician Gold, newly assigned to Brooklyn Dispatching on the 12 to 8 tour, receives a call from a Mr. Jones stating that the police in the 61st Precinct are involved in a parking conditions cover-up. Mr. Jones alleges that the officers in the precinct are not issuing tickets to vehicles illegally parked in the bus stop in front of Tuckley's Tavern at Nostrand Avenue and Avenue S. He insists that a unit from an adjoining precinct respond to the location immediately to issue tickets. Dispatcher Gold enters a job into the system as a 10-67S parking condition requesting that an adjoining resource respond.
    You, as the supervising dispatcher, should instruct Dispatcher Gold that she should have referred the caller to

    23._____

  A. the Special Corruptions number
  B. her supervisor so that a written report could be forwarded to the Civilian Complaint Review Board
  C. the Integrity Officer at the 61st Precinct since no particular police officer was named
  D. her supervisor so that a written report could be forwarded to the Internal Affairs Division

24. Police Communications Technician Furman receives a call from a Mrs. Cannon. She states that her husband, who has a history of mental illness, is acting violently and throwing furniture out of the window. Dispatcher Furman enters the job as a 10-54E1 at the caller's location. The job is brought to the attention of Supervising Dispatcher Simmons, and she instructs Dispatcher Furman that the 10-54E1 code must have an explicit route to *S* for assignment of an Emergency Service Unit. Which one of the following could Supervising Dispatcher Simmons use as another example of a code that would require an explicit route for an Emergency Service Unit?

    24._____

  A. 10-10Y2
  C. 10-54L1
                B. 10-20Q2
                D. None of the above

25. Mr. Ripple calls 911 and tells Police Communications
Technician Chips that Police Officer Newton, assigned to the 70th Precinct, goes to the
One Hundred and One Ice Cream Store on Ocean Avenue and Avenue M every day at
12 o'clock noon. He states that the manager always gives Officer Newton an extra
scoop of ice cream because the officer has an arrangement with the manager to give
special attention to his store. Dispatcher Chips refers the caller to you, the supervisor.
You should tell the caller

    A.   that this is not a justifiable complaint
    B.   to contact the Commanding Officer of the 70th Precinct
    C.   that you will contact the Internal Affairs Division
    D.   to contact the Civilian Complaint Review Board

25.____

KEY (CORRECT ANSWERS)

1.	B		11.	C
2.	C		12.	D
3.	A		13.	D
4.	A		14.	A
5.	B		15.	A
6.	A		16.	C
7.	C		17.	A
8.	D		18.	D
9.	D		19.	B
10.	C		20.	B

21.	A
22.	C
23.	D
24.	D
25.	C

OFFICE RECORD KEEPING

EXAMINATION SECTION

TEST 1

DIRECTIONS: Each question or incomplete statement is followed by several suggested answers or completions. Select the one that BEST answers the question or completes the statement. *PRINT THE LETTER OF THE CORRECT ANSWER IN THE SPACE AT THE RIGHT.*

Questions 1-5.

DIRECTIONS: Questions 1 through 5 are to be answered on the basis of the following chart to check for address and zip code errors.

     A. No errors
     B. Address only
     C. Zip code only
     D. Both

	Correct List Address	Zip Code	List to be Checked Address	Zip Code	
1.	44-A Western Avenue Bethesda, MD	65564	44-A Western Avenue Bethesda, MD	65654	1.____
2.	567 Opera Lane Jackson, MO	28218	567 Opera Lane Jacksen, MO	28218	2.____
3.	200 W. Jannine Dr. Missoula, MT	30707	200 W. Jannine Dr. Missoula, MT	30307	3.____
4.	28 Champaline Dr. Reno, NV	34101	28 Champaine Way Reno, NV	43101	4.____
5.	65156 Rodojo Parsimony, KY	44590-7326	65156 Rodojo Parsimony, KY	44590-7326	5.____

6. When alphabetized correctly, which of the following would be second?   6.____
   A. flame   B. herring   C. decadence   D. emoticon

7. Which one of the following letters is as far after E as K is before R in the alphabet? 7.____
   A. J   B. K   C. H   D. M

8. How many pairs of the following sets of numbers are exactly alike?   8.____
     134232   123456   432512   561343
     564643   432123   132439   438318

   A. 0   B. 2   C. 3   D. 4

9. When alphabetized correctly, which of the following would be FOURTH?   9._____
   A. microcosm   B. natural   C. lithe   D. nature

10. When alphabetized correctly, which of the following would be THIRD?   10._____
    A. exoskeleton   B. euthanize   C. Europe   D. eurythmic

11. Which one of the following letters is as far before T as S is after I in the   11._____
    alphabet?
    A. j   B. K   C. M   D. N

12. How many pairs of the following sets of letters are exactly ALIKE?   12._____
    GIHEKE   GIHEKE
    KIWNEB   KWINEB
    PQMZJI   PMQZJI
    OPZIBS   OBZIBS
    PONEHE   POENHE

    A. 0   B. 1   C. 2   D. 4

13. When alphabetized correctly, which of the following would be FIRST?   13._____
    A. Catalina   B. catcher   C. caustic   D. curious

14. Which of the following letters is as far after D as U is after B in the alphabet?   14._____
    A. R   B. V   C. W   D. Z

Questions 15-19.

DIRECTIONS: Use the following information and chart to complete Questions 15 through 19.

Every theft reported to an adjuster needs to be assigned a six-letter code containing the following:

    First Letter: Type of theft
    Second Letter: Witnesses
    Third Letter: Value of stolen item
    Fourth Letter: Location
    Fifth Letter: Time of theft
    Sixth Letter: Elapsed between theft and report

Type of Theft: Witnesses
A. Breaking and Entering   A. None
B. Retail Theft   B. 1 witness
C. Armed robbery   C. Multiple witnesses
D. Grand Theft Auto   D. Security camera

Location	Time Elapsed Between Theft and Report
A. Single Family Home	A. 0-1 hour
B. Apartment Building	B. 1-4 hours
C. Store	C. 4-12 hours
D. Office	D. 12-24 hours
E. Vehicle	E. 24 Hours
F. Public Space (Parking Garage, Park, etc.)	

Time of Theft	Value of Stolen Items
A. 7 AM – 1 PM	A. $0-$100
B. 1 PM – 6 PM	B. $101-$250
C. 6 PM – 11 PM	C. $251-$500
D. 11 PM – 3 AM	D. $500-$1000
E. 3 AM – 7 AM	E. $1001-$5000
	F. $5000 or more

15. At 9:30 PM, $175 worth of clothing was stolen from a store. The crime was reported right away by a single store associate. Which of the following would be the CORRECT code?

    A. BCCABB   B. BBBCCA   C. ACCBAB   D. CBCABB

15.____

16. A Crossover vehicle worth $4,500 was stolen from a park at approximately 6:45 AM this morning. It was reported stolen at 11:00 AM later that morning by the owner. There were no witnesses. What is the CORRECT code?

    A. DEECAF   B. CFECAE   C. DEFECA   D. DAEFEC

16.____

17. Although it was just reported, a breaking and entering occurred 5 days ago at 1:30 AM, according to security cameras that recorded the theft at the accounting firm. Although locks and doors were damaged, nothing was stolen. Which of the following would be the CORRECT code?

    A. ADDEEA   B. ADDDAE   C. ADADDE   D. ADEADE

17.____

18. Jill Wagner was held at knifepoint this morning at 11:30 AM when she was walking out of her apartment complex. The thief demanded money, and she gave him $54. She was the only witness and reported the crime immediately. Which of the following would be the CORRECT code?

    A. CBABAA   B. BBABAA   C. CBBABB   D. ABBBCA

18.____

19. An artifact worth $5,500 was stolen from the home of Chad Judea this early evening while he was out to dinner from 5:30 PM to 6 PM. When he arrived home at 6 PM, he immediately called the police. There were no witnesses. Which of the following would be the CORRECT code?

    A. AABBAF   B. AABFAF   C. AABABF   D. AAFABA

19.____

20. Diatribe means MOST NEARLY

    A. argument   B. cooperation   C. delicate   D. arrogance

20.____

21. Vitriolic means MOST NEARLY   21._____
    A. flammable   B. fearful   C. spiteful   D. asinine

22. Aplomb means MOST NEARLY   22._____
    A. self-righteous   B. respectable   C. dispirited   D. self-confidence

23. Pervicacious means MOST NEARLY   23._____
    A. rotten   B. immoral   C. stubborn   D. immortal

24. Detrimental means MOST NEARLY   24._____
    A. valuable   B. selfish   C. hopeless   D. harmful

25. Heinous means MOST NEARLY   25._____
    A. sweating   B. glorious   C. atrocious   D. moderate

KEY (CORRECT ANSWERS)

1.	C		11.	A
2.	B		12.	B
3.	C		13.	A
4.	D		14.	C
5.	A		15.	B
6.	D		16.	D
7.	B		17.	C
8.	A		18.	A
9.	D		19.	D
10.	B		20.	A

21.	C
22.	D
23.	C
24.	D
25.	C

TEST 2

DIRECTIONS: Each question or incomplete statement is followed by several suggested answers or completions. Select the one that BEST answers the question or completes the statement. *PRINT THE LETTER OF THE CORRECT ANSWER IN THE SPACE AT THE RIGHT.*

Questions 1-7.

DIRECTIONS: In answering Questions 1 through 7, you will be presented with analogies (known as word relationships). Select the answer choice that BEST completes the analogy.

1. Coordinated is related to movement as speech is related to   1._____
   A. predictive   B. rapid   C. prophetic   D. articulate

2. Pottery is related to shard as wood is related to   2._____
   A. acorn   B. chair   C. smoke   D. kiln

3. Poverty is related to money as famine is related to   3._____
   A. nourishment   B. infirmity   C. illness   D. care

4. Farmland is related to arable as waterway is related to   4._____
   A. impenetrable   B. maneuverable
   C. fertile   D. deep

5. 19 is related to 17 as 37 is related to   5._____
   A. 39   B. 36   C. 34   D. 31

6. Cup is related to lip as bird is related to   6._____
   A. beak   B. grass   C. forest   D. bush

7. ZRYQ is related to KCJB as PWOV is related to   7._____
   A. GBHA   B. ISJT   C. ELDK   D. EOFP

Questions 8-12.

DIRECTIONS: In answering Questions 8 through 12, each of the questions has a group. Find out which one of the given alternatives will be another member of that group.

8. Springfield, Sacramento, Tallahassee   8._____
   A. Buffalo   B. Bangor   C. Pittsburgh   D. Providence

9. Lock, Shut, Fasten   9._____
   A. Window   B. Iron   C. Door   D. Block

10. Pathology, Radiology, Ophthalmology   10._____
    A. Zoology   B. Hematology   C. Geology   D. Biology

11. Karate, Jujitsu, Boxing   11._____
    A. Polo   B. Pole-vault   C. Judo   D. Swimming

12. Newspaper, Hoarding, Television   12._____
    A. Press   B. Rumor   C. Media   D. Broadcast

Questions 13-18.

DIRECTIONS: Questions 13 through 18 are to be answered on the basis of the following pie
              chart.

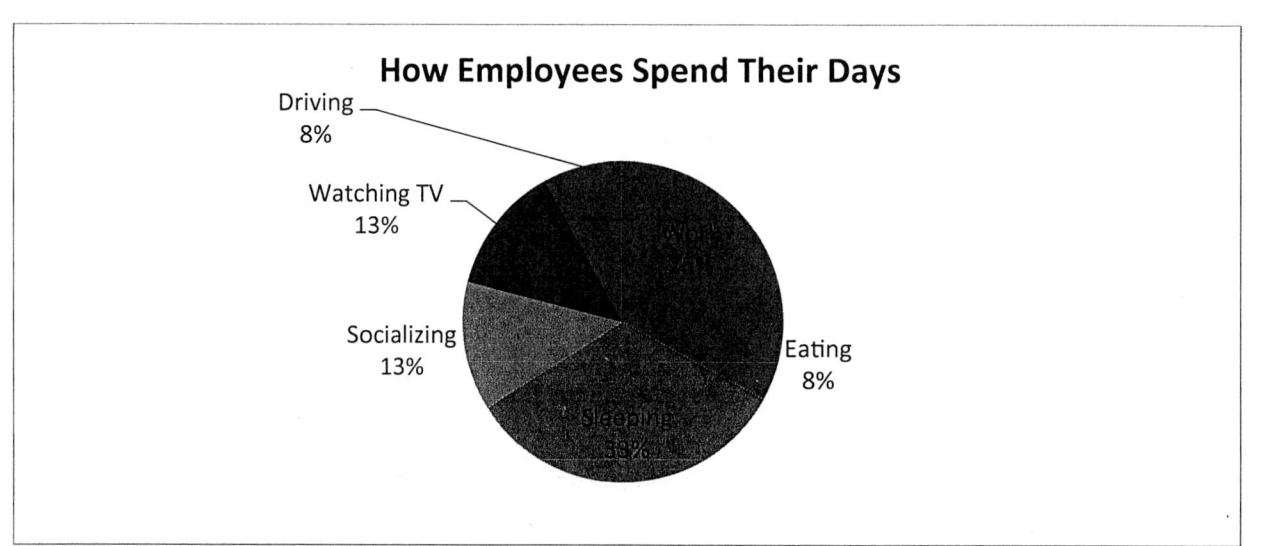

13. Approximately how many hours a day are spent eating?   13._____
    A. 2 hours   B. 5 hours   C. 1 hour   D. 30 minutes

14. According to the graph, for each 48 hour period, about how many hours are   14._____
    spent socializing and watching TV?
    A. 9 hours   B. 6 hours   C. 12 hours   D. 3 hours

15. If an employee ate two-thirds of their meals at a restaurant, what percentage   15._____
    of the total day is spent eating at home?
    A. 2.5%   B. 5.3%   C. 8%   D. 1.4%

16. About how many hours a day are spent working and sleeping?   16._____
    A. 7   B. 10   C. 12   D. 14

17. Which of the following equations could be used to figure out how much time   17._____
    an employee spends watching TV during a week? T equals the total amount of
    time watching TV during the week.
    A. T = 13% x 24 x 7   B. T = 24 x 13 x 7
    C. T = 24/13% x 7   D. T = 1.3 x 7 x 24

18. How many hours a week does the average employee spend socializing?   18._____
    A. 20   B. 22   C. 23   D. 24

Questions 19-25.

DIRECTIONS: Questions 19 through 25 are to be answered on the basis of the following charts.

DIAL DIRECT	WEEKDAY FULL RATE		EVENING 40% DISCOUNT		WEEKEND 60% DISCOUNT	
SAMPLE RATES FROM SEATTLE TO	FIRST MINUTE	EACH ADDITIONAL MINUTE	FIRST MINUTE	EACH ADDITIONAL MINUTE	FIRST MINUTE	EACH ADDITIONAL MINUTE
Savannah, GA	.52	.23	.31	.14	.21	.08
Providence, RI	.52	.223	.31	.14	.21	.08
Golden, CO	.52	.23	.31	.14	.21	.08
Indianapolis, IN	.48	.19	.29	.11	.19	.07
San Diego, CA	.54	.24	.32	.14	.22	.09
Tallahassee, FL	.54	.24	.32	.14	.22	.09
Milwaukee, WI	.57	.27	.34	.16	.23	.09
Minneapolis, MN	.49	.22	.29	.13	.20	.08
Baton Rouge, LA	.52	.23	.31	.14	.21	.08
Buffalo, NY	.52	.23	.31	.14	.21	.08
Annapolis, MD	.54	.24	.32	.14	.22	.09
Washington, DC	.52	.23	.31	.14	.21	.08

OPERATOR ASSISTED		
STATION-TO-STATION		PERSON-TO-PERSON
1 – 10 MILES	$.75	$3.00 FEE FOR ALL MILEAGES
11 - 22 MILES	$1.10	*NOTE: Add to this base charge – the minute rates from the above chart
23-3000 MILES	$1.55	

19. What is the price of a 6-minute dial direct call to Annapolis, MD when you call on a weekend?
   A. $0.59   B. $0.54   C. $0.67   D. $0.49

19.____

20. What is the difference in cost between a 10 minute dial direct to Buffalo, NY and a 10 minute person-to-person call to Buffalo, NY?
   A. $1.55   B. $3.00   C. $0.55   D. $4.55

20.____

21. What is the price of a 15-minute operator-assisted Station-to-Station call to Indianapolis, IN on a Monday at noon?
   A. $3.74   B. $7.80   C. $3.45   D. $4.69

21.____

22. What is the difference in price between an 11-minute dial direct call to Milwaukee, WI at 11:00 AM on a Wednesday and the same call made at 9 PM that night?
   A. $2.27   B. $3.00   C. $1.55   D. $1.336

22.____

23. Which of the following is NOT a type of charge for a dial direct call?
    A. Holiday   B. Evening   C. Weekend   D. Weekday

23.____

24. If a 3.5% tax applied to the total cost of any call, what would be the TOTAL cost of a 13-minute weekday, dial direct call to Golden, CO?
    A. $3.28   B. $3.39   C. $4.94   D. $6.39

24.____

25. What is the amount of discount from a dial direct, weekday call to Tallahassee, FL cost as compared to a dial direct, weekend call to Tallahassee?
    A. 45%   B. 30%   C. 60%   D. 20%

25.____

KEY (CORRECT ANSWERS)

1.	D		11.	C
2.	B		12.	D
3.	A		13.	A
4.	C		14.	C
5.	D		15.	A
6.	A		16.	D
7.	C		17.	A
8.	D		18.	B
9.	D		19.	C
10.	B		20.	B

21.	D
22.	D
23.	A
24.	B
25.	C

TEST 3

DIRECTIONS: Each question or incomplete statement is followed by several suggested answers or completions. Select the one that BEST answers the question or completes the statement. *PRINT THE LETTER OF THE CORRECT ANSWER IN THE SPACE AT THE RIGHT.*

Questions 1-7.

DIRECTIONS: Questions 1 through 7 are to be answered on the basis of the following graph.

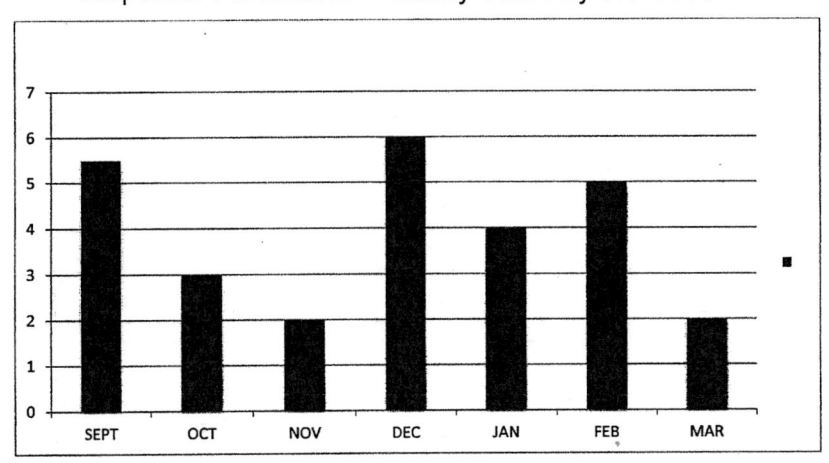

Corporate Fundraiser – Candy Sales by the Case

1. The vertical scale ranging from 0 to 7 represents the number of
   A. students selling candy
   B. candy sold in each case
   C. days each month that candy was sold
   D. cases of candy sold

1._____

2. Which two months had approximately the same amount of candy sold?
   A. November and March   B. September and February
   C. November and October   D. October and March

2._____

3. Which month showed a 100% increase in sales over the month of November?
   A. March   B. January   C. April   D. December

3._____

4. From month-to-month, which month saw an approximate 33% drop in sales from the previous month?
   A. March   B. September   C. January   D. October

4._____

5. The amount of candy sold in December is twice the amount of candy sold in which other month?
   A. October   B. March   C. January   D. September

5._____

6. What was the total amount of candy sold during the months shown on the graph?   6.____
   A. 44 cases   B. 35.5 cases   C. 23.5 cases   D. 27.5 cases

7. If the fundraiser extended the additional five months of the year and added   7.____
   an additional 65% in sales, approximately how many cases would be sold in
   total for an entire year?
   A. 40.5 cases   B. 37 cases   C. 45 cases   D. 27.5 cases

Questions 8-11.

DIRECTIONS: Questions 8 through 11 are to be answered on the basis of the following chart.

S = 10 students
s = 5 students

Mr. Hucklebee	S S S S s
Ms. Shopenhauer	S S S
Mr. White	S S S s
Mrs. Mulrooney	S S S

8. The size of Mr. White's class is _____ students.   8.____
   A. 30   B. 35   C. 40   D. 4

9. The total of all students in all four classes is _____ students.   9.____
   A. 150   B. 140   C. 125   D. 14

10. The average class size based on the above chart is _____ students.   10.____
    A. 140   B. 45   C. 35   D. 30

11. In order to ensure each teacher has the same amount of students in each   11.____
    class, how many students would need to transfer out of Mr. Hucklebee's class?
    A. 10
    B. 5
    C. 0
    d. 15 would need to transfer into his class

12. When alphabetized correctly, which of the following would be THIRD?   12.____
    A. box   B. departed   C. electrical   D. elemental

13. When alphabetized correctly, which of the following would be SECOND?   13.____
    A. polarize   B. omnipotent   C. polygraph   D. omniscient

14. When alphabetized correctly, which of the following would be THIRD?   14.____
    A. Macklemore, Jonathan   B. Mackelmore, J.
    C. DiCastro, Darian   D. Castro, Darren Henry

15. The group fought through the fog, *shambling* through the night, doing their
best to stay upright.
The word *shambling* means
   A. frozen in place   B. running
   C. walking awkwardly   D. shivering uncontrollably

15.____

16. Many doctors agree that Gen-aspirin is the best for fighting headaches. It
comes in different flavors and is easy to swallow.
Is this a valid or invalid argument?
   A. Invalid   B. Valid

16.____

Questions 17-21.

DIRECTIONS: Questions 17 through 21 are to be answered on the basis of the following
paragraph.

     Hospital workers and volunteers often ask Mr. Ansley to educate children who are
hospitalized with primary ciliary dyskinesia (PCD). As he goes through the precautionary
cleaning process (scrubbing, donning sterilized clothes, etc.) in order to see his students, Mr.
Ansley wonders why their parents add the stress and pressure of schooling and trying to play
catch-up because of the amount of time spent in the hospital and not in the classroom, which is
an unfortunate side effect of patients with PCD. These children go through so many painful
treatments on a given day that it seems punishing to subject them to schooling as normal
children do, especially with life expectancy being as short as it is.

17. What is meant by *precautionary* in the second sentence?
   A. Careful   B. Protective   C. Sterilizing   D. Medical

17.____

18. What is the MAIN idea of this passage?
   A. The preparation to visit a patient with primary ciliary dyskinesia is
      extensive.
   B. Children with PCD are unable to live normal lives.
   C. Children with PCD die young.
   D. Certain allowances should be made for children with PCD.

18.____

19. What is the author's purpose?
   A. To advise   B. To educate
   C. To establish credibility   D. To amuse

19.____

20. What is the author's tone?
   A. Cruel   B. Sympathetic
   C. Disbelieving   D. Cheerful

20.____

21. How is Mr. Ansley so familiar with the procedures used when visiting a child
with PCD?
   A. He has read about it
   B. He works in the hospital.
   C. His child has PCD.
   D. He tutors them on a regular basis.

21.____

Questions 22-25.

DIRECTIONS: One of the underlined words in Questions 22 through 25 should be changed. Select the one that should be changed and print the letter of the word that would change the underlined word.

22.   After we <u>washed</u> the fruit that had <u>growing</u> in the garden, we knew there <u>was</u>
a store that would buy them.
   A. washing   B. grown   C. is   D. No change

22.____

23.   When the temperature <u>drops</u> under 32 degrees (F), the water on the lake
<u>freezes</u>, which <u>allowed</u> children to skate across it.
   A. dropped   B. froze   C. allows   D. No change

23.____

24.   My friend's bulldog, while <u>chasing</u> cars in the street, always <u>manages</u> to
<u>knock</u> over our garbage bins.
   A. chased   B. manage   C. knocks   D. No change

24.____

25.   Some of the ice on the driveway <u>has melted</u>.
   A. having melted   B. have melted
   C. has melt   D. No change

25.____

—————

KEY (CORRECT ANSWERS)

1.	D		11.	A	
2.	A		12.	C	
3.	B		13.	D	
4.	C		14.	B	
5.	A		15.	C	
6.	D		16.	A	
7.	C		17.	C	
8.	B		18.	D	
9.	B		19.	A	
10.	C		20.	B	

21.	D
22.	B
23.	C
24.	D
25.	D

—————

TEST 4

DIRECTIONS: Each question or incomplete statement is followed by several suggested answers or completions. Select the one that BEST answers the question or completes the statement. *PRINT THE LETTER OF THE CORRECT ANSWER IN THE SPACE AT THE RIGHT.*

Questions 1-2.

DIRECTIONS: One of the underlined words in Questions 1 and 2 should be changed. Select the one that should be changed and print the letter of the word that would change the underlined word.

1. <u>You</u> can get to Martha's Vineyard by driving from Boston to Woods Hole. Once there, you can travel over on a boat, but <u>you</u> may find traveling by airplane to be more exciting.   1.____
   A. they   B. visitors   C. it   D. No change

2. When John wants to go to the store looking for <u>milk and eggs</u>, <u>you</u> must remember to bring <u>his</u> wallet.   2.____
   A. them   B. he   C. its   D. No change

3. An item that sells for $400 is put on sale at $145. What is the percentage of decrease?   3.____
   A. 25%   B. 28%   C. 64%   D. 36%

4. Two Junior College Mathematics courses have a total of 510 students. The 9:00 AM class has 60 more than the 12:30 PM class. How many students are in the 12:30 class?   4.____
   A. 225   B. 285   C. 255   D. 205

5. If a car gets 26 miles per gallon and it has driven 75,210 miles, approximately what is the number of gallons of gas that it has used?   5.____
   A. 3,000   B. 2,585   C. 165   D. 1,800

6. Which one of the following sentences about proper telephone usage is NOT always correct? When answering a telephone, you should   6.____
   A. know who you are speaking to
   B. give the caller your undivided attention
   C. identify yourself to the caller
   D. obtain the information your caller wishes before you do other work

7. You are part of the "Safety at Work" committee, which is dedicated to ensuring safety of employees. During your regular shift, you notice an employee in violation of one of your committee's rules. Which of the following actions should you take FIRST?
   A. Speak with the employee about the safety rules and mandate them to stop breaking the rules.
   B. Speak to the employee about safety rules and point out the rule they violated.
   C. Bring up the issue during the next committee meeting.
   D. Report the violation to the employee's superiors.

7._____

8. Part of your duties is overseeing employee confidential information. A friend and coworker of ours asks to obtain information concerning another employee. Which is the BEST action to take?
   A. Ask the coworker if you can share the information.
   B. Ask your supervisor if you can give the information to your friend.
   C. Refuse to give the information to your friend.
   D. Give the information to your friend.

8._____

9. Which of the following words means the OPPOSITE of protract?
   A. Extend   B. Hesitant   C. Curtail   D. Plethora

9._____

10. Which of the following words means the OPPOSITE of conserve?
    A. Relinquish   B. Waste   C. Proficient   D. Rigid

10._____

11. Which of the following words means the SAME as dissipate?
    A. Scatter   B. Emancipate
    C. Engage   D. Accumulate

11._____

12. Your office just purchased 14 fax machines. Each fax machine costs $79.99. How much did the 14 fax machines cost?
    A. $1,119.86   B. $1,108.77   C. $1,201.44   D. $1,788.22

12._____

Questions 13-19.

DIRECTIONS: Questions 13 through 19 are to be answered on the basis of the following chart.

Office City	Sales Rank	Production Materials Produced	Rank for Production	Damaged Materials	Employees	Percent of Profit	Sales Points	Weeks Without Injuries
Springfield	13.6	271	12	1	34	35	36	7
Philadelphia	17	274	4	3	25	41	20	4
Gary	16	260	10	5	34	34	21	3
Boulder	5	10	6	9	38	15	20	8
Miami	81	3	81	77	133	4	2	0
Houston	2	370	2	0	95	66	100	16
Battle Creek	82	290	82	81	91	13	9	2

13. Between Philadelphia and Battle Creek, how many damaged materials were there?   13.____
    A. 84   B. 78   C. 45   D. 86

14. How many offices have had 5 or more weeks without injuries?   14.____
    A. 3   B. 4   C. 2   D. 0

15. What was the TOTAL number of damaged materials for the offices in Boulder, Miami, Houston, and Springfield offices?   15.____
    A. 91   B. 87   C. 80   D. 77

16. What were the TOTAL sales points of Houston, Battle Creek, and Gary?   16.____
    A. 115   B. 145   C. 160   D. 130

17. Which of the offices had the LOWEST number of weeks without an injury?   17.____
    A. Battle Creek   B. Miami   C. Gary   D. Philadelphia

18. If worker efficiency is a percentage based on the number of workers at an office and the amount of materials produced, which office has the GREATEST worker efficiency?   18.____
    A. Philadelphia   B. Springfield   C. Boulder   D. Gary

19. If the company was looking to close a facility, which of the following factors would NOT be a reason to close the Miami office?   19.____
    A. Weeks without injury   B. Sales rank
    C. Production materials produced   D. Employees

Questions 20-25.

DIRECTIONS: In answering Questions 20 through 25, select the sentence in which the underlined word is used correctly.

20. A. Jon needs to increase his <u>capitol</u> by 30% to invest in my business.   20.____
    B. The organization is reevaluating <u>it's</u> decision to purchase the building.
    C. The office supply store sells computer paper and <u>stationery</u>.
    D. The quarterback and running back left <u>there</u> helmets on the bus.

21. A. The police sergeant <u>sited</u> me for disorderly conduct and driving without a license.   21.____
    B. The votes have <u>already</u> been counted.
    C. The professor's theory contradicts the <u>principals</u> of Einstein and Newton.
    D. <u>Who's</u> glass of water is on the table?

22. A. The board of trustees decided to <u>accept</u> the CEO's resignation.   22.____
    B. <u>Lose</u> hats will help keep your head from hurting.
    C. She <u>complemented</u> me on my exquisite dinner tastes.
    D. Jamaal offered him some sound <u>advise</u>.

23. A. In class today, Maya <u>lead</u> us in the reciting of the pledge.
    B. Doctors worry about the <u>affects</u> of drinking red wine right before bed.
    C. The workers used sledge hammers to <u>break</u> up the pavement.
    D. The teacher gave her students wise <u>council</u>.

23.____

24. A. This building was <u>formerly</u> the site of one of the city's oldest department stores.
    B. In his position, Albert must be very <u>discrete</u> in handling confidential information.
    C. He was <u>to</u> tired to continue the race.
    D. Each of his mortgage payments as about evenly divided between <u>principle</u> and interest.

24.____

25. A. The police spent several hours at the <u>cite</u> of the accident.
    B. A majority of the public support <u>capitol</u> punishment.
    C. The magician used mirrors to create a convincing <u>illusion</u>.
    D. The heiress <u>flouted</u> her wealth by wearing expensive jewelry.

25.____

KEY (CORRECT ANSWERS)

1.	D		11.	A
2.	B		12.	D
3.	C		13.	A
4.	A		14.	C
5.	A		15.	B
6.	D		16.	D
7.	B		17.	B
8.	C		18.	A
9.	C		19.	D
10.	B		20.	C

21.	B
22.	A
23.	C
24.	A
25.	C

CODING
EXAMINATION SECTION

COMMENTARY

An ingenious question-type called coding, involving elements of alphabetizing, filing, name and number comparison, and evaluative judgement and application, has currently won wide acceptance in testing circles for measuring clerical aptitude and general ability, particularly on the senior (middle) grades (levels).

While the directions for this question usually vary in detail, the candidate is generally asked to consider groups of names, codes, and numbers, and then, according to a given plan, to arrange codes in alphabetic order; to arrange these in numerical sequence; to re-arrange columns of names and numbers in correct order; to espy errors in coding; to choose the correct coding arrangement in consonance with the given directions and examples, etc.

This question-type appears to have few parameters in respect to form, substance, or degree of difficulty.

Accordingly acquaintance with, and practice in, the coding question is recommended for the serious candidate.

TEST 1

DIRECTIONS: Answer questions 1 through 8 an the basis of the code table and the instructions given below.

Code Letter for Traffic Problem	B	H	Q	J	F	L	M	I
Code Number for Action Taken	1	2	3	4	5	6	7	8

Assume that each of the capital letters on the above chart is a radio code for a particular traffic problem and that the number immediately below each capital letter is the radio code for the correct action to be taken to deal with the problem. For instance, "1" is the action to be taken to deal with problem "B", "2" is the action to be taken to deal with problem "H", and so forth.

In each question, a series of code letters is given in Column 1. Column 2 gives four different arrangements of code numbers. You are to pick the answer (A, B, C, or D) in Column 2 that gives the code numbers that match the code letters in the same order

SAMPLE QUESTION

Column 1
BHLFMQ

Column 2
A. 125678
B. 216573
C. 127653
D. 126573

According to the chart, the code numbers that correspond to these code letters are as follows: B - 1, M - 2, L- 6, F - 5, M - 7, Q - 3. Therefore, the right answer is 126573. This answer is D in Column 2.

Column 1	Column 2	
1. BHQLMI	A. 123456 B. 123567 C. 123678 D. 125678	1.___
2. HBJQLF	A. 214365 B. 213456 C. 213465 D. 214387	2.___
3. QHMLFJ	A. 321654 B. 345678 C. 327645 D. 327654	3.___
4. FLQJIM	A. 543287 B. 563487 C. 564378 D. 654378	4.___
5. FBIHMJ	A. 518274 B. 152874 C. 528164 D. 517842	5.___
6. MIHFQB	A. 872341 B. 782531 C. 782341 D. 783214	6.___
7. JLFHQIM	A. 465237 B. 456387 C. 4652387 D. 4562387	7.___
8. LBJQIFH	A. 6143852 B. 6134852 C. 61437852 D. 61431852	8.___

KEY (CORRECT ANSWERS)

1.	C	5.	A
2.	A	6.	B
3.	D	7.	C
4.	B	8.	A

TEST 2

DIRECTIONS: Questions 1 through 5 are based on the following list showing the name and number of each of nine inmates.

1.	Johnson	4.	Thompson	7.	Gordon
2.	Smith	5.	Frank	8.	Porter
3.	Edwards	6.	Murray	9.	Lopez

Each question consists of 3 sets of numbers and letters. Each set should consist of the numbers of three inmates and the first letter of each of their names. The letters should be in the same order as the numbers. In at least two of the three choices, there will be an error. On your answer sheet, mark only that choice in which the letters correspond with the numbers and are in the same order. If all three sets are wrong, mark choice D in your answer space.

SAMPLE QUESTION
A.   386 EPM
B.   542 FST
C.   474 LGT

Since 3 corresponds to E for Edwards, 8 corresponds to P for Porter, and 6 corresponds to M for Murray, choice A is correct and should be entered in your answer space. Choice B is wrong because letters T and S have been reversed. Choice C is wrong because the first number, which is 4, does *NOT* correspond with the first letter of choice C, which is L. It should have been T. If choice A were also wrong, then D would be the correct answer.

1.	A.	382 EGS	B.	461 TMJ	C.	875 PLF	1._____
2.	A.	549 FLT	B.	692 MJS	C.	758 GSP	2._____
3.	A.	936 LEM	B.	253 FSE	C.	147 JTL	3._____
4.	A.	569 PML	B.	716 GJP	C.	842 PTS	4._____
5.	A.	356 FEM	B.	198 JPL	C.	637 MEG	5._____

Questions 6-10

DIRECTIONS: Answer questions 6 through 10 on the basis of the following information:

In order to make sure stock is properly located, incoming units are stored as follows:

STOCK NUMBERS			BIN NUMBERS	
00100	-	39999	D30,	L44
40000	-	69999	I4L,	D38
70000	-	99999	41L,	80D
100000 and over			614,	83D

Using the above table, choose the answer A, B, C, or D, which lists the correct Bin Number for the Stock Number given

6. 17243

   A. 41L   B. 83D   C. I4L   D. D30   6._____

7. 9219

   A. D38   B. L44   C. 614   D. 41L   7._____

8. 90125

   A. 41L   B. 614   C. D38   D. D30   8._____

9. 10001

   A. L44   B. D38   C. 80D   D. 83D   9._____

10. 200100

   A. 41L   B. I4L   C. 83D   D. D30   10._____

KEY (CORRECT ANSWERS)

1. B
2. D
3. A
4. C
5. C

6. D
7. B
8. A
9. A
10. C

TEST 3

DIRECTIONS: Assume that the Police Department is planning to conduct a statistical study of individuals who have been convicted of crimes during a certain year. For the purpose of this study, identification numbers are being assigned to individuals in the following manner:

The first two digits indicate the age of the individual:
The third digit indicates the sex of the individual:
    1.   male
    2.   female

The fourth digit indicates the type of crime involved:
    1.   criminal homicide
    2.   forcible rape
    3.   robbery
    4.   aggravated assault
    5.   burglary
    6.   larceny
    7.   auto theft
    8.   other

The fifth and sixth digits indicate the month in which the conviction occurred:
    01.   January
    02.   February, etc.

Answer questions 1 through 9 *SOLELY* on the basis of the above information and the following list of individuals and identification numbers.

Abbott, Richard	271304	Morris, Chris	212705
Collins, Terry	352111	Owens, William	231412
Elders, Edward	191207	Parker, Leonard	291807
George, Linda	182809	Robinson, Charles	311102
Hill, Leslie	251702	Sands, Jean	202610
Jones , Jackie	301106	Smith, Michael	421308
Lewis, Edith	402406	Turner, Donald	191601
Mack, Helen	332509	White, Barbara	242803

1.   The number of women on the above list is   1.____

    A. 6   B. 7   C. 8   D. 9

2.   The two convictions which occurred during February were for the crimes of   2.____

    A.   aggravated assault and auto theft
    B.   auto theft and criminal homicide
    C.   burglary and larceny
    D.   forcible rape and robbery

3.   The *ONLY* man convicted of auto theft was   3.____

    A.   Richard Abbott   B.   Leslie Hill
    C.   Chris Morris   D.   Leonard Parker

4. The number of people on the list who were 25 years old or older is   4._____

    A. 6   B. 7   C. 8   D. 9

5. The *OLDEST* person on the list is   5._____

    A. Terry Collins   B. Edith Lewis
    C. Helen Mack   D. Michael Smith

6. The two people on the list who are the same age are   6._____

    A. Richard Abbott and Michael Smith
    B. Edward Elders and Donald Turner
    C. Linda George and Helen Mack
    D. Leslie Hill and Charles Robinson

7. A 28-year-old man who was convicted of aggravated assault in October would have iden-   7._____
tification number

    A. 281410   B. 281509   C. 282311   D. 282409

8. A 33-year-old woman convicted in April of criminal homicide would have identification   8._____
number

    A. 331140   B. 331204   C. 332014   D. 332104

9. The number of people on the above list who were convicted during the first six months of   9._____
the year is

    A. 6   B. 7   C. 8   D. 9

Questions 10-19.

DIRECTIONS: The following is a list of patients who were referred by various clinics to the laboratory for tests. After each name is a patient identification number. Answer questions 10 through 19 based on the information contained in this list and the explanation accompanying it.

The *first digit* refers to the clinic which made the referral:

    1. Cardiac   6. Hematology
    2. Renal   7. Gynecology
    3. Pediatrics   8. Neurology
    4. Opthalmology   9. Gastroenterology
    5. Orthopedics

The *second digit* refers to the sex of the patient:

    1. male   2. female

The *third* and *fourth digits* give the age of the patient.

The *last two digits give* the day of the month the laboratory tests were performed.

LABORATORY REFERRALS DURING JANUARY

Adams, Jacqueline	320917	Miller, Michael	511806
Black, Leslie	813406	Pratt, William	214411
Cook, Marie	511616	Rogers, Ellen	722428
Fisher, Pat	914625	Saunders, Sally	310229
Jackson, Lee	923212	Wilson, Jan	416715
James, Linda	624621	Wyatt, Mark	321326
Lane, Arthur	115702		

10. According to the list, the number of women referred to the laboratory during January was   10.____

    A. 4   B. 5   C. 6   D. 7

11. The clinic from which the MOST patients were referred was   11.____

    A. Cardiac   B. Gynecology
    C. Opthamology   D. Pediatrics

12. The YOUNGEST patient referred from any clinic other than Pediatrics was   12.____

    A. Leslie Black   B. Marie Cook
    C. Arthur Lane   D. Sally Saunders

13. The number of patients whose laboratory tests were performed on or before January 16 was   13.____

    A. 7   B. 8   C. 9   D. 10

14. The number of patients referred for laboratory tests who are under age 45 is   14.____

    A. 7   B. 8   C. 9   D. 10

15. The OLDEST patient referred to the clinic during January was   15.____

    A. Jacqueline Adams   B. Linda James
    C. Arthur Lane   D. Jan Wilson

16. The ONLY patient treated in the Orthopedics clinic was   16.____

    A. Marie Cook   B. Pat Fisher
    C. Ellen Rogers   D. Jan Wilson

17. A woman, age 37, was referred from the Hematology clinic to the laboratory. Her laboratory tests were performed on January 9. Her identification number would be   17.____

    A. 610937   B. 623709   C. 613790   D. 623790

18. A man was referred for lab tests from the Orthopedics clinic. He is 30 years old and his tests were performed on January 6. His identification number would be   18.____

    A. 413006   B. 510360   C. 513006   D. 513060

19. A 4 year old boy was referred from Pediatrics clinic to have laboratory tests on January 23. His identification number was   19.____

    A. 310422   B. 310423   C. 310433   D. 320403

KEY (CORRECT ANSWERS)

1.	B	11.	D
2.	B	12.	B
3.	B	13.	A
4.	D	14.	C
5.	D	15.	D
6.	B	16.	A
7.	A	17.	B
8.	D	18.	C
9.	C	19.	B
10.	B		

TEST 4

DIRECTIONS: Questions 1 through 10 are to be answered on the basis of the information and directions given on the following page.

Assume that you are a Senior Stenographer assigned to the personnel bureau of a city agency. Your supervisor has asked you to classify the employees in your agency into the following five groups:

    A.   employees who are college graduates, who are at least 35 years of age but less than 50, and who have been employed by the. city for five years or more;

    B.   employees who have been employed by the City for less than five years, who are not college graduates, and who earn at least $32,500 a year but less than $34,500;

    C.   employees who have been city employees for five years or more, who are at least 21 years of age but less than 35, and who are not college graduates;

    D.   employees who earn at least $34,500 a year but less than $36,000 who are college graduates, and who have been employed by the city for less than five years;

    E.   employees who are not included in any of the foregoing groups.

NOTE: In classifying these employees you are to compute age and period of service as of <u>January 1, 2003</u>. In all cases, it is to be assumed that each employee has been employed continuously in City service. <u>In each question, consider only the information which will assist you in classifying each employee. Any information which is of no assistance in classifying an employee should not be considered.</u>

SAMPLE: Mr. Brown, a 29-year-old veteran, was appointed to his present position of Clerk on June 1, 2000. He has completed two years of college. His present salary is $33,050.

The correct answer to this sample is B, since the employee has been employed by the city for less than five years, is not a college graduate, and earns at least $32,500 a year but less than $34,500 .

DIRECTIONS: Questions 1 to 10 contain excerpts from the personnel records of 10 employees in the agency. In the correspondingly numbered space on the right print the capital letter preceding the appropriate group into which you would place each employee,

1.   Mr. James has been employed by the city since 1993, when he was graduated from a local college. Now 35 years of age, he earns $36,000 a year.

1.____

2.   Mr. Worth began working in city service early in 1999. He was awarded his college degree in 1994, at the age of 21.
As a result of a recent promotion, he now earns $34,500 a year.

2.____

3.   Miss Thomas has been a City employee since August 1, 1998. Her salary is $34,500 a year. Miss Thomas, who is 25 years old, has had only three years of high school training.

3.____

4.   Mr. Williams has had three promotions since entering city service on January 1, 1991. He was graduated from college with honors in 1974, when he was 20 years of age. His present salary is $37,000 a year.

4.____

5. Miss Jones left college after two years of study to take an appointment to a position in the city service paying $33,300 a year. She began work on March 1, 1997 when she was 19 years of age.

   5.____

6. Mr. Smith was graduated from an engineering college with honors in January 1998 and became a city employee three months later. His present yearly salary is $35,810 . Mr. Smith was born in 1976.

   6.____

7. Miss Earnest was born on May 31, 1979. Her education consisted of four years of high school and one year of business school. She was appointed as a typist in a city agency on June 1, 1997. Her annual salary is $33,500.

   7.____

8. Mr. Adams, a 24-year-old clerk, began his city service on July 1, 1999, soon after being discharged from the U.S.
Army. A college graduate, his present annual salary is $33,200

   8.____

9. Miss Charles attends college in the evenings, hoping to obtain her degree in 2004, when she will be 30 years of age. She has been a city employee since April 1998,and earns $33,350.

   9.____

10. Mr. Dolan was just promoted to his present position after six years of city service. He was graduated from high school in 1982, when he was 18 years of age, but did not go on to college, Mr. Dolan's present salary is $33,500.

   10.____

KEY (CORRECT ANSWERS)

1. A
2. D
3. E
4. A
5. C

6. D
7. C
8. E
9. B
10. E

TEST 5

Questions 1 through 4 each contain five numbers that should be arranged in numerical order. The number with the lowest numerical value should be first and the number with the highest numerical value should be last. Pick that option which indicates the *correct* order of the numbers.

Examples:
A.   9; 18; 14; 15; 27
B.   9; 14; 15; 18; 27
C. 14; 15; 18; 27;   9
D.   9; 14; 15; 27; 18

The correct answer is B, which indicates the proper arrangement of the five numbers.

1.   A.   20573; 20753; 20738; 20837; 20098   1.____
     B.   20098; 20753; 20573; 20738; 20837
     C.   20098; 20573; 20753; 20837; 20738
     D.   20098; 20573; 20738; 20753; 20837

2.   A.   113492; 113429; 111314; 113114; 131413   2.____
     B.   111314; 113114; 113429; 113492; 131413
     C.   111314; 113429; 113492; 113114; 131413
     D.   111314; 113114; 131413; 113429; 113492

3.   A.   1029763; 1030421; 1035681; 1036928; 1067391   3.____
     B.   1030421; 1029763; 1035681; 1067391; 1036928
     C.   1030421; 1035681; 1036928; 1067391; 1029763
     D.   1029763; 1039421; 1035681; 1067391; 1036928

4.   A.   1112315; 1112326; 1112337; 1112349; 1112306   4.____
     B.   1112306; 1112315; 1112337; 1112326; 1112349
     C.   1112306; 1112315; 1112326; 1112337; 1112349
     D.   1112306; 1112326; 1112315; 1112337; 1112349

KEY (CORRECT ANSWERS)

1. D
2. B
3. A
4. C

TEST 6

DIRECTIONS: The phonetic filing system is a method of filing names in which the alphabet is reduced to key code letters. The six key letters and their equivalents are as follows:

KEY LETTERS	EQUIVALENTS
b	p, f, v
c	s, k, g, j , q, x, z
d	t
l	none
m	n
r	none

A key letter represents itself.
Vowels (a, e, i, o and u) and the letters w, h, and y are omitted.
For example, the name GILMAN would be represented as follows:
G is represented by the key letter C.
I is a vowel and is omitted.
L is a key letter and represents itself.
M is a key letter and represents itself.
A is a vowel and is omitted.
N is represented by the key letter M.

Therefore, the phonetic filing code for the name GILMAN is CLMM.
Answer questions 1 through 10 based on the information on the previous page.

1. The phonetic filing code for the name FITZGERALD would be   1.____

   A. BDCCRLD   B. BDCRLD   C. BDZCRLD   D. BTZCRLD

2. The phonetic filing code CLBR may represent any one of the following names EXCEPT   2.____

   A. Calprey   B. Flower   C. Glover   D. Silver

3. The phonetic filing code LDM may represent any one of the following names EXCEPT   3.____

   A. Halden   B. Hilton   C. Walton   D. Wilson

4. The phonetic filing code for the name RODRIGUEZ would be   4.____

   A. RDRC   B. RDRCC   C. RDRCZ   D. RTRCC

5. The phonetic filing code for the name MAXWELL would be   5.____

   A. MCLL   B. MCWL   C. MCWLL   D. MXLL

6. The phonetic filing code for the name ANDERSON would be   6.____

   A. AMDRCM   B. ENDRSM   C. MDRCM   D. NDERCN

7. The phonetic filing code for the name SAVITSKY would be   7.____

   A. CBDCC   B. CBDCY   C. SBDCC   D. SVDCC

8. The phonetic filing code CMC may represent any one of the following names EXCEPT   8.____

    A. James   B. Jayes   C. Johns   D. Jones

9. The *ONLY* one of the following names that could be represented by the phonetic filing   9.____
code CDDDM would be

    A. Catalano   B. Chesterton   C. Cittadino   D. Cuttlerman

10. The *ONLY* one of the following names that could be represented by the phonetic filing   10.____
code LLMCM would be

    A. Ellington   B. Hallerman   C. Inslerman   D. Willingham

---

KEY (CORRECT ANSWERS)

1. A
2. B
3. D
4. B
5. A

6. C
7. A
8. B
9. C
10. D

EXAMINATION SECTION
TEST 1

DIRECTIONS: Each question or incomplete statement is followed by several suggested answers or completions. Select the one that BEST answers the question or completes the statement. *PRINT THE LETTER OF THE CORRECT ANSWER IN THE SPACE AT THE RIGHT.*

1. Following are three statements concerning on-the-job training:
    I.   On-the-job training is rarely used as a method of training employees.
    II. On-the-job training is often carried on with little or no planning.
    III. On-the-job training is often less expensive than other types.
Which of the following BEST classifies the above statements into those that are correct and those that are not?

    A. I is correct, but II and III are not
    B. II is correct, but I and III are not
    C. I and II are correct, but III is not
    D. II and III are correct, but I is not

1._____

2. The one of the following which is NOT a valid principle for a supervisor to keep in mind when talking to a subordinate about his performance is:

    A. People frequently know when they deserve criticism
    B. Supervisors should be prepared to offer suggestions to subordinates about how to improve their work
    C. Good points should be discussed before bad points
    D. Magnifying a subordinate's faults will get him to improve faster

2._____

3. In many organizations information travels quickly through the *grapevine*.
Following are three statements concerning the *grapevine*:
    I.   Information a subordinate does not want to tell her supervisor may reach the supervisor through the *grapevine*.
    II. A supervisor can often do her job better by knowing the information that travels through the *grapevine*.
    III. A supervisor can depend on the *grapevine* as a way to get accurate information from the employees on his staff
Which one of the following *correctly* classifies the above statements into those which are generally CORRECT and those which are NOT?

    A. II is correct, but I and III are not
    B. III is correct, but I and II are not
    C. I and II are correct, but III is not
    D. I and III are correct, but II is not

3._____

4. Following are three statements concerning supervision:
    I.   A supervisor knows he is doing a good job if his subordinates depend upon him to make every decision.
    II. A supervisor who delegates authority to his subordinates soon finds that his subordinates begin to resent him.
    III. Giving credit for good work is frequently an effective method of getting subordinates to work harder.

4._____

Which one of the following *correctly* classifies the above statements into those that are CORRECT and those that are NOT?

A. I and II are correct, but III is not
B. II and III are correct, but I is not
C. II is correct, but I and III are not
D. III is correct, but I and II are not

5. Of the following, the LEAST appropriate action for a supervisor to take in preparing a disciplinary case against a subordinate is to

5.___

A. keep careful records of each incident in which the subordinate has been guilty of misconduct or incompetency, even though immediate disciplinary action may not be necessary
B. discuss with the employee each incident of misconduct as it occurs so the employee knows where he stands
C. accept memoranda from any other employees who may have been witnesses to acts of misconduct
D. keep the subordinate's personnel file confidential so that he is unaware of the evidence being gathered against him

6. Praise by a supervisor can be an important element in motivating subordinates. Following are three statements concerning a supervisor's praise of subordinates:

6.___

    I. In order to be effective, praise must be lavish and constantly restated.
    II. Praise should be given in a manner which meets the needs of the individual subordinate.
    III. The subordinate whose work is praised should believe that the praise is earned.

Which of the following *correctly* classifies the above statements into those that are CORRECT and those that are NOT?

A. I is correct, but II and III are not
B. II and III are correct, but I is not
C. III is correct, but I and II are not
D. I and II are correct, but III is not

7. A supervisor feels that he is about to lose his temper while reprimanding a subordinate. Of the following, the BEST action for the supervisor to take is to

7.___

A. postpone the reprimand for a short time until his self-control is assured
B. continue the reprimand because a loss of temper by the supervisor will show the subordinate the seriousness of the error he made
C. continue the reprimand because failure to do so will show that the supervisor does not have complete self-control
D. postpone the reprimand until the subordinate is capable of understanding the reason for the supervisor's loss of temper

8. Following are three statements concerning various ways of giving orders to subordi- 8._____
   nates:
       I.   An implied order or suggestion is usually appropriate for the inexperienced
          employee.
       II. A polite request is less likely to upset a sensitive subordinate than a direct
          order.
       III. A direct order is usually appropriate in an emergency situation.
   Which of the following correctly classifies the above statements into those that are
   CORRECT and those that are NOT?

      A. I is correct, but II and III are not
      B. II and III are correct, but I is not
      C. III is correct, but I and II are not
      D. I and II are correct, but III is not

9. The one of the following which is NOT an acceptable reason for taking disciplinary action 9._____
   against a subordinate guilty of serious violations of the rules is that

      A. the supervisor can "*let off steam*" against subordinates who break rules frequently
      B. a subordinate whose work continues to be unsatisfactory may be terminated
      C. a subordinate may be encouraged to improve his work
      D. an example is set for other employees

10. At the first meeting with your staff after appointment as a supervisor, you find consider- 10._____
    able indifference and some hostility among the participants.
    Of the following, the *most appropriate* way to handle this situation is to

       A. disregard the attitudes displayed and continue to make your presentation until you
          have completed it
       B. discontinue your presentation but continue the meeting and attempt to find out the
          reasons for their attitudes
       C. warm up your audience with some good natured statements and anecdotes and
          then proceed with your presentation
       D. discontinue the meeting and set up personal interviews with the staff members to
          try to find out the reason for their attitude

11. Use a written rather than oral communication to amend any previous written communica- 11._____
    tion.
    Of the following, the BEST justification for this statement is that

       A. oral changes will be considered more impersonal and thus less important
       B. oral changes will be forgotten or recalled indifferently
       C. written communications are clearer and shorter
       D. written communications are better able to convey feeling tone

12. Assume that a certain supervisor, when writing important communications to his subordi-   12.___
nates, often repeats certain points in different words.
This technique is *generally*

    A. *ineffective;* it tends to confuse rather than help
    B. *effective;* it tends to improve understanding by the subordinates
    C. *ineffective;* it unnecessarily increases the length of the communication and may
       annoy the subordinates
    D. *effective;* repetition is always an advantage in communications

13. In preparing a letter or a report, a supervisor may wish to persuade the reader of the cor-   13.___
rectness of some idea or course of action.
The BEST way to accomplish this is for the supervisor to

    A. encourage the reader to make a prompt decision
    B. express each idea in a separate paragraph
    C. present the subject matter of the letter in the first paragraph
    D. state the potential benefits for the reader

14. Effective communications, a basic necessity for successful supervision is a two-way   14.___
street. A good supervisor needs to listen to, as well as disseminate, information and he
must be able to encourage his subordinates to communicate with him. Which of the following suggestions will contribute LEAST to improving the *listening power* of a supervisor?

    A. Don't assume anything; don't anticipate, and don't let a subordinate think you know
       what he is going to say
    B. Don't interupt; let him have his full say even if it requires a second session that day
       to get the full story
    C. React quickly to his statements so that he knows you are interested, even if you
       must draw some conclusions prematurely
    D. Try to understand the real need for his talking to you even if it is quite different from
       the subject under discussion

15. Of the following, the MOST useful approach for the supervisor to take toward the informal   15.___
employee communications network know as the *grapevine* is to

    A. remain isolated from it, but not take any active steps to eliminate it
    B. listen to it, but not depend on it for accurate information
    C. use it to disseminate confidential information
    D. eliminate it as diplomatically as possible

16. If a supervisor is asked to estimate the number of employees that he believes he will   16.___
need in his unit in the coming fiscal year, the supervisor should FIRST attempt to learn
the

    A. nature and size of the workload his unit will have during that time
    B. cost of hiring and training new employees
    C. average number of employee absences per year
    D. number of employees needed to indirectly support or assist his unit

17. An important supervisory responsibility is coordinating the operations of the unit. This   17._____
may include setting work schedules, controlling work quality, establishing interim due
dates, etc. In order to handle this task it has been divided into the following five stages:
   I. <u>Determine the steps</u> or sequence required for the tasks to be performed.
   II. <u>Give the orders,</u> either written or oral, to begin work on the Tasks.
   III. <u>check up</u> by following each task to make sure it is proceeding according to
      plan.
   IV. <u>Schedule the jobs</u> by setting a time for each task of operation to begin and
      end.
   V. <u>Control the process</u> by correcting conditions which interfere with the plan.
The MOST logical sequence in which these planning steps should be
performed is

   A. I, II, III, IV, V   B. II, I, V, III, IV
   C. I, IV, II, III, V   D. IV, I, II, III, V

18. Assume that a supervisor calls a meeting with the staff under his supervision in order to   18._____
discuss several proposals. After some discussion, he realizes that he strongly disagrees
with one proposal that four of the staff have rather firmly favored.
At this point, he could BEST handle the situation by saying

   A. *I have the responsibility for this decision, and I must disagree.*
   B. *I am just reminding you that I have had a great deal more experience in these
      matters.*
   C. *You have presented some good points, but perhaps we could look at it another
      way.*
   D. *The only way that this proposal can be disposed of is to defer it for further discus-
      sion.*

19. As far as the social activities and groups of his subordinates are concerned, a supervisor   19._____
in a large organization can BEST strengthen his tools of leadership by

   A. emphasizing the organization as a whole and forbidding the formation of groups
   B. ignoring the groups as much as possible and dealing with each subordinate as an
      individual
   C. learning about the status structure of employee groups and their values
   D. avoiding any relationship with groups

20. If a subordinate asks you, his supervisor, for advice in planning his career in the depart-   20._____
ment you *should*

   A. encourage him to feel that he can easily reach the top of his occupational ladder
   B. discourage him from setting his hopes too high
   C. discuss career opportunities realistically with him
   D. explain that you have no control over his opportunities for advancement

21. A supervisor's evaluation of an employee is usually based upon a combination of objec-   21._____
tive facts and subjective judgments or opinions.
Which of the following aspects of an employee's work or performance is *most likely* to
be subjectively evaluated?

   A. Quantity   B. Accuracy   C. Attitude   D. Attendance

22. Of the following possible characteristics of supervisors, the one *most likely* to lead to failure as a supervisor is   22.___

    A. a tendency to seek several opinions before making decisions in complex matters
    B. lack of a strong desire to advance to a top position in management
    C. little formal training in human relations skills
    D. poor relations with subordinates and other supervisory personnel

23. People who break rules do so for a number of reasons. However, employees will break rules *less* often if   23.___

    A. the supervisor uses his own judgment about work methods
    B. the supervisor pretends to act strictly, but isn't really serious about it
    C. they greatly enjoy their work
    D. they have completed many years of service

24. Assume that an employee under your supervision has become resentful and generally noncooperative after his request for transfer to another office closer to his place of residence was denied. The request was denied primarily because of the importance of his current assignment. The employee has been a valued worker, but you are now worried that his resentful attitude will have a detrimental effect. Of the following, the MOST desirable way for you to handle this situation is to   24.___

    A. arrange for the employee's transfer to the office he originally requested
    B. arrange for the employee's transfer to another office, but not the one he originally requested
    C. attempt to re-focus the employee's attention on those aspects of his current assignment which will be most rewarding and satisfying to him
    D. explain to the employee that, while you are sympathetic to his request, department rules will not allow transfers for reasons of personal convenience

25. Of the following, it would be LEAST advisable for a supervisor to use his administrative authority to affect the behavior and activities of his subordinates when he is trying to   25.___

    A. change the way his subordinates perform a particular task
    B. establish a minimum level of conformity to established rules
    C. bring about change in the attitudes of his subordinates
    D. improve the speed with which his subordinates respond to his orders

26. Assume that a supervisor gives his subordinate instructions which are appropriate and clear. The subordinate thereupon refuses to follow these instructions.
Of the following, it would then be MOST appropriate for the supervisor to   26.___

    A. attempt to find out what it is that the employee objects to
    B. take disciplinary action that same day
    C. remind the subordinate about supervisory authority and threaten him with discipline
    D. insist that the subordinate carry out the order immediately

27. Of the following, the MOST effective way to identify training needs resulting from gradual changes in procedure is to

    27._____

    A. monitor on a continuous basis the actual jobs performed and the skills required
    B. periodically send out a written questionnaire asking personnel to identify their needs
    C. conduct interviews at regular intervals with selected employees
    D. consult employees' personnel records

28. Assume that you, as a supervisor, have had a new employee assigned to you. If the duties of his position can be broken into independent parts, which of the following is usually the BEST way to train this new employee?
Start with

    28._____

    A. the easiest duties and progressively proceed to the most difficult
    B. something easy; move to something difficult; then back to something easy
    C. something difficult; move to something easy; then to something difficult
    D. the most difficult duties and progressively proceed to the easiest

29. The oldest and most commonly used training technique is on-the-job training. Instruction is given to the worker by his supervisor or by another employee. Such training is essential in most jobs, although it is not always effective when used alone.
This technique, however, *can* be effectively used alone if

    29._____

    A. the skills involved can be learned quickly
    B. a large number of people are to be trained at one time
    C. other forms of training have not been previously used with the people involved
    D. the skills to be taught are mental rather than manual

30. It is generally agreed that the learning process is facilitated in proportion to the amount of feedback that the learner is given about his performance.
Following are three statements concerning the learning process:

    30._____

    I. The more specific the learner's knowledge of how he performed, the more rapid his improvement and the higher his level of performance.
    II. Giving the learner knowledge of his results does not affect his motivation to learn .
    III. Learners who are not given feedback will set up subjective criteria and evaluate their own performance.

Which of the following choices lists ALL of the above statements that are *generally* correct?

    A. I and II *only*
    B. I and III *only*
    C. II and III *only*
    D. I, II and III

KEY (CORRECT ANSWERS)

1.	D	11.	B	21.	C
2.	D	12.	B	22.	D
3.	C	13.	D	23.	C
4.	D	14.	C	24.	C
5.	D	15.	B	25.	C
6.	B	16.	A	26.	A
7.	A	17.	C	27.	A
8.	B	18.	C	28.	A
9.	A	19.	C	29.	A
10.	D	20.	C	30.	B

TEST 2

DIRECTIONS: Each question or incomplete statement is followed by several suggested answers or completions. Select the one that BEST answers the question or completes the statement. *PRINT THE LETTER OF THE CORRECT ANSWER IN THE SPACE AT THE RIGHT.*

Questions 1–6.

DIRECTIONS: Questions 1 through 6 are to be answered SOLELY on the basis of the information given in the following paragraph.

The use of role-playing as a training technique was developed during the past decade by social scientists, particularly psychologists, who have been active in training experiments. Originally, this technique was applied by clinical psychologists who discovered that a patient appears to gain understanding of an emotionally disturbing situation when encouraged to act out roles in that situation. As applied in government and business organizations, the purpose of role-playing is to aid employees to understand certain work problems involving interpersonal relations and to enable observers to evaluate various reactions to them. Thus, for example, on the problem of handling grievances, two individuals from the group might be selected to act out extemporaneously the parts of subordinate and supervisor. When this situation is enacted by various pairs among the class and the techniques and results are discussed, the members of the group are presumed to reach conclusions about the most effective means of handling similar situations. Often the use of role reversal, where participants take parts different from their actual work roles, assists individuals to gain more insight into other people's problems and viewpoints. Although role-playing can be a rewarding training device, the trainer must be aware of his responsibilities. If this technique is to be successful, thorough briefing of both actors and observers as to the situation in question, the participants' roles, and what to look for, is essential.

1. The role-playing technique was FIRST used for the purpose of

    A. measuring the effectiveness of training programs
    B. training supervisors in business organizations
    C. treating emotionally disturbed patients
    D. handling employee grievances

1._____

2. When role-playing is used in private business as a training device, the CHIEF aim is to

    A. develop better relations between supervisor and subordinate in the handling of grievances
    B. come up with a solution to a specific problem that has arisen
    C. determine the training needs of the group
    D. increase employee understanding of the human relation factors in work situations

2._____

3. From the above passage, it is MOST reasonable to conclude that when role-playing is used, it is preferable to have the roles acted out by

    A. only one set of actors
    B. no more than two sets of actors
    C. several different sets of actors
    D. the trainer or trainers of the group

3._____

4. Based on the above passage, a trainer using the technique of role reversal in a problem   4.___
of first-line supervision should assign a senior employee to play the part of a(n)

    A. new employee   B. senior employee
    C. principal employee   D. angry citizen

5. It can be inferred from the above passage that a limitation of role-play as a training   5.___
method is that

    A. many work situations do not lend themselves to role-play
    B. employees are not experienced enough as actors to play the roles realistically
    C. only trainers who have psychological training can use it successfully
    D. participants who are observing and not acting do not benefit from it

6. To obtain good results from the use of role-play in training, a trainer should give partici-   6.___
pants

    A. a minimum of information about the situation so that they can act spontaneously
    B. scripts which illustrate the best method for handling the situation
    C. a complete explanation of the problem and the roles to be acted out
    D. a summary of work problems which involve interpersonal relations

7. Of the following, the MOST important reason for a supervisor to prepare good written   7.___
reports is that

    A. a supervisor is rated on the quality of his reports
    B. decisions are often made on the basis of the reports
    C. such reports take less time for superiors to review
    D. such reports demonstrate efficiency of department operations

8. Of the following, the BEST test of a good report is whether it   8.___

    A. provides the information needed
    B. shows the good sense of the writer
    C. is prepared according to a proper format
    D. is grammatical and neat

9. When a supervisor writes a report, he can BEST show that he has an understanding of   9.___
the subject of the report by

    A. including necessary facts and omitting non-essential details
    B. using statistical data
    C. giving his conclusions but not the data on which they are based
    D. using a technical vocabulary

10. Suppose you and another supervisor on the same level are assigned to work together on   10.___
a report. You disagree strongly with one of the recommendations the other supervisor
wants to include in the report but you cannot change his views.
Of the following, it would be BEST that

    A. you refuse to accept responsibility for the report
    B. you ask that someone else be assigned to this project to replace you
    C. each of you state his own ideas about this recommendation in the report
    D. you give in to the other supervisor's opinion for the sake of harmony

11. Standardized forms are often provided for submitting reports.
Of the following, the MOST important advantage of using standardized forms for reports is that

    A. they take less time to prepare than individually written reports
    B. necessary information is less likely to be omitted
    C. the responsibility for preparing these reports can be delegated to subordinates
    D. the person making the report can omit information he considers unimportant

11._____

12. A report which may BEST be classed as a *periodic* report is one which

    A. requires the same type of information at regular intervals
    B. contains detailed information which is to be retained in permanent records
    C. is prepared whenever a special situation occurs
    D. lists information in graphic form

12._____

13. Which one of the following is NOT an important reason for keeping accurate records in an office?

    A. Facts will be on hand when decisions have to be made.
    B. The basis for past actions can be determined.
    C. Information needed by other bureaus can be furnished.
    D. Filing is easier when records are properly made out.

13._____

14. Suppose you are preparing to write a report recommending a change in a certain procedure. You learn that another supervisor made a report a few years ago suggesting a change in this same procedure, but that no action was taken.
Of the following, it would be MOST desirable for you to

    A. avoid reading the other supervisor's report so that you will write with a more up-to-date point of view
    B. make no recommendation since management seems to be against any change in the procedure
    C. read the other report before you write your report to see what bearing it may have on your recommendations
    D. avoid including in your report any information that can be obtained by referring to the other report

14._____

15. If a report you are preparing to your superior is going to be a very long one, it would be DESIRABLE to include a summary of your basic conclusions

    A. at the end of the report
    B. at the beginning of the report
    C. in a separate memorandum
    D. right after you present the supporting data

15._____

16. Suppose that some bureau and department policies must be very frequently applied by   16.___
your subordinates while others rarely come into use.
As a supervising employee, a GOOD technique for you to use in fulfilling your responsibility of seeing to it that policies are adhered to is to

    A. ask the director of the bureau to issue to all employees an explanation in writing of
all policies
    B. review with your subordinates every week those policies which have daily applica-
tion
    C. follow up on and explain at regular intervals the application of those policies which
are not used very often by your subordinates
    D. recommend to your superiors that policies rarely used be changed or dropped

17. The BASIC purpose behind the principle of delegation of authority is to   17.___

    A. give the supervisor who is delegating a chance to acquire skills in higher level func-
tions
    B. free the supervisor from routine tasks in order that he may do the important parts
of his job
    C. prevent supervisors from overstepping the lines of authority which have been
established
    D. place the work delegated in the hands of those employees who can perform it best

18. A district commander can BEST assist management in long-range planning by   18.___

    A. reporting to his superiors any changing conditions in the district
    B. maintaining a neat and efficiently run office
    C. scheduling work so that areas with a high rate of non-compliance get more inten-
sive coverage
    D. properly training new personnel assigned to his district

19. Suppose that new quarters have been rented for your district office.   19.___
Of the following, the LEAST important factor to be considered in planning the layout of
the office is the

    A. need for screening confidential activities from unauthorized persons
    B. relative importance of the various types of work
    C. areas of noise concentration
    D. convenience with which communication between sections of the office can be
achieved

20. Of the following, the MOST basic effect of organizing a department so that lines of   20.___
authority are clearly defined and duties are specifically assigned is to

    A. increase the need for close supervision
    B. decrease the initiative of subordinates
    C. lessen the possibility of duplication of work
    D. increase the responsibilities of supervisory personnel

21. An accepted management principle is that decisions should be delegated to the lowest   21.____
point in the organization at which they can be made effectively.
The one of the following which is MOST likely to be a result of the application of this
principle is that

    A. no factors will be overlooked in making decisions
    B. prompt action will follow the making of decisions
    C. decisions will be made more rapidly
    D. coordination of decisions that are made will be simplified

22. Suppose you are a supervisor and need some guidance from a higher authority.   22.____
In which one of the following situations would it be PERMISSIBLE for you to bypass
the regular upward channels of communication in the chain of command?

    A. In an emergency when your superior is not available
    B. When it is not essential to get a quick reply
    C. When you feel your immediate superior is not understanding of the situation
    D. When you want to obtain information that you think your superior does not have

23. Of the following, the CHIEF limitation of the organization chart as it is generally used in   23.____
business and government is that the chart

    A. makes lines of responsibility and authority undesirably definite and formal
    B. is often out of date as soon as it is completed
    C. does not show human factors and informal working relationships
    D. is usually too complicated

24. The *span of control* for any supervisor is the   24.____

    A. number of tasks he is expected to perform himself
    B. amount of office space he and his subordinates occupy
    C. amount of work he is responsible for getting out
    D. number of subordinates he can supervise effectively

25. Of the following duties performed by a supervising employee, which would be considered   25.____
a LINE function rather than a staff function?

    A. Evaluation of office personnel
    B. Recommendations for disciplinary action
    C. Initiating budget requests for replacement of equipment
    D. Inspections, at irregular times, of conditions and staff in the field

KEY (CORRECT ANSWERS)

1.	C		11.	B
2.	D		12.	A
3.	C		13.	D
4.	A		14.	C
5.	A		15.	B
6.	C		16.	C
7.	B		17.	B
8.	A		18.	A
9.	A		19.	B
10.	C		20.	C

21.	B
22.	A
23.	C
24.	D
25.	D

———

EXAMINATION SECTION
TEST 1

DIRECTIONS: Each question or incomplete statement is followed by several suggested answers or completions. Select the one that BEST answers the question or completes the statement. *PRINT THE LETTER OF THE CORRECT ANSWER IN THE SPACE AT THE RIGHT.*

1. A supervisor was given a booklet that showed a new work method that could save time. He didn't tell his men because he thought that they would get the booklet anyway. For the supervisor to have acted like this is a   1.____

    A. *good* idea because he saves the time and bother of talking to the men
    B. *bad* idea because he should make sure his men know about better work methods
    C. *good* idea because the men would rather read about it themselves
    D. *bad* idea because a supervisor should always show his men every memo he gets from higher authority

2. A supervisor found it necessary to discipline two subordinates. One man had been operating his equipment in a wrong way, while the other man came to work late for three days in a row. The supervisor decided to talk to both men together. For the supervisor to deal with the problems in this way is a   2.____

    A. *good* idea because each man will learn about the difficulties of the other person and how to solve such difficulties
    B. *bad* idea because the supervisor should wait until he can bring a larger group together and save time in discussing such questions
    C. *good* idea because he will be able to get the men to see that their problems are related
    D. *bad* idea because he should meet with each man separately and give him his full attention

3. A supervisor should try to make his men feel their jobs are important in order to   3.____

    A. get the men to say good things about their supervisor to his own superior
    B. get the men to think in terms of advancing to better jobs
    C. let higher management in the agency know that the supervisor is efficient
    D. help the men to be able to work more efficiently and enthusiastically

4. A supervisor should know approximately how long it takes to do a particular kind of job CHIEFLY because he   4.____

    A. will know how much time to take if he has to do it himself
    B. will be able to tell his men to do it even faster
    C. can judge the performance of the person doing the job
    D. can retrain experienced employees in better work habits

5. Supervisors often get their employees' opinions about better work methods because   5.____

    A. the men will know that they are respected
    B. the men would otherwise lose all their confidence in the supervisor
    C. the supervisor might find in this way a good suggestion he could use
    D. this is the best method for improvement of work methods

6. Right after you have trained your subordinates in doing a new job, you find that they   6.___
   seem to be doing all right, but that it will take them several days to finish. You also have
   several groups of men working at other locations. The MOST efficient way for you to
   make sure that the men continue doing the new job properly is to

   A. stay on that job with the men until it is finished just in case trouble develops
   B. visit the men every half hour until the job is done
   C. stay away from their job that day and visit the men the next day to ask them if they
       had any problems
   D. visit the men a few times each day until they finish the new job

7. Assume that one of your new employees is older than you are. You also think that he   7.___
   may be hard to get along with because he is older than you. The BEST way for you to
   avoid any problems with the older worker is for you to

   A. lay down the law immediately and tell the man he better not cause you any trouble
   B. treat the man just the way you would any other worker
   C. always ask the older worker for advice in the presence of all the men
   D. ignore the man entirely until he realizes that you are the boss

8. Assume that you have tried a new method suggested by one of your employees and find   8.___
   that it is easier and cheaper than the method you had been using.
   The proper thing for you to do NEXT is to

   A. say nothing to anyone but train your men to use the new method
   B. train your men to use the new method and tell your crew that you got the idea from
       one of the men
   C. continue using the old method because a supervisor should not use suggestions of
       his men
   D. have your crew learn the new method and take credit for the idea since you are the
       boss

9. Suppose you are a supervisor and your superior tells you that the way your men are   9.___
   doing a certain procedure is wrong and that you should re-train your men as soon as
   possible.
   When you begin to re-train the men, the FIRST thing you should do is

   A. tell your men that a wrong procedure had been used and that a new method must
       be learned as a result
   B. train your employees in the new method with no explanation since you are the boss
   C. tell the crew that your superior has just decided that everyone should learn a new
       method
   D. tell the crew that your superior says your method is wrong but that you don't agree
       with this

10. It is BAD practice to criticize a man in front of the other men because   10.___

    A. people will think you are too strict
    B. it is annoying to anyone who walks by
    C. it is embarrassing to the man concerned
    D. it will antagonize the other men

11. A supervisor decides not to put his two best men on a work detail because he knows that   11._____
    they won't like it.
    For the supervisor to make the work assignment this way is a

    A. *good* idea because it is only fair to give your best men a break once in a while
    B. *bad* idea because you should treat all of your men fairly and not show favoritism
    C. *good* idea because you save the strength of these men for another job
    D. *bad* idea because more of the men should be exempted from the assignment

12. Suppose you are a supervisor and you find it inconvenient to obey an established proce-   12._____
    dure set by your agency. You think another procedure would be better.
    The BEST thing to do first about this procedure that you don't like is for you to

    A. obey the procedure even if you don't want to and suggest your idea to your own
       supervisor
    B. disregard the procedure because a supervisor is supposed to have some privi-
       leges
    C. follow the procedure some of the time but ignore it when the men are not watching
    D. organize a group of other supervisors to get the procedure changed

13. A supervisor estimated that it would take his crew one workday per week to do a certain   13._____
    job each week. However, after a month he noticed that the job averaged two and a half
    days a week and this delayed other jobs that had to be done.
    The FIRST thing that the supervisor should do in this case is to

    A. call his men together and warn them that they will get a poor work evaluation if they
       do not work harder
    B. talk to each man personally, asking him to work harder on the job
    C. go back and study the maintenance job by himself to see if more men should be
       assigned to the job
    D. write his boss a report describing in detail how much time it is taking the men to do
       the job

14. An employee complains to you that some of his work assignments are too difficult to do   14._____
    alone.
    Which of the following is the BEST way for you to handle this complaint?

    A. Go with him to see exactly what he does and why he finds it so difficult.
    B. Politely tell the man that he has to do the job or be brought up on charges.
    C. Tell the man to send his complaint to the head of your agency.
    D. Sympathize with the man and give him easier jobs.

15. The BEST way for a supervisor to keep control of his work assignments is to   15._____

    A. ask the men to report to him immediately when their jobs are finished
    B. walk around the buildings once a week and get a firsthand view of what is being
       done
    C. keep his ears open for problems and complaints, but leave the men alone to do the
       work
    D. write up a work schedule and check it periodically against the actual work done

16. A supervisor made a work schedule for his men. At the bottom of it, he wrote, *No changes or exceptions will be made in this schedule for any reason.*
For the supervisor to have made this statement is

    A. *good* because the men will respect the supervisor for his attitude
    B. *bad because* there are emergencies and special situations that occur
    C. *good* because each man will know exactly what is expected of him
    D. *bad* because the men should expect that no changes will ever be made in the work schedule without written permission

16.____

17. Which one of the following would NOT be a result of a well-planned work schedule?
The schedule

    A. makes efficient use of the time of the staff
    B. acts as a check list for an important job that might be left out
    C. will give an idea of the work to a substitute supervisor
    D. shows at a glance who the best men are

17.____

18. A new piece of equipment you have ordered is delivered. You are familiar with it, but the men under you who will use it do not know the equipment. Of the following methods, which is the BEST to take in explaining to them how to operate this equipment?

    A. Ask the men to watch other crews using the equipment.
    B. Show one reliable man how to operate the equipment and ask him to teach the other men.
    C. Ask the men to read the instructions in the manual for the equipment.
    D. Call the men together and show them how to operate the equipment.

18.____

19. One supervisor assigns work to his men by calling his crew together each week and describing what has to be done that week. He then tells them to arrange individual assignments among themselves and to work as a team during the week.
This method of scheduling work is a

    A. *good* idea because this guarantees that the men will work together
    B. *bad* idea because responsibility for doing the job is poorly fixed
    C. *good* idea because the men will finish the job in less time, working together
    D. *bad* idea because the supervisor should always stay with his men

19.____

20. Suppose that an employee came to his supervisor with a problem concerning his assignment.
For the supervisor to listen to this problem is a

    A. *good* idea because a supervisor should always take time off to talk when one of his men wants to talk
    B. *bad* idea because the supervisor should not be bothered during the work day
    C. *good* idea because it is the job of the supervisor to deal with problems of job assignment
    D. *bad* idea because the employee could start annoying the supervisor with all sorts of problems

20.____

21. Suppose that on the previous afternoon you were looking for an experienced employee   21.____
in order to give him an emergency job and he was missing from his job location. The next
morning, he tells you that he got sick suddenly and had to go home, but could not tell you
since you were not around. He has never done this before.
What should you do?

    A. Tell the man he is excused and that in such circumstances he did the wisest thing.
    B. Bring the man up on charges because whatever he says he could still have notified
you.
    C. Have the man examined by a doctor to see if he really was sick the day before.
    D. Explain to the man that he should make every effort to tell you or to get a message
to you if he must leave.

22. An employee had a grievance and went to his supervisor about it. The employee was not   22.____
satisfied with the way the supervisor tried to help him and told him so. Yet, the supervisor
had done everything he could under the circumstances.
The PROPER action for the supervisor to take at this time is to

    A. politely tell the employee that there is nothing more for the supervisor to do about
the problem
    B. let the employee know how he can bring his complaint to a higher authority
    C. tell the employee that he must solve the problem on his own since he did not want
to follow the supervisor's advice
    D. suggest to the employee that he ask another supervisor for assistance

23. In which of the following situations is it BEST to give your men spoken rather than written   23.____
orders?

    A. You want your men to have a record of the instructions.
    B. Spoken instructions are less likely to be forgotten.
    C. An emergency situation has arisen in which there is no time to write up instruc-
tions.
    D. There are instructions on time and leave regulations which are complicated.

24. One of your employees tells you that a week ago he had a small accident on the job but   24.____
he did not bother telling you because he was able to continue working.
For the employee not to have told his supervisor about the accident was

    A. *good* because the accident was a small one
    B. *bad* because all accidents should be reported, no matter how small
    C. *good* because the supervisor should be bothered only for important matters
    D. *bad* because having an accident is one way to get excused for the day

25. For a supervisor to deal with each of his subordinates in exactly the same manner is   25.____

    A. *poor* because each man presents a different problem and there is no one way of
handling all problems
    B. *good* because once a problem is handled with one man, he can handle another
man with the same problem
    C. *poor* because the men will resent it if they are not handled each in a better way
than others
    D. *good* because this assures fair and impartial treatment of each subordinate

KEY (CORRECT ANSWERS)

1.	B		11.	B
2.	D		12.	A
3.	D		13.	C
4.	C		14.	A
5.	C		15.	D
6.	D		16.	B
7.	B		17.	D
8.	B		18.	D
9.	A		19.	B
10.	C		20.	C

21.	D
22.	B
23.	C
24.	B
25.	A

———

TEST 2

DIRECTIONS: Each question or incomplete statement is followed by several suggested answers or completions. Select the one that BEST answers the question or completes the statement. *PRINT THE LETTER OF THE CORRECT ANSWER IN THE SPACE AT THE RIGHT.*

1. Jim Johnson has been on your staff for over four years. He has always been a conscientious and productive worker. About a month ago, his wife died; and since that time, his work performance has been very poor.
   As his supervisor, which one of the following is the BEST way for you to deal with this situation?

   A. Allow Jim as much time as he needs to overcome his grief and hope that his work performance improves.
   B. Meet with Jim to discuss ways to improve his performance.
   C. Tell Jim directly that you are more concerned with his work performance than with his personal problem.
   D. Prepare disciplinary action on Jim as soon as possible.

   1.____

2. You are responsible for the overall operation of a storehouse which is divided into two sections. Each section has its own supervisor. You have decided to make several complex changes in the storekeeping procedures which will affect both sections.
   Of the following, the BEST way to make sure that these changes are understood by the two supervisors is for you to

   A. meet with both supervisors to discuss the changes
   B. issue a memorandum to each supervisor explaining the changes
   C. post the changes where the supervisors are sure to see them
   D. instruct one supervisor to explain the changes to the other supervisor

   2.____

3. You have called a meeting of all your subordinates to tell them what has to be done on a new project in which they will all be involved. Several times during the meeting, you ask if there are any questions about what you have told them.
   Of the following, to ask the subordinates whether there are any questions during the meeting can BEST be described as

   A. *inadvisable* because it interferes with their learning about the new project
   B. *advisable* because you will find out what they don't understand and have a chance to clear up any problems they may have
   C. *inadvisable* because it makes the meeting too long and causes the subordinates to lose interest in the new project
   D. *advisable* because it gives you a chance to learn which of your subordinates are paying attention to what you say

   3.____

4. As a supervisor, you are responsible for seeing to it that absenteeism does not become a problem among your subordinates.
   Which one of the following is NOT an acceptable way of controlling the problem of excessive absences?

   A. Distribute a written statement to your staff on the policies regarding absenteeism in your organization.
   B. Arrange for workers who have the fewest absences to talk to those workers who have the most absences.
   C. Let your subordinates know that a record is being kept of all absences.
   D. Arrange for counseling of those employees who are frequently absent.

   4.____

5. One of your supervisors has been an excellent worker for the past two years. There are   5.__
    no promotion opportunities for this worker in the foreseeable future. Due to the city's
    present budget crisis, a salary increase is not possible.
    Under the circumstances, which one of the following actions on your part would be
    MOST likely to continue to motivate this worker?

    A. Tell the worker that times are bad all over and jobs are hard to find.
    B. Give the worker less work and easier assignments.
    C. Tell the worker to try to look for a better paying job elsewhere.
    D. Seek the worker's advice often and show that the suggestions provided are appre-
        ciated.

6. As a supervisor in a warehouse, it is important that you use your available work force to   6.__
    its fullest potential. Which one of the following actions on your part is MOST likely to
    increase the effectiveness of your work force?

    A. Assigning more workers to a job than the number actually needed.
    B. Eliminating all job training to allow more time for work output.
    C. Using your best workers on jobs that average workers can do.
    D. Making sure that all materials and equipment used are maintained in good working
        order.

7. You learn that your storage area will soon be undergoing changes which will affect the   7.__
    work of your subordinates. You decide not to tell your subordinates about what is to hap-
    pen.
    Of the following, your action can BEST be described as

    A. wise because your subordinates will learn of the changes for themselves
    B. unwise because your subordinates should be advised about what is to happen
    C. wise because it is better for your subordinates to continue working without being
        disturbed by such news
    D. unwise because the work of your subordinates will gradually slow down

8. In making plans for the operation of your unit, you are MOST likely to see these plans   8.__
    carried out successfully if you

    A. allow your staff to participate in developing these plans
    B. do not spend any time on the minor details of these plans
    C. base these plans on the past experiences of others
    D. allow these plans to interact with outside activities in other units

9. As a supervisor in charge of the total operation of a food supply warehouse, you find   9.__
    vandalism to be a potentially serious problem. On occasion, trespassers have gained
    entrance into the facility by climbing over an unprotected 8-foot fence surrounding the
    warehouse whose dimensions measure 100 feet by 100 feet.
    Assuming that all of the following would be equally effective ways in preventing these
    breaches in security in the situation described above, which one would be LEAST
    costly?

    A. Using two trained guard dogs to roam freely throughout the facility at night.
    B. Hiring a security guard to patrol the facility after working hours.
    C. Installing tape razor wire on top of the fence surrounding the facility.
    D. Installing an electronic burglar alarm system requiring the installation of a new
        fence.

10. The area for which you have program responsibility has undergone recent changes. Your   10.____
staff is now required to perform many new tasks, and morale is low.
The LEAST effective way for you to improve long-term staff morale would be to

    A. develop support groups to discuss problems
    B. involve staff in job development
    C. maintain a comfortable social environment within the group
    D. adequately plan and give assignments in a timely manner

11. As a supervisor in a large office, one of your subordinate supervisors stops you in the   11.____
middle of the office and complains loudly that he is being treated unfairly. The rest of the
staff ceases work and listens to the complaint. The MOST appropriate action for you to
take in this situation is to

    A. ignore this unprofessional behavior and continue on your way
    B. tell the supervisor that his behavior is unprofessional and he should learn how to
conduct himself
    C. explain to the supervisor why you believe he is not being treated unfairly
    D. ask the supervisor to come to your office at a specific time to discuss the matter

12. You are told that one of your subordinates is distributing literature which attempts to   12.____
recruit individuals to join a particular organization. Several workers complain that their
rights are being violated. Of the following, the BEST action for you to take FIRST is to

    A. ignore the situation because no harm is being done
    B. discuss the matter further with your supervisor
    C. ask the worker to stop distributing the literature
    D. tell the workers that they do not have to read the material

13. You have been assigned to develop a short training course for a recently issued proce-   13.____
dure.
In designing this course, which of the following statements is the LEAST important for
you to consider?

    A. The learning experience must be interesting and meaningful in terms of the staff
member's job.
    B. The method of teaching must be strictly followed in order to develop successful
learning experiences.
    C. The course content should incorporate the rules and regulations of the agency.
    D. The procedure should be consistent with the agency's objectives.

14. As a supervisor, there are several newly-promoted employees under your supervision.   14.____
Each of these employees is subject to a probationary period PRIMARILY to

    A. assess the employee's performance to see if the employee should be retained or
removed from the position
    B. give the employee the option to return to his former employment if the employee is
unhappy in the new position
    C. give the employee an opportunity to learn the duties and responsibilities of the
position
    D. judge the employee's potential for upward mobility in the future

15. An employee under your supervision rushes into your office to tell you he has just received a telephone bomb threat.
As the administrative supervisor, the FIRST thing you should do is

   A. evacuate staff from the floor
   B. call the police and building security
   C. advise your administrator
   D. do a preliminary search

16. After reviewing the Absence Control form for a unit under your supervision, you find that one of your staff members has a fifth undocumented sick leave within a six-month period.
In this situation, the FIRST action you should take is to

   A. discuss the seriousness of the matter with the staff member when he returns to work and fully document the details of the discussion
   B. review the case with the location director and warn the staff member that future use of sick leave will be punished
   C. submit the proper disciplinary forms to ensure that the staff member is penalized for excessive absences
   D. request that the timekeeper put the staff member on doctor's note restriction

17. A subordinate supervisor recently assigned to your office begins his first conference with you by saying that he has learned something that another supervisor is doing that you should know about.
After hearing this statement, of the following, the BEST approach for you to take is to

   A. explain to the supervisor that the conference is to discuss his work and not that of his co-workers
   B. tell the supervisor that you do not encourage a spy *system* among the staff you supervise
   C. tell the supervisor that you will listen to his report only if the other supervisor is present
   D. allow the supervisor to continue talking until you have enough information to make a decision on how best to respond

18. Assume that you are a supervisor recently assigned to a new unit. You notice that, for the past few days, one of the employees in your unit whose work is about average has been stopping work at about four o'clock and has been spending the rest of the afternoon relaxing at his desk.
The BEST of the following actions for you to take in this situation is to

   A. assign more work to this employee since it is apparent that he does not have enough work to keep him busy
   B. observe the employee's conduct more closely for about ten days before taking any more positive action
   C. discuss the matter with the employee, pointing out to him how he can use the extra hour daily to raise the level of his job performance
   D. question the previous supervisor in charge of the unit in order to determine whether he had sanctioned such conduct when he supervised that unit

15.__

16.__

17.__

18.__

19. A new supervisor was assigned to your program four months ago. Although he tries   19.____
    hard, he has been unable to meet certain standards because he still has a lot to learn. As
    his supervisor, you are required to submit performance evaluations within a few days.
    How would you rate this employee on the tasks where he fails to meet standards
    because of lack of experience?

    A. Satisfactory   B. Conditional
    C. Unsatisfactory   D. Unratable

20. You find that there is an important procedural error in a memo which you distributed to   20.____
    your staff several days ago. The BEST approach for you to take at this time is to

    A. send a corrected memo to the staff, indicating what prior error was made
    B. send a corrected memo to the staff without mentioning the prior error
    C. tell the staff about the error at the next monthly staff meeting
    D. place the corrected memo on the office bulletin board

21. Your superior asks you, a supervisor, about the status of the response to a letter from a   21.____
    public official concerning a client's case. When you ask the subordinate who was
    assigned to prepare the response to give you the letter, the subordinate denies that it
    was given to him. You are certain that the subordinate has the letter, but is withholding it
    because the response has not yet been prepared.
    Of the following, in order to secure the letter from the subordinate, you should FIRST

    A. accuse the subordinate of lying and demand that the letter be given to you immedi-
        ately
    B. say that you would consider it a personal favor if the subordinate would find the let-
        ter
    C. continue to question the subordinate until he admits to having been given the letter
    D. offer a face-saving solution, such as asking the subordinate to look again for the
        letter

22. As a supervisor, you have been assigned to write a few paragraphs to be included in the   22.____
    agency's annual report, describing a public service agency department this year as com-
    pared to last year.
    Which of the following elements basic to the agency is LEAST likely to have changed
    since last year?

    A. Mission   B. Structure
    C. Technology   D. Personnel

23. As a supervisor, you have been informed that a grievance has been filed against you,   23.____
    accusing you of assigning a subordinate to out-of-title tasks. Of the following, the BEST
    approach for you to take is to

    A. waive the grievance so that it will proceed to a Step II hearing
    B. immediately change the subordinate's assignment to avoid future problems
    C. respond to the grievance, giving appropriate reasons for the assignment
    D. review the job description to ensure that the subordinate's tasks are not out-of-title

24. Which of the following is NOT a correct statement about agency group training programs in a public service agency?

    24.__

    A. Training sessions continue for an indefinite period of time.
    B. Group training sessions are planned for designated personnel.
    C. Training groups are organized formally through administrative planning.
    D. Group training is task-centered and aimed toward accomplishing specific educational goals.

25. As a supervisor, you have submitted a memo to your superior requesting a conference to discuss the performance of a manager under your supervision. The memo states that the manager has a good working relationship with her staff; however, she tends to interpret agency policy too liberally and shows poor administrative skills by missing some deadlines and not keeping proper controls.
Which of the following steps should NOT be taken in order to prepare for this conference with your superior?

    25.__

    A. Collect and review all your notes regarding the manager's prior performance.
    B. Outline your agenda so that you will have sufficient time to discuss the situation.
    C. Tell the manager that you will be discussing her performance with your superior.
    D. Clearly define objectives which will focus on improving the manager's performance.

KEY (CORRECT ANSWERS)

1.	B		11.	D
2.	A		12.	C
3.	B		13.	B
4.	B		14.	A
5.	D		15.	B
6.	D		16.	A
7.	B		17.	D
8.	A		18.	C
9.	C		19.	B
10.	C		20.	A

21.	D
22.	A
23.	C
24.	A
25.	C

PHILOSOPHY, PRINCIPLES, PRACTICES AND TECHNICS
OF
SUPERVISION, ADMINISTRATION, MANAGEMENT AND ORGANIZATION

TABLE OF CONTENTS

TABLE OF CONTENTS (CONTINUED)

PHILOSOPHY, PRINCIPLES, PRACTICES, AND TECHNICS
OF
SUPERVISION, ADMINISTRATION, MANAGEMENT AND ORGANIZATION

I. MEANING OF SUPERVISION

The extension of the democratic philosophy has been accompanied by an extension in the scope of supervision. Modern leaders and supervisors no longer think of supervision in the narrow sense of being confined chiefly to visiting employees, supplying materials, or rating the staff. They regard supervision as being intimately related to all the concerned agencies of society, they speak of the supervisor's function in terms of "growth", rather than the "improvement," of employees.

This modern concept of supervision may be defined as follows:

Supervision is leadership and the development of leadership within groups which are cooperatively engaged in inspection, research, training, guidance and evaluation.

II. THE OLD AND THE NEW SUPERVISION

TRADITIONAL
1. Inspection
2. Focused on the employee
3. Visitation
4. Random and haphazard
5. Imposed and authoritarian
6. One person usually

MODERN
1. Study and analysis
2. Focused on aims, materials, methods, supervisors, employees, environment
3. Demonstrations, intervisitation, workshops, directed reading, bulletins, etc.
4. Definitely organized and planned (scientific)
5. Cooperative and democratic
6. Many persons involved (creative)

III THE EIGHT (8) BASIC PRINCIPLES OF THE NEW SUPERVISION

1. *PRINCIPLE OF RESPONSIBILITY*
   Authority to act and responsibility for acting must be joined.
   a. If you give responsibility, give authority.
   b. Define employee duties clearly.
   c. Protect employees from criticism by others.
   d. Recognize the rights as well as obligations of employees.
   e. Achieve the aims of a democratic society insofar as it is possible within the area of your work.
   f. Establish a situation favorable to training and learning.
   g. Accept ultimate responsibility for everything done in your section, unit, office, division, department.
   h. Good administration and good supervision are inseparable.

2. *PRINCIPLE OF AUTHORITY*
The success of the supervisor is measured by the extent to which the power of authority is not used.

    a. Exercise simplicity and informality in supervision.
    b. Use the simplest machinery of supervision.
    c. If it is good for the organization as a whole, it is probably justified.
    d. Seldom be arbitrary or authoritative.
    e. Do not base your work on the power of position or of personality.
    f. Permit and encourage the free expression of opinions.

3. *PRINCIPLE OF SELF-GROWTH*
The success of the supervisor is measured by the extent to which, and the speed with which, he is no longer needed.

    a. Base criticism on principles, not on specifics.
    b. Point out higher activities to employees.
    c. Train for self-thinking by employees, to meet new situations.
    d. Stimulate initiative, self-reliance and individual responsibility.
    e. Concentrate on stimulating the growth of employees rather than on removing defects.

4. *PRINCIPLE OF INDIVIDUAL WORTH*
Respect for the individual is a paramount consideration in supervision.

    a. Be human and sympathetic in dealing with employees.
    b. Don't nag about things to be done.
    c. Recognize the individual differences among employees and seek opportunities to permit best expression of each personality.

5. *PRINCIPLE OF CREATIVE LEADERSHIP*
The best supervision is that which is not apparent to the employee.

    a. Stimulate, don't drive employees to creative action.
    b. Emphasize doing good things.
    c. Encourage employees to do what they do best.
    d. Do not be too greatly concerned with details of subject or method.
    e. Do not be concerned exclusively with immediate problems and activities.
    f. Reveal higher activities and make them both desired and maximally possible.
    g. Determine procedures in the light of each situation but see that these are derived from a sound basic philosophy.
    h. Aid, inspire and lead so as to liberate the creative spirit latent in all good employees.

6. *PRINCIPLE OF SUCCESS AND FAILURE*
There are no unsuccessful employees, only unsuccessful supervisors who have failed to give proper leadership.

    a. Adapt suggestions to the capacities, attitudes, and prejudices of employees.
    b. Be gradual, be progressive, be persistent.
    c. Help the employee find the general principle; have the employee apply his own problem to the general principle.
    d. Give adequate appreciation for good work and honest effort.
    e. Anticipate employee difficulties and help to prevent them.
    f. Encourage employees to do the desirable things they will do anyway.
    g. Judge your supervision by the results it secures.

7. *PRINCIPLE OF SCIENCE*
Successful supervision is scientific, objective, and experimental. It is based on facts, not on prejudices.

   a. Be cumulative in results.
   b. Never divorce your suggestions from the goals of training.
   c. Don't be impatient of results.
   d. Keep all matters on a professional, not a personal level.
   e. Do not be concerned exclusively with immediate problems and activities.
   f. Use objective means of determining achievement and rating where possible.

8. *PRINCIPLE OF COOPERATION*
Supervision is a cooperative enterprise between supervisor and employee.

   a. Begin with conditions as they are.
   b. Ask opinions of all involved when formulating policies.
   c. Organization is as good as its weakest link.
   d. Let employees help to determine policies and department programs.
   e. Be approachable and accessible - physically and mentally.
   f. Develop pleasant social relationships.

IV. WHAT IS ADMINISTRATION?

Administration is concerned with providing the environment, the material facilities, and the operational procedures that will promote the maximum growth and development of supervisors and employees. (Organization is an aspect, and a concomitant, of administration.)

There is no sharp line of demarcation between supervision and administration; these functions are intimately interrelated and, often, overlapping. They are complementary activities.

1. *PRACTICES COMMONLY CLASSED AS "SUPERVISORY"*
   a. Conducting employees conferences
   b. Visiting sections, units, offices, divisions, departments
   c. Arranging for demonstrations
   d. Examining plans
   e. Suggesting professional reading
   f. Interpreting bulletins
   g. Recommending in-service training courses
   h. Encouraging experimentation
   i. Appraising employee morale
   j. Providing for intervisitation

2. *PRACTICES COMMONLY CLASSIFIED AS "ADMINISTRATIVE"*
   a. Management of the office
   b. Arrangement of schedules for extra duties
   c. Assignment of rooms or areas
   d. Distribution of supplies
   e. Keeping records and reports
   f. Care of audio-visual materials
   g. Keeping inventory records
   h. Checking record cards and books
   i. Programming special activities
   j. Checking on the attendance and punctuality of employees

3. *PRACTICES COMMONLY CLASSIFIED AS BOTH "SUPERVISORY" AND "ADMINISTRATIVE"*
   a. Program construction
   b. Testing or evaluating outcomes
   c. Personnel accounting
   d. Ordering instructional materials

V. RESPONSIBILITIES OF THE SUPERVISOR

A person employed in a supervisory capacity must constantly be able to improve his own efficiency and ability. He represents the employer to the employees and only continuous self-examination can make him a capable supervisor.

Leadership and training are the supervisor's responsibility. An efficient working unit is one in which the employees work with the supervisor. It is his job to bring out the best in his employees. He must always be relaxed, courteous and calm in his association with his employees. Their feelings are important, and a harsh attitude does not develop the most efficient employees.

VI. COMPETENCIES OF THE SUPERVISOR

1. Complete knowledge of the duties and responsibilities of his position.
2. To be able to organize a job, plan ahead and carry through.
3. To have self-confidence and initiative.
4. To be able to handle the unexpected situation and make quick decisions.
5. To be able to properly train subordinates in the positions they are best suited for.
6. To be able to keep good human relations among his subordinates.
7. To be able to keep good human relations between his subordinates and himself and to earn their respect and trust.

VII. THE PROFESSIONAL SUPERVISOR-EMPLOYEE RELATIONSHIP

There are two kinds of efficiency: one kind is only apparent and is produced in organizations through the exercise of mere discipline; this is but a simulation of the second, or true, efficiency which springs from spontaneous cooperation. If you are a manager, no matter how great or small your responsibility, it is your job, in the final analysis, to create and develop this involuntary cooperation among the people whom you supervise. For, no matter how powerful a combination of money, machines, and materials a company may have, this is a dead and sterile thing without a team of willing, thinking and articulate people to guide it.

The following 21 points are presented as indicative of the exemplary basic relationship that should exist between supervisor and employee:

1. Each person wants to be liked and respected by his fellow employee and wants to be treated with consideration and respect by his superior.
2. The most competent employee will make an error. However, in a unit where good relations exist between the supervisor and his employees, tenseness and fear do not exist. Thus, errors are not hidden or covered up and the efficiency of a unit is not impaired.
3. Subordinates resent rules, regulations, or orders that are unreasonable or unexplained.
4. Subordinates are quick to resent unfairness, harshness, injustices and favoritism.
5. An employee will accept responsibility if he knows that he will be complimented for a job well done, and not too harshly chastised for failure; that his supervisor will check the cause of the failure, and, if it was the supervisor's fault, he will assume the blame therefore. If it was the employee's fault, his supervisor will explain the correct method or means of handling the responsibility.

6. An employee wants to receive credit for a suggestion he has made, that is used. If a suggestion cannot be used, the employee is entitled to an explanation. The supervisor should not say "no" and close the subject.
7. Fear and worry slow up a worker's ability. Poor working environment can impair his physical and mental health. A good supervisor avoids forceful methods, threats and arguments to get a job done.
8. A forceful supervisor is able to train his employees individually and as a team, and is able to motivate them in the proper channels.
9. A mature supervisor is able to properly evaluate his subordinates and to keep them happy and satisfied.
10. A sensitive supervisor will never patronize his subordinates.
11. A worthy supervisor will respect his employees' confidences.
12. Definite and clear-cut responsibilities should be assigned to each executive.
13. Responsibility should always be coupled with corresponding authority.
14. No change should be made in the scope or responsibilities of a position without a definite understanding to that effect on the part of all persons concerned.
15. No executive or employee, occupying a single position in the organization, should be subject to definite orders from more than one source.
16. Orders should never be given to subordinates over the head of a responsible executive. Rather than do this, the officer in question should be supplanted.
17. Criticisms of subordinates should, whoever possible, be made privately, and in no case should a subordinate be criticized in the presence of executives or employees of equal or lower rank.
18. No dispute or difference between executives or employees as to authority or responsibilities should be considered too trivial for prompt and careful adjudication.
19. Promotions, wage changes, and disciplinary action should always be approved by the executive immediately superior to the one directly responsible.
20. No executive or employee should ever be required, or expected, to be at the same time an assistant to, and critic of, another.
21. Any executive whose work is subject to regular inspection should, whever practicable, be given the assistance and facilities necessary to enable him to maintain an independent check of the quality of his work.

VIII. MINI-TEXT IN SUPERVISION, ADMINISTRATION, MANAGEMENT, AND ORGANIZATION

A. BRIEF HIGHLIGHTS

Listed concisely and sequentially are major headings and important data in the field for quick recall and review.

1. *LEVELS OF MANAGEMENT*

Any organization of some size has several levels of management. In terms of a ladder the levels are:

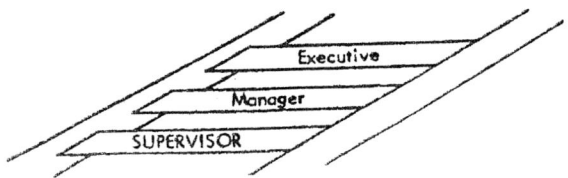

The first level is very important because it is the beginning point of management leadership.

2. *WHAT THE SUPERVISOR MUST LEARN*

A supervisor must learn to:
- (1) Deal with people and their differences
- (2) Get the job done through people
- (3) Recognize the problems when they exist
- (4) Overcome obstacles to good performance
- (5) Evaluate the performance of people
- (6) Check his own performance in terms of accomplishment

3. *A DEFINITION OF SUPERVISOR*

The term supervisor means any individual having authority, in the interests of the employer, to hire, transfer, suspend, lay-off, recall, promote, discharge, assign, reward, or discipline other employees or responsibility to direct them, or to adjust their grievances, or effectively to recommend such action, if, in connection with the foregoing, exercise of such authority is not of a merely routine or clerical nature but requires the use of independent judgment.

4. *ELEMENTS OF THE TEAM CONCEPT*

What is involved in teamwork? The component parts are:

(1) Members	(3) Goals	(5) Cooperation
(2) A leader	(4) Plans	(6) Spirit

5. *PRINCIPLES OF ORGANIZATION*

- (1) A team member must know what his job is.
- (2) Be sure that the nature and scope of a job are understood.
- (3) Authority and responsibility should be carefully spelled out.
- (4) A supervisor should be permitted to make the maximum number of decisions affecting his employees.
- (5) Employees should report to only one supervisor.
- (6) A supervisor should direct only as many employees as he can handle effectively.
- (7) An organization plan should be flexible.
- (8) Inspection and performance of work should be separate.
- (9) Organizational problems should receive immediate attention.
- (10) Assign work in line with ability and experience.

6. *THE FOUR IMPORTANT PARTS OF EVERY JOB*

- (1) Inherent in every job is the *accountability* for results.
- (2) A second set of factors in every job is *responsibilities*.
- (3) Along with duties and responsibilities one must have the *authority* to act within certain limits without obtaining permission to proceed.
- (4) No job exists in a vacuum. The supervisor is surrounded by key *relationships*.

7. *PRINCIPLES OF DELEGATION*

Where work is delegated for the first time, the supervisor should think in terms of these questions:
- (1) Who is best qualified to do this?
- (2) Can an employee improve his abilities by doing this?
- (3) How long should an employee spend on this?
- (4) Are there any special problems for which he will need guidance?
- (5) How broad a delegation can I make?

8. PRINCIPLES OF EFFECTIVE COMMUNICATIONS
      (1) Determine the media
      (2) To whom directed?
      (3) Identification and source authority
      (4) Is communication understood?

9. PRINCIPLES OF WORK IMPROVEMENT
      (1) Most people usually do only the work which is assigned to them
      (2) Workers are likely to fit assigned work into the time available to perform it
      (3) A good workload usually stimulates output
      (4) People usually do their best work when they know that results will be reviewed or inspected
      (5) Employees usually feel that someone else is responsible for conditions of work, workplace layout, job methods, type of tools/equipment, and other such factors
      (6) Employees are usually defensive about their job security
      (7) Employees have natural resistance to change
      (8) Employees can support or destroy a supervisor
      (9) A supervisor usually earns the respect of his people through his personal example of diligence and efficiency

10. AREAS OF JOB IMPROVEMENT
The areas of job improvement are quite numerous, but the most common ones which a supervisor can identify and utilize are:

(1) Departmental layout	(5) Work methods
(2) Flow of work	(6) Materials handling
(3) Workplace layout	(7) Utilization
(4) Utilization of manpower	(8) Motion economy

11. SEVEN KEY POINTS IN MAKING IMPROVEMENTS
      (1) Select the job to be improved
      (2) Study how it is being done now
      (3) Question the present method
      (4) Determine actions to be taken
      (5) Chart proposed method
      (6) Get approval and apply
      (7) Solicit worker participation

12. CORRECTIVE TECHNIQUES OF JOB IMPROVEMENT

Specific Problems	General Improvement	Corrective Techniques
(1) Size of workload	(1) Departmental layout	(1) Study with scale model
(2) Inability to meet schedules	(2) Flow of work	(2) Flow chart study
(3) Strain and fatigue	(3) Work plan layout	(3) Motion analysis
(4) Improper use of men and skills	(4) Utilization of manpower	(4) Comparison of units produced to standard allowance
(5) Waste, poor quality, unsafe conditions	(5) Work methods	(5) Methods analysis
(6) Bottleneck conditions that hinder output	(6) Materials handling	(6) Flow chart & equipment study
(7) Poor utilization of equipment and machine	(7) Utilization of equipment	(7) Down time vs. running time
(8) Efficiency and productivity of labor	(8) Motion economy	(8) Motion analysis

13. A *PLANNING CHECKLIST*

(1) Objectives	(6) Resources	(11) Safety
(2) Controls	(7) Manpower	(12) Money
(3) Delegations	(8) Equipment	(13) Work
(4) Communications	(9) Supplies and materials	(14) Timing of improvements
(5) Resources	(10) Utilization of time	

14. *FIVE CHARACTERISTICS OF GOOD DIRECTIONS*

In order to get results, directions must be:

(1) Possible of accomplishment	(3) Related to mission	(5) Unmistakably clear
(2) Agreeable with worker interests	(4) Planned and complete	

15. *TYPES OF DIRECTIONS*

(1) Demands or direct orders	(3) Suggestion or implication
(2) Requests	(4) Volunteering

16. *CONTROLS*

A typical listing of the overall areas in which the supervisor should establish controls might be:

(1) Manpower	(3) Quality of work	(5) Time	(7) Money
(2) Materials	(4) Quantity of work	(6) Space	(8) Methods

17. *ORIENTING THE NEW EMPLOYEE*

(1) Prepare for him	(3) Orientation for the job
(2) Welcome the new employee	(4) Follow-up

18. *CHECKLIST FOR ORIENTING NEW EMPLOYEES*   Yes   No

(1) Do your appreciate the feelings of new employees when they first report for work? ____ ____

(2) Are you aware of the fact that the new employee must make a big adjustment to his job? ____ ____

(3) Have you given him good reasons for liking the job and the organization? ____ ____

(4) Have you prepared for his first day on the job?

(5) Did you welcome him cordially and make him feel needed?

(6) Did you establish rapport with him so that he feels free to talk and discuss matters with you? ____ ____

(7) Did you explain his job to him and his relationship to you? ____ ____

(8) Does he know that his work will be evaluated periodically on a basis that is fair and objective? ____ ____

(9) Did you introduce him to his fellow workers in such a way that they are likely to accept him? ____ ____

(10) Does he know what employee benefits he will receive?

(11) Does he understand the importance of being on the job and what to do if he must leave his duty station? ____ ____

(12) Has he been impressed with the importance of accident prevention and safe practice? ____ ____

(13) Does he generally know his way around the department? ____ ____

(14) Is he under the guidance of a sponsor who will teach the right ways of doing things? ____ ____

(15) Do you plan to follow-up so that he will continue to adjust successfully to his job? ____ ____

19. *PRINCIPLES OF LEARNING*
       (1) Motivation   (2) Demonstration or explanation   (3) Practice

20. *CAUSES OF POOR PERFORMANCE*
       (1) Improper training for job
       (2) Wrong tools
       (3) Inadequate directions
       (4) Lack of supervisory follow-up
       (5) Poor communications
       (6) Lack of standards of performance
       (7) Wrong work habits
       (8) Low morale
       (9) Other

21. *FOUR MAJOR STEPS IN ON-THE-JOB INSTRUCTION*
       (1) Prepare the worker
       (2) Present the operation
       (3) Tryout performance
       (4) Follow-up

22. *EMPLOYEES WANT FIVE THINGS*
       (1) Security (2) Opportunity (3) Recognition (4) Inclusion (5) Expression

23. *SOME DON'TS IN REGARD TO PRAISE*
       (1) Don't praise a person for something he hasn't done
       (2) Don't praise a person unless you can be sincere
       (3) Don't be sparing in praise just because your superior withholds it from you
       (4) Don't let too much time elapse between good performance and recognition of it

24. *HOW TO GAIN YOUR WORKERS' CONFIDENCE*
Methods of developing confidence include such things as:
       (1) Knowing the interests, habits, hobbies of employees
       (2) Admitting your own inadequacies
       (3) Sharing and telling of confidence in others
       (4) Supporting people when they are in trouble
       (5) Delegating matters that can be well handled
       (6) Being frank and straightforward about problems and working conditions
       (7) Encouraging others to bring their problems to you
       (8) Taking action on problems which impede worker progress

25. *SOURCES OF EMPLOYEE PROBLEMS*
On-the-job causes might be such things as:
       (1) A feeling that favoritism is exercised in assignments
       (2) Assignment of overtime
       (3) An undue amount of supervision
       (4) Changing methods or systems
       (5) Stealing of ideas or trade secrets
       (6) Lack of interest in job
       (7) Threat of reduction in force
       (8) Ignorance or lack of communications
       (9) Poor equipment
      (10) Lack of knowing how supervisor feels toward employee
      (11) Shift assignments

Off-the-job problems might have to do with:
       (1) Health   (2) Finances   (3) Housing   (4) Family

26. *THE SUPERVISOR'S KEY TO DISCIPLINE*
There are several key points about discipline which the supervisor should keep in mind:
    (1) Job discipline is one of the disciplines of life and is directed by the supervisor.
    (2) It is more important to correct an employee fault than to fix blame for it.
    (3) Employee performance is affected by problems both on the job and off.
    (4) Sudden or abrupt changes in behavior can be indications of important employee problems.
    (5) Problems should be dealt with as soon as possible after they are identified.
    (6) The attitude of the supervisor may have more to do with solving problems than the techniques of problem solving.
    (7) Correction of employee behavior should be resorted to only after the supervisor is sure that training or counseling will not be helpful.
    (8) Be sure to document your disciplinary actions.
    (9) Make sure that you are disciplining on the basis of facts rather than personal feelings.
    (10) Take each disciplinary step in order, being careful not to make snap judgments, or decisions based on impatience.

27. *FIVE IMPORTANT PROCESSES OF MANAGEMENT*
    (1) Planning   (2) Organizing   (3) Scheduling
    (4) Controlling   (5) Motivating

28. *WHEN THE SUPERVISOR FAILS TO PLAN*
    (1) Supervisor creates impression of not knowing his job
    (2) May lead to excessive overtime
    (3) Job runs itself -- supervisor lacks control
    (4) Deadlines and appointments missed
    (5) Parts of the work go undone
    (6) Work interrupted by emergencies
    (7) Sets a bad example
    (8) Uneven workload creates peaks and valleys
    (9) Too much time on minor details at expense of more important tasks

29. *FOURTEEN GENERAL PRINCIPLES OF MANAGEMENT*

(1) Division of work	(8) Centralization
(2) Authority and responsibility	(9) Scalar chain
(3) Discipline	(10) Order
(4) Unity of command	(11) Equity
(5) Unity of direction	(12) Stability of tenure of personnel
(6) Subordination of individual interest to general interest	(13) Initiative
(7) Remuneration of personnel	(14) Esprit de corps

30. *CHANGE*
Bringing about change is perhaps attempted more often, and yet less well understood, than anything else the supervisor does. How do people generally react to change? (People tend to resist change that is imposed upon them by other individuals or circumstances.

Change is characteristic of every situation. It is a part of every real endeavor where the efforts of people are concerned.

A. Why do people resist change?
People may resist change because of:
(1) Fear of the unknown
(2) Implied criticism
(3) Unpleasant experiences in the past
(4) Fear of loss of status
(5) Threat to the ego
(6) Fear of loss of economic stability

B. How can we best overcome the resistance to change?
In initiating change, take these steps:
(1) Get ready to sell
(2) Identify sources of help
(3) Anticipate objections
(4) Sell benefits
(5) Listen in depth
(6) Follow up

B. BRIEF TOPICAL SUMMARIES

I. WHO/WHAT IS THE SUPERVISOR?
1. The supervisor is often called the "highest level employee and the lowest level manager."
2. A supervisor is a member of both management and the work group. He acts as a bridge between the two.
3. Most problems in supervision are in the area of human relations, or people problems.
4. Employees expect: Respect, opportunity to learn and to advance, and a sense of belonging, and so forth.
5. Supervisors are responsible for directing people and organizing work. Planning is of paramount importance.
6. A position description is a set of duties and responsibilities inherent to a given position.
7. It is important to keep the position description up-to-date and to provide each employee with his own copy.

II. THE SOCIOLOGY OF WORK
1. People are alike in many ways; however, each individual is unique.
2. The supervisor is challenged in getting to know employee differences. Acquiring skills in evaluating individuals is an asset.
3. Maintaining meaningful working relationships in the organization is of great importance.
4. The supervisor has an obligation to help individuals to develop to their fullest potential.
5. Job rotation on a planned basis helps to build versatility and to maintain interest and enthusiasm in work groups.
6. Cross training (job rotation) provides backup skills.
7. The supervisor can help reduce tension by maintaining a sense of humor, providing guidance to employees, and by making reasonable and timely decisions. Employees respond favorably to working under reasonably predictable circumstances.
8. Change is characteristic of all managerial behavior. The supervisor must adjust to changes in procedures, new methods, technological changes, and to a number of new and sometimes challenging situations.
9. To overcome the natural tendency for people to resist change, the supervisor should become more skillful in initiating change.

III. PRINCIPLES AND PRACTICES OF SUPERVISION

1. Employees should be required to answer to only one superior.
2. A supervisor can effectively direct only a limited number of employees, depending upon the complexity, variety, and proximity of the jobs involved.
3. The organizational chart presents the organization in graphic form. It reflects lines of authority and responsibility as well as interrelationships of units within the organization.
4. Distribution of work can be improved through an analysis using the "Work Distribution Chart."
5. The "Work Distribution Chart" reflects the division of work within a unit in understandable form.
6. When related tasks are given to an employee, he has a better chance of increasing his skills through training.
7. The individual who is given the responsibility for tasks must also be given the appropriate authority to insure adequate results.
8. The supervisor should delegate repetitive, routine work. Preparation of recurring reports, maintaining leave and attendance records are some examples.
9. Good discipline is essential to good task performance. Discipline is reflected in the actions of employees on the job in the absence of supervision.
10. Disciplinary action may have to be taken when the positive aspects of discipline have failed. Reprimand, warning, and suspension are examples of disciplinary action.
11. If a situation calls for a reprimand, be sure it is deserved and remember it is to be done in private.

IV. DYNAMIC LEADERSHIP

1. A style is a personal method or manner of exerting influence.
2. Authoritarian leaders often see themselves as the source of power and authority.
3. The democratic leader often perceives the group as the source of authority and power.
4. Supervisors tend to do better when using the pattern of leadership that is most natural for them.
5. Social scientists suggest that the effective supervisor use the leadership style that best fits the problem or circumstances involved.
6. All four styles -- telling, selling, consulting, joining -- have their place. Using one does not preclude using the other at another time.
7. The theory X point of view assumes that the average person dislikes work, will avoid it whenever possible, and must be coerced to achieve organizational objectives.
8. The theory Y point of view assumes that the average person considers work to be as natural as play, and, when the individual is committed, he requires little supervision or direction to accomplish desired objectives.
9. The leader's basic assumptions concerning human behavior and human nature affect his actions, decisions, and other managerial practices.
10. Dissatisfaction among employees is often present, but difficult to isolate. The supervisor should seek to weaken dissatisfaction by keeping promises, being sincere and considerate, keeping employees informed, and so forth.
11. Constructive suggestions should be encouraged during the natural progress of the work.

V. PROCESSES FOR SOLVING PROBLEMS

1. People find their daily tasks more meaningful and satisfying when they can improve them.
2. The causes of problems, or the key factors, are often hidden in the background. Ability to solve problems often involves the ability to isolate them from their backgrounds. There is some substance to the cliché that some persons "can't see the forest for the trees."
3. New procedures are often developed from old ones. Problems should be broken down into manageable parts. New ideas can be adapted from old ones.

4. People think differently in problem-solving situations. Using a logical, patterned approach is often useful. One approach found to be useful includes these steps:

(a) Define the problem	(d) Weigh and decide
(b) Establish objectives	(e) Take action
(c) Get the facts	(f) Evaluate action

VI. TRAINING FOR RESULTS

1. Participants respond best when they feel training is important to them.
2. The supervisor has responsibility for the training and development of those who report to him.
3. When training is delegated to others, great care must be exercised to insure the trainer has knowledge, aptitude, and interest for his work as a trainer.
4. Training (learning) of some type goes on continually. The most successful supervisor makes certain the learning contributes in a productive manner to operational goals.
5. New employees are particularly susceptible to training. Older employees facing new job situations require specific training, as well as having need for development and growth opportunities.
6. Training needs require continuous monitoring.
7. The training officer of an agency is a professional with a responsibility to assist supervisors in solving training problems.
8. Many of the self-development steps important to the supervisor's own growth are equally important to the development of peers and subordinates. Knowledge of these is important when the supervisor consults with others on development and growth opportunities.

VII. HEALTH, SAFETY, AND ACCIDENT PREVENTION

1. Management-minded supervisors take appropriate measures to assist employees in maintaining health and in assuring safe practices in the work environment.
2. Effective safety training and practices help to avoid injury and accidents.
3. Safety should be a management goal. All infractions of safety which are observed should be corrected without exception.
4. Employees' safety attitude, training and instruction, provision of safe tools and equipment, supervision, and leadership are considered highly important factors which contribute to safety and which can be influenced directly by supervisors.
5. When accidents do occur they should be investigated promptly for very important reasons, including the fact that information which is gained can be used to prevent accidents in the future.

VIII. EQUAL EMPLOYMENT OPPORTUNITY

1. The supervisor should endeavor to treat all employees fairly, without regard to religion, race, sex, or national origin.
2. Groups tend to reflect the attitude of the leader. Prejudice can be detected even in very subtle form. Supervisors must strive to create a feeling of mutual respect and confidence in every employee.
3. Complete utilization of all human resources is a national goal. Equitable consideration should be accorded women in the work force, minority-group members, the physically and mentally handicapped, and the older employee. The important question is: "Who can do the job?"
4. Training opportunities, recognition for performance, overtime assignments, promotional opportunities, and all other personnel actions are to be handled on an equitable basis.

IX. IMPROVING COMMUNICATIONS

1. Communications is achieving understanding between the sender and the receiver of a message. It also means sharing information -- the creation of understanding.
2. Communication is basic to all human activity. Words are means of conveying meanings; however, real meanings are in people.
3. There are very practical differences in the effectiveness of one-way, impersonal, and two-way communications. Words spoken face-to-face are better understood. Telephone conversations are effective, but lack the rapport of person-to-person exchanges. The whole person communicates.
4. Cooperation and communication in an organization go hand in hand. When there is a mutual respect between people, spelling out rules and procedures for communicating is unnecessary.
5. There are several barriers to effective communications. These include failure to listen with respect and understanding, lack of skill in feedback, and misinterpreting the meanings of words used by the speaker. It is also common practice to listen to what we want to hear, and tune out things we do not want to hear.
6. Communication is management's chief problem. The supervisor should accept the challenge to communicate more effectively and to improve interagency and intra-agency communications.
7. The supervisor may often plan for and conduct meetings. The planning phase is critical and may determine the success or the failure of a meeting.
8. Speaking before groups usually requires extra effort. Stage fright may never disappear completely, but it can be controlled.

X. SELF-DEVELOPMENT

1. Every employee is responsible for his own self-development.
2. Toastmaster and toastmistress clubs offer opportunities to improve skills in oral communications.
3. Planning for one's own self-development is of vital importance. Supervisors know their own strengths and limitations better than anyone else.
4. Many opportunities are open to aid the supervisor in his developmental efforts, including job assignments; training opportunities, both governmental and non-governmental -- to include universities and professional conferences and seminars.
5. Programmed instruction offers a means of studying at one's own rate.
6. Where difficulties may arise from a supervisor's being away from his work for training, he may participate in televised home study or correspondence courses to meet his self-develop- ment needs.

XI. TEACHING AND TRAINING

A. The Teaching Process

Teaching is encouraging and guiding the learning activities of students toward established goals. In most cases this process consists in five steps: preparation, presentation, summarization, evaluation, and application.

1. Preparation

Preparation is twofold in nature; that of the supervisor and the employee.

Preparation by the supervisor is absolutely essential to success. He must know what, when, where, how, and whom he will teach. Some of the factors that should be considered are:

(1) The objectives	(5) Employee interest
(2) The materials needed	(6) Training aids
(3) The methods to be used	(7) Evaluation
(4) Employee participation	(8) Summarization

Employee preparation consists in preparing the employee to receive the material. Probably the most important single factor in the preparation of the employee is arousing and maintaining his interest. He must know the objectives of the training, why he is there, how the material can be used, and its importance to him.

2. Presentation

In presentation, have a carefully designed plan and follow it.
The plan should be accurate and complete, yet flexible enough to meet situations as they arise. The method of presentation will be determined by the particular situation and objectives.

3. Summary

A summary should be made at the end of every training unit and program. In addition, there may be internal summaries depending on the nature of the material being taught. The important thing is that the trainee must always be able to understand how each part of the new material relates to the whole.

4. Application

The supervisor must arrange work so the employee will be given a chance to apply new knowledge or skills while the material is still clear in his mind and interest is high. The trainee does not really know whether he has learned the material until he has been given a chance to apply it. If the material is not applied, it loses most of its value.

5. Evaluation

The purpose of all training is to promote learning. To determine whether the training has been a success or failure, the supervisor must evaluate this learning.

In the broadest sense evaluation includes all the devices, methods, skills, and techniques used by the supervisor to keep him self and the employees informed as to their progress toward the objectives they are pursuing. The extent to which the employee has mastered the knowledge, skills, and abilities, or changed his attitudes, as determined by the program objectives, is the extent to which instruction has succeeded or failed.

Evaluation should not be confined to the end of the lesson, day, or program but should be used continuously. We shall note later the way this relates to the rest of the teaching process.

B. Teaching Methods

A teaching method is a pattern of identifiable student and instructor activity used in presenting training material.

All supervisors are faced with the problem of deciding which method should be used at a given time.

As with all methods, there are certain advantages and disadvantages to each method.

1. Lecture

The lecture is direct oral presentation of material by the supervisor. The present trend is to place less emphasis on the trainer's activity and more on that of the trainee.

2. Discussion

Teaching by discussion or conference involves using questions and other techniques to arouse interest and focus attention upon certain areas, and by doing so creating a learning situation. This can be one of the most valuable methods because it gives the employees 'an opportunity to express their ideas and pool their knowledge.

3. Demonstration

The demonstration is used to teach how something works or how to do something. It can be used to show a principle or what the results of a series of actions will be. A well-staged demonstration is particularly effective because it shows proper methods of performance in a realistic manner.

4. Performance

Performance is one of the most fundamental of all learning techniques or teaching methods. The trainee may be able to tell how a specific operation should be performed but he cannot be sure he knows how to perform the operation until he has done so.

5. Which Method to Use

Moreover, there are other methods and techniques of teaching. It is difficult to use any method without other methods entering into it. In any learning situation a combination of methods is usually more effective than anyone method alone.

Finally, evaluation must be integrated into the other aspects of the teaching-learning process.

It must be used in the motivation of the trainees; it must be used to assist in developing understanding during the training; and it must be related to employee application of the results of training.

This is distinctly the role of the supervisor.

POLICE COMMUNICATIONS & TELETYPE OPERATIONS

TABLE OF CONTENTS

POLICE COMMUNICATIONS & TELETYPE OPERATIONS

I. COMMUNICATIONS

A. RADIOS IN AUTOMOBILES

It is an Unclassified misdemeanor for any person who is not a peace officer to either equip an automobile with or knowingly use an automobile equipped with a radio receiving set capable of receiving signals on the frequencies allocated to police use. Excepted are holders of Federal amateur radio operator's licenses operating a receiver in connection with a mobile transmitter (V&T Sec. 397).

B. POLICE RADIO MESSAGES

It is a like misdemeanor to in any way knowingly interfere with the transmission of radio messages by police without first having secured a permit to do so from the person authorized to issue such a permit by the local municipal governing body or board. Offenses are punishable by fine not over $1,000, imprisonment not more than 6 months, or both (V&T Sec. 397).

The law excepts persons who hold a valid amateur radio operator's license issued by the Federal Communications Commission and who operate a duly licensed portable transmitter-receiver on frequencies allocated by the Federal Communications Commission to licensed radio amateurs (V&T Sec. 397).

C. TAMPERING WITH PRIVATE COMMUNICATIONS

A person is guilty of Tampering with Private Communications when, knowing that he does not have the consent of the sender or receiver, he obtains or attempts to obtain from an employee, officer or representative, of a telephone or telegraph corporation, by connivance, deception, intimidation or in any other manner, information with respect to the contents or nature thereof of a telephonic or telegraphic communication (P.L. Sec. 250.25, subd. 3).

A person is also guilty of Tampering with Private Communications when, knowing that he does not have the consent of the sender or receiver, and being an employee, officer or representative of a telephone or telegraph corporation, he knowingly divulges to another person the contents or nature thereof of a telephonic or telegraphic communication. The provisions of this subdivision do not apply to such person when he acts to report a criminal communication under the requirements of Penal Law Section 250.35 (see next paragraph) (P.L. Sec. 250.25, subd. 4). Tampering with Private Communications is a Class B misdemeanor.

D. FAILING TO REPORT CRIMINAL TELEPHONE OR TELEGRAPH COMMUNICATIONS

It is the duty of a telephone or telegraph corporation and of any employee, officer or representative thereof having knowledge that the facilities of such corporation are being used to conduct any criminal business, traffic or transaction, to furnish or attempt to furnish to an appropriate law enforcement officer or agency, all pertinent information within his possessionrelating to such matter, and to cooperate fully with any law enforcement officer or agency investigating such matter. A person is guilty of Failing to Report Criminal Communications when he knowingly violates any duty prescribed in this section (P.L. Sec. 250.35).

Failing to Report Criminal Communications is a Class B misdemeanor.

The prohibitions in Section 250.25, Penal Law do not apply to a law enforcement officer who obtains information from a telephone or telegraph corporation pursuant to Section 250.35 of the Penal Law (P.L. Sec. 250.25, subd.3).

E. UNLAWFULLY OBTAINING COMMUNICATIONS INFORMATION

A person is guilty of Unlawfully Obtaining Communications Information when, knowing that he does not have the authorization of a telephone or telegraph corporation, he obtains or attempts to obtain, by deception, stealth or in any other manner, from such corporation or from any employee, officer or representative thereof:

1. Information concerning identification or location of any wires, cables, lines, terminals or other apparatus used in furnishing telephone or telegraph service; or
2. Information concerning a record of any communication passing over telephone or telegraph lines of any such corporation (P.L. Sec. 250.30).

Unlawfully Obtaining Communications Information is a Class B misdemeanor.

F. TAMPERING WITH LETTERS, MAIL, ETC.

A person is guilty of Tampering with Private Communications when:

1. Knowing that he does not have the consent of the sender or receiver, he opens or reads a sealed letter or other sealed private communication (P.L. Sec. 250.25, subd. 1); or
2. Knowing that a sealed letter or other sealed private communication has been opened or read in violation of subdivision one of this section, he divulges, without the consent of the sender or receiver, the contents of such letter or communication, in whole or in part, or a resume of any portion of the contents thereof (P.L. Sec. 250.25, subd. 2).

Tampering with Private Communications is a Class B misdemeanor.

It is a Federal crime, punishable by $2,000 fine or 5 years imprisonment or both, to take a letter, postcard or package out of any post office or authorized depository or from a mail carrier or to take such thing which has been in the mails before it is delivered to a person to whom directed, with intent to obstruct the correspondence or to pry into the business or secrets of another. This violation includes taking mail left by the carrier, including from private mail boxes where deposited by the carrier.

It is also a Federal violation to steal or obtain mail by fraud from the post office or any postal facility.

These Federal violations are investigated by U.S. Postal Inspectors, who should be promptly notified of offenses (Title 18 U.S. Code, Secs. 1703, 1708).

II. OFFENSES IN USE OF COMMUNICATION MEDIA

A. PARTY LINES

A person commits the crime of Unlawfully Refusing to Yield a Party Line when being informed that a party line is needed for an emergency call, he refuses to immediately relinquish the line (P.L. Sec 270.15, subd. 2).

Unlawfully Refusing to Yield a Party Line is a Class B misdemeanor. A "party line" is a subscriber's line telephone circuit, consisting of two or more main telephone stations connected therewith, each station with a distinctive ring or telephone number (P.L. Sec. 270.15, subd. 1-a). An "emergency call" is a telephone call to a police or fire department, or for medical aid or ambulance service, necessitated by a situation in which human life or property is in jeopardy and prompt summoning of aid is essential (P.L. Sec. 270.15, subd. 1-b).

B. ANNOYING OR ALARMING COMMUNICATIONS

It is the crime of Aggravated Harassment to communicate with a person anonymously or otherwise, by telephone, telegraph, mail or any other form of communication, in a manner likely to cause annoyance or alarm, with intent to harass, annoy or alarm another (P.L. Sec. 240.30, subd.1). Aggravated Harassment is a Class A misdemeanor.

C. JAMMING, OTHER NON-LEGITIMATE PHONE CALLS
It is also Aggravated Harassment for any person to make a telephone call, whether or not a conversation ensues, with no purpose of legitimate communication and with intent to harass, annoy or alarm another (P.L. Sec. 240.30, subd. 2).

D. THEFT OF SERVICES (TELEPHONE, TELEGRAPH)
A person is guilty of Theft of Services when, with intent to avoid payment by himself or another person of the lawful charge for any telecommunications service, he obtains or attempts to avoid payment therefor by himself or another person by means of:
1. Tampering or making connection with the equipment of the supplier, whether by mechanical, electrical, acoustical, or other means, or
2. Any misrepresentation of fact which he knows to be false, or
3. Any other artifice, trick,deception, code or device (P.L. Sec. 165.15, subd. 4).

Theft of Services is a Class A misdemeanor. It includes use of illicit credit cards

III. INVESTIGATIONS

In any case involving police-frequency radio in automobiles, care must be taken to ensure that an actual test of the illicit receiver is made, to establish receipt of police frequencies. In addition, an expert in radio matters should make an examination of the radio, for expert testimony that the radio could receive police frequencies.

In taking complaints dealing with Tampering with Private Communications, the officer must be certain to pin down specific facts and details of the matter divulged, with exact times, dates and facts as to identification of violators.

In cases involving *"jamming"* telephones, it is proper to take detailed written statements from complaints, setting down the time and date of the calls and specific words said. Any factual information the victim may have to identify the offender should be obtained in detail. Where positive proof of identity is lacking, obtain permission to monitor the victim's telephone and consider obtaining an order to monitor the telephone of any suspect. Telephone companies may be able to offer valuable technical assistance in respect to crimes of this kind and the possibilities should be explored with ranking telephone company officals in proper cases.

In party line telephone cases, the officer must establish that the offender was in fact informed that the line was needed for an emergency call and that the emergency met the terms of the statute. A factor of identification of the offender is always present and if the complainant is not familiar with the offender, arrangements may be made for telephone and personal confrontation of the complainant and each potential user of the party line who could be the offender, for identification purposes. Officers should not overlook the value of proper interrogation of suspects in this kind of case.
In cases involving Theft of Services, officers should always work closely with telephone company sections assigned responsibility for attempting to determine to whom calls should properly be billed, since these persons are frequently able to make associations of persons and numbers which cannot be done by anyone not constantly working with such things.

IV. POLICE RADIO COMMUNICATIONS

Police radio transmitters must be licensed by the Federal Communications Commission (FCC). Each Base Station transmitter must be licensed. All mobile stations are included under the main license. The FCC will assign appropriate frequencies and call letters. Police radio falls in the category of "Public Safety Radio Services" in FCC terminology and is covered by FCC Rules and Regulations, Part 89.

All adjustments and tests which may affect the proper operation of police radios must be made only by holders of first or second class commercial radio operator's licenses. Such license holders may be either a department member or an outsider, such as a radio shop owner or employee.

Police officers and dispatchers broadcasting over police voice radios are not required to have individual licenses.

FCC Rules and Regulations, Sec. 89.151, require that all police transmissions, regardless of their nature, shall be restricted to the minimum practical transmission time.

In all police agencies with radio broadcasting systems, clear general instructions should be in effect to ensure that the headquarters transmitter is in charge of the air and may order other units silenced for priority messages, regardless of the rank of persons using mobile equipment, including radio cars, in the field.

In an emergency, the headquarters transmitter can temporarily transfer command of the air to a ranking officer in the field. This should be a rare occasion and should be done on a formal basis. There should be no informal monopolizing of the air by mobile units in the field.

A list of emergency telephone numbers should be maintained at the dispatcher's desk. The list should be regularly checked and kept current and complete. It should include hospitals, ambulance service, doctors available for emergencies, fire departments, coroner and medical examiners, garages, etc.

A. GENERAL REQUIREMENTS FOR PROPER TRANSMISSIONS

All transmission must be clearly enunicated. The microphone should be held exactly in front of the speaker's lips and about two inches away. The voice should always be free of emotion or stress. The speaker must be certain that a very brief pause is made after pressing the transmitter button and before speaking and that another very brief pause is made before releasing the button after speaking, to avoid chopping off parts of the transmission.

Inexperienced officers commonly fail to clearly enunciate and often chop off parts of their transmissions by pressing or releasing the transmitter button too late or too soon. All officers using any transmitter should receive substantial training to ensure that they use it properly. (A microphone-amplifier-loudspeaker or a tape recorder set-up should be used in training and not any actual radio transmissions.)

Training should include practice in the use of established radio procedure of the department and in brief, clear wording of transmissions, whether information messages, requests for information or instructions.

Headquarters radio transmitters are distinguishable by sound from the mobile transmitters. It is thus not necessary for headquarters to always identify itself. FCC rules require only that the main station shall identify itself with its assigned call letters at least once each thirty minutes during each period of operation. Mobile transmitters (radio cars, walkie-talkies, etc.) must identify themselves with the geographic name of the governmental subdivision under whose name the main station is licensed (e.g., car two of the Southton, N.Y., Police Department would call itself "Southton two").

A usual, clear and brief routine would thus be: "Car two" (from headquarters); "Southton two" (from the mobile unit), "Compliant, Mrs. John Doe, one Main Street, family disturbance" (from Headquarters); "Southton two okay" (from the mobile unit). With these brief messages, headquarters has located car two "in service," issued instructions to investigate a family disturbance based on a complaint, given the identity of the complainant and the location of the disturbance and has been informed by car two that the message was understood and that the instructions would be complied with.

Established procedures should also include routing for mobile units to inform headquarters when they go into service at the beginning of a tour of duty and when they go out of service from time to time during the tour. The initial call at the beginning of the tour will automatically give a check of the operating condition of the mobile units' radio equipment. The officer or officers using the equipment during the tour should be identified in this initial call.

A usual routing would be: "Southton two" (from the mobile unit); "Car two" (from headquarters); "In service, occupant 113" (from the mobile unit); "'Okay two" (acknowledgment from headquarters, specifying which car is being acknowledged).

"Occupant 113" identifies the officers in Southton Car two in the preceding example. It is best to use numbers, usually badge or shield numbers, to identify officers on the air. It is more secure against unauthorized listeners and is more accurate and brief than using names. The headquarters radioman should of course have a complete list of officers' names and numbers, arranged in numerical sequence and also in name order. He should record the mobile units in use and the officers using them, as they call in.

In larger departments, where air-time is limited, due to the large number of mobile units requiring air-time, it is desirable to use a code to save time on the air. The "ten-signal" code is widely used. It provides codes for a major part of the information constituting police radio traffic, thus cutting down words and saving substantial amounts of air-time. Some departments may add security to their use of radio by assigning numbers "post numbers") to key locations in their territory and then describing locations by giving distance and direction from a post number. The following are frequently used "ten-signals" of the system recommended by the Associated Public Safety Communications Officers, Inc. (APCO);

TEN-SIGNAL CODE

Code	Meaning	Code	Meaning
10-1	Unable to copy, change your location	10-8	In Service
		10-9	Repeat, please
10-2	Signals good	10-10	Fight in progress at
10-3	Stop transmitting	10-11	Dog case (describe - e.g., "fight," "biting," "rabid")
10-4	Acknowledgment		
10-5	Relay		
10-6	Busy, stand by unless urgent	10-12	Stand by (or "stop")
		10-13	Weather and road
10-7	Out of service atreport (give location or telephone number)	10-14	Report of prowler at
		10-15	Civil disturbance at
10-16	Domestic trouble at	10-48	Traffic standard needs repairs at
10-17	Meet complainant at		
10-18	Complete assignment quickly	10-49	Traffic light out at
		10-50	Accident (Kind, location)
10-19	Return to		
10-20	My location is (or what is your location)	10-51	Wrecker needed at

10-21	Call by telephone	10-52	Ambulance needed at
10-22	Disregard	10-53	Road blocked at
10-23	Arrived at scene	10-54	Livestock on highway
10-24	Assignment completed	10-55	Intoxicated driver
10-25	Report in person to (meet)	10-56	Intoxicated pedestrian
10-26	Holding subject - expedite reply	10-57	Hit-and-run (fatal personal injury, property damage)
10-27	Diver's license information	10-58	Direct traffic at
10-29	Check records for wanted	10-59	Convoy or escort (specify)
10-30	Illegal use of radio	10-62	Reply to message
10-31	Crime in progress at	10-63	Prepare to make written copy
10-32	Man with gun at		
10-33	Emergency	10-64	Message for local delivery
10-36	Correct time is		
10-37	Investigate suspicious vehicle (describe)	10-65	Net message assignment
10-38	Stopping suspicious vehicle (Give description and location before stopping)	10-66	Message cancellation
		10-67	Clear to read net message
		10-68	Dispatch information
		10-69	Message received
10-41	Beginning tour of duty	10-70	Fire alarm at
10-42	Ending tour of duty	10-74	Negative
10-43	Inform me about	10-75	In contact with
10-44	Request permission to leave patrol for	10-76	En Route
		10-77	Estimated time of arrival
10-45	Animal carcass in lane at	10-78	Need assistance at
10-46	Assist motorist at	10-90	Bank alarm at
10-47	Emergency road repairs needed at or stolen	10-94	Drag racing at
		10-96	Mental subject
		10-99	Records indicate wanted

Accuracy is of prime importance in radio work. Names should be spelled out in any instance where a file check is required or it is otherwise important that the correct spelling be known. Names should be spelled with a word-code by the officer transmitting. The following word code is good:

WORD CODE

A	Adam	I	Ida	R	Robert
B	Boy	J	John	S	Sam
C	Charles	K	King	T	Tom
D	David	L	Lincoln	U	Union
E	Edward	M	Mary	V	Victor
F	Frank	N	Nora	W	William
G	George	O	Ocean	X	X-ray
H	Henry	P	Paul	Y	Young
		Q	Queen	Z	Zebra

In using the word-code for spelling, transmit as follows:

"... JONES, J-JOHN, O-OCEAN, N-NORA, E-EDWARD, S-SAM." Do not say: "J AS IN JOHN" or "J LIKE IN JOHN" or similar wordy recitals.

In cases where numbers must be transmitted, such as license and serial numbers, the receiving officer should repeat each completed number on the air so that the sending officer can verify that it was correctly heard and understood.

B. HEADQUARTERS TRANSMISSIONS

A ranking officer should always be in command of headquarters radio. A dispatcher trained in radio procedures may be permitted to send out routine complaints or other items as received, but all important messages, including instructions to make arrests, alarms of major crimes and similar things should be screened by the ranking officer to insure that proper instructions are issued, that important instructions are not overlooked and that problems of identification, force to be used, road blocks and similar matters requiring police skill and experience are correctly handled. It should be the ranking officer's duty to also coordinate closely the work of the radio dispatcher and any complaint desk or officer, if complaint duties are not handled by the radio dispatcher.

C. FIELD TRANSMISSIONS

In order to keep transmission brief, officers should eliminate the use of unnecessary expressions or formal courtesies, such as "Roger," "Wilco," "Over and out," "Do you want to," "Will you please," "Yes, sir," "Thank you," and so on. Transmissions must be brief, businesslike and impersonal.

D. LISTENERS

It must always be remembered that police frequencies may be overheard by anyone on a large number of radio receivers purchasable almost anywhere. Consequently, matters of a confidential nature should not be put over the air except in extreme emergencies.

E. AUTHORITY

Standing instructions should exist in all departments having radio as to the authority of the headquarters dispatcher to make assignments of mobile units and officers and procedures for instances where mobile units have current assignments when they are called by the dispatcher to take a new assignment, or to take some police action of higher priority.

Generally speaking, the dispatcher should have final and complete authority as to assignments and all should understand that he is working closely with and expressing the instructions of the ranking officer in charge of communications.

The dispatcher should log all assignments as made and the exact time, for immediate reference and for a permanent record.

F. RADIO LOGS

Federal Communications Commission rules require that a radio log be maintained at each base (fixed) station from which transmissions are made (Federal Communications Commission Rules and Regulations, Section 89.175). Maintaining a log is also in accordance with proper police practice and procedure. Logs maintained by police agencies should include all transmissions and messages received and the exact time of each. Abbreviations may be used to reduce the work involved. These logs should also contain notations of exact time station identifying call letters were broadcast, and the full signature of the operator, showing time at beginning and end of his period of responsibility or tour of duty.

Mobile unit operators should not be required to keep radio logs. It is dangerous, since they will often be driving while receiving or transmitting.

V. POLICE TELETYPE NETWORKS

Chapter 533, Laws of 1931, established a basic system of coordinated teletype-writer communications, "for the purpose of prompt collection and distribution of information throughout the State of New York as the police problems of the state may require" (Exec. L. Sec. 217).

The Superintendent of State Police is responsible for the system's installation, operation and maintenance. The system is available for use by any department or division of the government of New York State, or by any municipal, county, town, village, railroad or other special police department lawfully maintained by any New York corporation (Exec. L. Sec. 219).

The original "basic system" has been expanded over the years since it was established. The current system is operated in conjunction with computers which do both data recording and message routing. Its modern and current name is "Computer Oriented Police information System," and it is commonly referred to by police officers as "COPS."

The COPS teletype network connects with and is part of the Nationwide Law Enforcement Teletype System (known to police as "LETS" or "N-LETS"). LETS covers the 48 continental states (not Alaska or Hawaii).

COPS is also directly connected to the National Crime Information Center ("NCIC") operated by the FBI in Washington, DC, and the NCIC computers. These computers store crime data from throughout the United States.

A. DESCRIPTION OF "COPS"

The Computer Oriented Police-information System of New York is a teletype network divided into districts, under the control of New York State Police Headquarters. Each district is generally co-extensive with the territory assigned to the various State Police stations. State and Troop Headquarters are "control points."

"Control points" control the teletypewriter circuits in the geographical area assigned them. The individual circuits have varying numbers of teletype machines and stations. All circuits terminate in the computer located at State Police Headquarters in Albany. The teletypewriter stations are located in municipal police departments, sheriff's offices, and other law enforcement agencies, including, of course, New York State Police installations.

All teletypewriter machines on the COPS system are equipped with "selective coding equipment" which permits each teletype machine to receive only those messages addressed to it.

Messages to police departments and other law enforcement agencies not on the COPS network are sent to the station nearest or most accessible to the department to which directed, to be forwarded by telephone or personal delivery. No special instructions in messages are required to secure this service. However, it will only be done in case of messages sent direct to or for the attention of a particular department. An "All Points Bulletin" ("APB") will be sent only to stations on the COPS network. If it is desired that one or more police agencies not on COPS receive an alarm, an individual direction to such agency(ies) is necessary.

B. COMPUTER CONTROL

The entire COPS network is under the control of its computer in Albany. All messages are transmitted by the computer exactly as received from the sending machines. It is thus essential that every person preparing teletype messages for sending via a COPS teletypewriter shall make certain that only correct messages are delivered to communications personnel for sending.

1.   Through selective coding and automatic switching by the computer, the various teletype machines receive only messages addressed to them, except that "control points" receive also all messages on the "circuits" which they control.

2.   The computer is designed to hold up and store teletype traffic for any station when the station is out of service due to routine maintenance, mechanical or electronic trouble, change of paper, etc. It will then send the traffic when the station returns to service.

C.   OPERATING RULES AND PROCEDURES

Operating rules and detailed procedures for sending messages on the basic system are set out in the COPS Operating Manual. Copies may be obtained from the New York State Police. Operating rules and procedures must be strictly adhered to. Unless there is exact adherence to proper message construction and to proper codes, the computer will not accept or will misdirect messages.

1.   Officers must be familiar with and comply with the following basic Regulations:
   a.   Message traffic shall be brief and in the form prescribed.
   b.   No message may be sent without proper authorization.
   c.   All message traffic must be official business.
   d.   Only the messages of duly authorized member agencies shall be transmitted.
   e.   Member stations shall transmit official messages without charge for State Police personnel and for members of police departments without teletypewriter service.
   f.   Requests of military authorities for use of system to report the arrest of deserters or other military personnel shall be honored.
   g.   All messages are confidential and shall not be divulged to unauthorized persons.
   h.   The official time of the system is Eastern Standard except that Daylight Saving Time shall be used whenever it is officially in effect.

D.   TELETYPE MESSAGES REQUIRED BY LAW

When any peace officer or police agency in New York receives a complaint that a felony has been committed and if the perpetrator thereof has not been apprehended within five hours after such complaint was received, such police agency must cause information of such felony to be dispatched over the police communications system. Police agencies not connected with basic system must transmit such information to the nearest or most convenient teletypewriter station, from where it will be immediately dispatched in conformity with the regulations governing the system (Exec. L. Sec. 221).

1.   The paramount consideration in respect to the messages sent in compliance with this law is that they shall accurately inform all police agencies that criminals are abroad and could be in any one of their jurisdictions.

2.   Any classification of teletype which conforms to COPS regulations will comply with this law.

E.   PERSONS WANTED

Section 173 of the Criminal Procedure Law provides that when a warrant has been issued in New York for the arrest of a person for a crime or offense, any officer having received a communication in the official course of business of the existence of such warrant may arrest such person, although the officer does not have the warrant in his possession at the time of arrest, if the arrest would otherwise have been proper if the officer had the warrant in his possession. The officer must advise the person arrested of the crime or offense charged and of the fact that a warrant has been issued.

Any officer originating any communication in the official course of business involving the commission of a misdemeanor or lesser offense must include therein the fact that a warrant of arrest has or has not been issued and further indicate, when appropriate, that the warrant has been endorsed for "nighttime" and Sunday execution."

Messages on persons wanted from police agencies in states other than New York are covered by Section 843 of the Criminal Procedure Law, which permits arrest without a warrant upon reasonable information that the defendant stands charged in the courts of another state with a crime punishable by death or imprisonment for a term exceeding one year. The official teletype message will constitute "reasonable information."

1. Messages on persons wanted from Canada or any foreign country must be handled in accordance with Federal law. Defendants can only be extradited by Canada or other foreign countries through the government of the United States, in accordance with Federal statute, treaties and conventions. Section 3184 of Title 18, United States Code, provides that any justice or judge of the United States, any United States Commissioners authorized by a US District Court or any New York judge of a court of record of general jurisdiction may, on complaint made under oath, issue a warrant of arrest for a person charged with a crime in the jurisdiction of any foreign government, if the crime is one provided for by treaty or convention between the United States and that foreign government. The teletype message may be used as the basis for complaint by New York officers in such cases.

F. WARRANT AND EXTRADITION

All messages on persons wanted (whether File 5, or other classifications) must state whether a warrant has been issued or facts justifying arrest without a warrant. If no warrant has been issued and one is required, the message must state "CHECKING ON WARRANT."

1. If a message is directed outside New York State, it must also state whether the requesting authority will extradite (e.g., "WARRANT ISSUED, WILL EXTRA-DITE," or "WAREX") and, if this fact has not been determined, must state "CHECKING ON EXTRADITION."
2. No message concerning a person wanted will be relayed outside New York State unless it has a statement as to warrant and extradition.
3. An "ADDED INFORMATION" message should be directed to the same points as the original message as soon as the facts have been ascertained as to warrant and extradition if the original message stated "CHECKING ON WARRANT" or "CHECKING ON WARRANT AND EXTRADITION" or "WARRANT ISSUED, CHECKING ON EXTRADITION."
4. Wording such as "HOLD FOR INVESTIGATION," "DETAIN FOR THIS DEPARTMENT," etc., cannot be used in any messages on persons wanted, and messages containing such phrases will not be forwarded.

Messages on persons wanted should include all available information required to accurately identify the persons to be taken into custody, including the exact time of the crime or incident, when known, in order to protect arresting officers.

1. When the fingerprint classification (abbreviated "FPC") of a wanted person is known, it must be included in the person wanted message.
2. Such messages shall also include any information known that wanted persons are armed with a dangerous weapon or are otherwise dangerous or have suicidal tendencies.

G. RETENTION OF TELETYPE MESSAGE COPIES

The printed message or "printout" which teletype machines produce (both inquiries of and answers from the computer or other agencies) is a necessary link in establishing "probable cause" warranting the arrest of an individual and should be preserved with the case file. It is not critical whether the document preserved is the original or the copy, but the original is best. The printout should go directly into the file of the agency taking arrest action, to be preserved for any necessary future use.

If a police agency having no teletypewriter terminal of its own has an officer who stops a suspicious car and the officer communicates with a police agency which has a terminal, and is told moments later that he has a "hit," the terminal employee who answers the officer's inquiry should note in writing on the printout sheet how, when and to whom he furnished the information. He should initial his notation, and then forward the printout to the inquiring officer's agency for retention in that agency's case file. This establishes a chain of evidence for the official police communication.

There is no set time as to how long a message printout should be retained. It should be retained as long as there is any chance the defendant will raise a question on the probable cause for his arrest. Some persons arrested and prosecuted in state courts, after arrest on a printout, may receive long sentences and be confined in a penitentiary for several years. Subsequently they may decide to raise the question of arrest in Federal Court on an appeal of some kind. Permanent retention of the printout would seem to be the most desirable rule in any case where an actual arrest is made based on the message.

H. CASES INVOLVING PROPERTY

In any case involving property in which the complainant's only or primary interest is recovery of the property, a message must not be sent unless a warrant has been issued. This rule is for the protection of arresting officers.

I. STOLEN CARS

Whenever a stolen car is reported by a message on the basic system, and is recovered, it should not be released to any person unless and until a full cancellation of the message reporting it stolen has been sent by the department which originated the stolen message and has been received by the department which recovered the car.

J. EMERGENCY MESSAGES

Emergency messages may include only matters requiring immediate transmission and attention, such as hit-and-run, armed robbery, temporary whereabouts of wanted persons, or other urgent matters.

K. CRIMINAL RECORD REQUESTS

New York State Identification and Intelligence System (NYSIIS). - Requests directed to NYSIIS for record information will be sent to and handled by NYSHS, day or night, seven days a week.

1. NYSIIS does its utmost to handle teletypewriter messages requesting information on an immediate basis. It is an imposition to request and in most cases, an impossibility for them to check and reply to a long list of names on a teletype request. Except in a rare case of extreme emergency, lengthy lists of names to be checked should be sent by mail or otherwise and not over the "COPS" system.

L. FIREARMS RECORDS

New York State Police Headquarters (Pistol Permit Section) maintains records of all pistol licenses issued in New York. It also keeps a lost or stolen weapons file, licensed pistol registration file and records of weapons purchased and sold by gun dealers (except gun dealers' records on purchases and sales in New York City). These files will be searched on request. Messages should be directed to "SP ALBANY, ATTN: PISTOL PERMIT SECTION." Requests to check New York City files on gun dealers' purchases and sales should be directed to the New York City Police Department.

M. DEFINITIONS

A full list of definitions applicable to all phases of operation of the basic system is published in the COPS Manual; however, the following teletype terms should be understood by all officers:

ACKNOWLEDGMENT - act by which an operator or machine signifies that a message has been received.

ADDED INFORMATION - message sent to supplement an original message and referred thereto.

APB (ALL POINTS BULLETIN) - a general alarm, to all terminals.

AUTHORITY - person responsible for the origination of a message.

BROADCAST - the transmission of a message on all circuits.

CANCELLATION - a message sent to cancel an original alarm.

CDC (CALL DIRECTING CODE) - directs message to its proper destination.

CORRECTION - a message sent to amend a previous message.

DIRECT MESSAGE - a message addressed to a specific agency or receiver.

EMERGENCY CANCELLATION - a message sent to cancel, without delay, previous message.
FINGERPRINT CLASSIFICATION - a listing of the kinds of fingerprint patterns, ridge counts and tracings and missing fingers in a subject's fingerprints, using a code notation for each of the ten fingers.

JUNK - any message or part thereof which is unintelligible by reason of mechanical or electrical difficulties.

MESSAGE NUMBER - numerals in the upper left-hand corner of a teletypewriter communication to distinguish it from other communications having the same point of origin.

MESSAGE TIME - the figures placed on a message after the sender's name, to indicate the time the typing was completed. Time based on the conventional time designator of ante meridian (AM) and post meridian (PM) (noon and midnight designated as 12-00 N and 12-00 MID, respectively). Eastern Standard Time used except when Daylight Saving Time is in effect.

PART CANCELLATION - a message sent by the originating station to cancel some portion of an original and/or previous message, using a new message number and the same file classification as the original.

REFERENCE - data by which an original message is identified, i.e., the message and file numbers, place and date of origin, message direction and subject.

REPLY - a message that answers a previous teletype message; must refer to the original and be designated by the word "REPLY."

SENDER - surname of operator who originally transmits a message.

N. AUTHORIZED ABBREVIATIONS
   The following abbreviations may be used in teletype messages:

AA	Control Point, Troop "A," Batavia
ADDED INFO	Added information
AKA	Also known as
AM	Ante Meridian - (Between Midnight and Noon)
APB	All Points Bulletin
ASSIGN	Assignment
ASST	Assistant
ATL	Attempt to locate
ATTN	Attention
AUTH	Message sent on authority of
BB	Control Point, Troop "B," Malone
BCI	Bureau of Criminal Investigation
BLD	Build
BLK	Black
BRN	Brown
CC	Control Point, Troop "C," Sidney
C (in description)	Chinese
CANCEL	Cancellation
CAPT	Captain
CCT	Circuit
CHIEF INSPR	Chief Inspector
CODE SIG	Code Signal
COL	Colonel
COMP	Complexion
CORRECT	Correction
CP	Chief of Police
CPL	Corporal
CT/SGT	Chief Technical Sergeant
DD	Control Point, Troop "D," Oneida
DATA	We request owner's name, address, make of car, motor number, etc., on the following registration
DCT	Direct
DEP	Deputy
DK	Dark
DMV	Department of Motor Vehicles, Albany, NY
DOA	Dead on arrival
DOB	Date of birth
EE	Control Point, Troop "E," Canandaigua

ETA	Estimated time of arrival
F	Female
FF	Control Point, Troop "F." Middletown
FILE	File classification number
F/SGT	First Sergeant
FOA	For other authorities
FPC	Fingerprint classification
GG	Control Point, Troop "G," Loudonville
HQ	Division Headquarters, Albany
I	Indian
INV	Investigator
INSPR	Inspector
J	Japanese
KK	Control Point, Troop "K," Hawthorne
LETS	Nationwide Law Enforcement Teletype System
LIC	License number
LIEUT	Lieutenant
M	Male
MAJ	Major
MED	Medium
MESA	Referring to your message
MEX	Mexican
MID	Midnight
MOT	Motor
NCIC	National Crime Information Center
NFC	Negative file check
NYSIIS	New York State Identification and Intelligence System
NMN	No middle name
NYS	New York State
O (in description)	Other (meaning any other racial abbreviation not listed herein)
OFF	Officer
OPR	Operator
PART CANCEL	Partial cancellation
PD	Municipal Police Department
PD NYC	Police Department, City of New York
PM	Post Meridian (Between Noon and Midnight)
PTL	Patrolman
QQ	Control Point, Division Headquarters, Albany
REF	Please refer to our message
REG	Registration number
ROIR	Reply only if record
RP	Message repeated by
SER	Serial
SGT	Sergeant
SO	Sheriff
SP	State Police
SR INV	Senior Investigator
S/SGT	Staff Sergeant
SUPT	Superintendent
TT	Control Point, Troop "T," Elsmere
TOT	Turned over to
TPR	Trooper
T/SGT	Technical Sergeant
TWX	Teletypewriter Exchange System

UNK	Unknown
VIN	Vehicle Identification Number
VOID	Cancel our message
W	White
WAREX	Warrant issued will extradite
Z/SGT	Zone Sergeant

The permissible abbreviations for states of the United States, and for foreign countries, Canadian Provinces and Mexican states are set out In the COPS manual, phone book and postal directory.

VI.   PREPARING TELETYPE MESSAGES

All messages for transmission over the basic system must be in the prescribed form and as brief as possible without losing clarity. Conformance with instructions for message construction set out in the COPS Manual is not only essential for use on the basic system of New York State but also permits the message to be correctly carried to other states in the continental United States over the Nationwide Law Enforcement Teletype System (LETS) and to the National Crime Information Center (NCIC) computers at the FBI in Washington, DC.

COPS Manuals may be found at all stations on the basic system, including local police stations as well as State Police stations and may be procured from the New York State Police at Albany.

A.   MESSAGE FORM

Messages which do not conform (in construction or content) to the requirements set out in the COPS Manual will not be sent but will be returned to the point of origin for correction. Conformity is necessary so that every department in the state may operate with a minimum of delay and to give maximum protection to the individual officer who acts on the basis of information received in a teletype message over the basic system.

B.   MESSAGE EXAMPLE

All messages on the basic system must have a heading, a body, an authority and a sender, in the form indicated by the following example:

```
EXAMPLE:
Line 1 ... NYAZ
Line 2 ... 6214 FILE 12 PD NYC APR 4-10 REPLY
Line 3 ... TO PD JAMESTOWN NY CODE 77
Line 4 ...
Line 5 ... MESA 381 FILE APR 3-10 APB UNK W M
Line 6 ... SUSPECT HARRY ROE WAS AT QUEENS COUNTY ADDRESS FROM
          8-30 AM TO 12-00 MID APR 2-10 ACCORDING TO RELIABLE WIT-
          NESSESNO FURTHER INVESTIGATION BEING CONDUCTED. WRIT-
          TEN REPORT FOLLOWS.
2nd line below
body ..... AUTH LT MURPHY BROWN 6-17 PM
3rd line below
body ..... NY03030
```

1. File 1 Messages (Stolen Motor Vehicles, Trailers or Motorcycles) and File 16 Messages (Lost and Stolen License Plates) are the only exceptions to the preceding rule as to form of teletype messages. They must be prepared in a special format, as shown later in this ongoing section.

2. All departments have been assigned NCIC code numbers, whether or not they have teletype facilities on the basic system are assigned two-letter call directing codes ("CDC's"). Both NCIC codes and CDC's are listed in the COPS Manual.

3. The individual lines of the sample message were prepared in accordance with the following rules:

   a. Line 1 contains a message's "call directing codes" (or "CDC's"). These are the means by which the computer determines the destination of the message. The police officer preparing the message must decide on its destination and use. It is the responsibility of the teletype operator to translate these into the proper CDC's (and "Function Codes," if any -the Function Codes give instructions as to computer activity in respect to the message). CDC's and Function Codes are all set out in the COPS Manual.

      (1) The first two letters in the example, on Line 1, are the CDC for the agency originating the message (i.e,. NY for New York City Police Department). The next two letters are the CDC for the department to which the message is destined (i.e. AZ for Jamestown Police Department). The correct CDC must always be ascertained from the COPS Manual

      (2) The CDC "SP" will send the message to all New York State Police teletype stations. The CDC "PD" will send it to all police agencies and sheriff's offices in New York. If a message is to go out of New York to an out-of-state law enforcement agency, the CDC for out-of-state is "IS" and must be followed by the CDC for the out-of-state destination.

      (3) If a message has an inquiry of or information for the New York State Identification and Intelligence System (NYSIIS), the proper CDC for NYSIIS is "QC."

   b. Lines 2 and 3 constitute the "heading" of the message. They show the identity of the message and its origin and destinations, spelled out in words and abbreviations. In the example, the message is the 6,214th message sent by the Police Department, New York City. It is a "File 12" (message concerning homicide). Line 3 (the second line of the heading) shows the message's destination and the code signal for special handling desired ("Code 77").

      (1) Every message must be designated by a number (in the example, "6214"). For every teletype station on the basic system, message numbering always begins with "1" for the first message sent after midnight of December 31 annually and messages are thereafter numbered consecutively throughout the year, straight through the last message sent on the following December 31st.

   c. Line 4 is always left blank

   d. Line 5 is always the reference line, if a reference is required and shows to what prior message, if any, the message relates.

   e. Line 6 and following are the body of the message. The body always begins on line 6 unless there is no reference, when it begins on line 5.

   f. The authority, sender and time sent are the next to last line of every message (in the example, this line is marked "2nd line below body" to show its placement when teletyped). The "authority" is the identity and rank of the officer who authorized the message, "Lt. Murphy" in the example. "Brown" in the example is the teletype operator who sent the message.

 g. The last line of the message is the "NCIC Code" of the sending agency. Frequently a sending agency is not one with a station on the basic system and thus has no CDC. The NCIC code will be its identifier. In the example this is "NY 03030," marked "3rd. line below body" to show its placement when typed on the teletype machine.

C. FILE 1 AND FILE 16 MESSAGES

  File 1 (Stolen Motor Vehicles, Trailers, and Motorcycles) and File 16 (Lost or Stolen License Plates) messages have a special format of their own. All the data on the stolen or lost item which the message sets out are automatically entered in the memory banks of the computer the instant the teletype message is received by it when the proper function code is included with the call directing codes (CDC's). Examples of a proper File 1 and a proper File 16 original message are as follows:

  EXAMPLE, File 1:
  Line 1 ... KORESPPDQLQJNX
  Line 2 ... 235 FILE 1 SP CLAVERACK NY MAY 1-10
  Line 3 ... TO APB
  Line 4 ...
  Line 5 ... 4A7528.NY.10..
  Line 6 ... 09ME44217CO.
  Line 7 ... 09.MERC.COU.2T. GRN/LGR
  Line 8 ... 050170
  Line 9 ... NY11001
  Line 10 .. K0235.
  Line 11 .. STOLEN GHENT NY 9 TO 11 PM-OWNER CHARLES A. DOE-
    1 MAIN-CLAVERACK NY 2nd line below
  body ..... AUTH SGT ROE GREEN 11-50 PM
  3rd line below body ..... NY 11001

EXPLANATION

 1. The above message concerns a 2009 Mercury Cougar, color top green over light green body, hardtop, two-door, 2010 New York license plates 4A7528, owned by Charles A. Doe, 1 Main Street, Claverack, NY, and stolen at Ghent, NY, sometime between 9:00 and 11:00 PM on May 1, 2010. The individual lines of the example were prepared under the following rules:

  a. Line 1 contains the "CDC's" and "KO" is the CDC for the State Police at Claverack. In addition, this line has the function code "RE," a direction to the computer to include the data in the message in the computer memory bank. Function code "RE" is the same for all File 1 messages. "SP" is the CDC for all State Police installations with teletype. "PD" is the CDC for all police and sheriffs' offices with teletype installations. "QL" is the CDC for the New York State Motor Vehicle Department at Albany; "QJ" is the CDC for New York State Police Communications Headquarters, Albany, and "NX" is the CDC for the National Auto Theft Bureau (NATB) in New York City.

  b. Line 2 is the same as any other message and carries the message number, the "file, originating agency and date sent."

c. Line 3 is the same as any other message, showing the distribution desired - in the example, APB (the abbreviation for "all points bulletin" to all teletype installations on the basic system).

d. Line 4 is left blank as in other messages.

e. Line 5 gives the license plate data. These are always set out in this order: plate number, issuing state and year, followed by two periods for a private plate or an appropriate abbreviation from the COPS Manual for any other kind of plate (e.g., "DL" for dealers' plates, "OB" for passenger bus plates, "TK" for truck plates, etc.). Only private passenger automobile plates are represented solely by two periods, as in the example.

f. Line 6 gives the stolen vehicle's identification number its "VIN."

g. Line 7 sets out the description of the vehicle, using the codes set out in the COPS Manual for motor vehicles, always in the following order: year, make, model, style, color. In the example, these are: "09," "Merc" for Mercury, "COU" for Cougar model, "2T" for two-door hardtop style, and GRN/LGR for green top, light green body. Periods must be used in line 7 just as shown in the example (see paragraph on "Punctuation" later in this section).

h. Line 8 is the date of occurrence of the incident . The date must be set out with numerals for month, day and year. If the month or day is a single numeral it is preceded by 0. February third would thus be entered 0203, followed by the year or "020304" for February 3, 2004. October 20, 2004, would be "102004."

i. Line 9 carries the NCIC code of the originating police agency (SP Claverack is "NY 11001").

j. Line 10 is always the CDC of the originating agency and the message number (KO is the CDC for SP Claverack and the message number is 235).

k. Line 11 carries any pertinent information desired as to the theft, such as owner, time of theft, place of theft. Such data are restricted to a total of 42 characters and nothing past the 42 characters will be entered into the computer, although anything past 42 characters will be transmitted to all receiving an actual copy of the message. This is similar to the "body" of other teletype messages. Any readily recognizable abbreviations pertinent and suitable may be used in the 42 characters, contrary to the general rules that only authorized abbreviations may be used in other messages.

   (1) To include material information in 42 characters requires some thought and economy of phrasing but is not difficult. For example, the characters "ARMED V M" indicate an armed white male, the characters "STOLEN 32 CAL COLT REV GLV COMPT" indicate a .32 caliber Colt revolver which was in the glove compartment was stolen.

l. Second line below the body is the same as other messages, showing the authority for the message and the sender.

m. Third line below the body is also the same as in other messages, carrying the NCIC Code for the originating agency (same as Line 9 of File 1's).

EXAMPLE, File 16:

Line 1 ... KORGQLQJ
Line 2 ... 236 FILE 16 SP CLAVERACK NY MAY 1-10
Line 3 ... TO APB
Line 4 ...
Line 5 ... .2A2314.NY.10..1.
Line 6 ... 050110
Line 7 ... NY11001.
Line 8 ... K0236
Line 9 ... STOLEN GHENT
2nd line below
body ..... AUTH SGT ROE GREEN 11-52 PM
3rd line below body NY11001

EXPLANATION

1. The above message concerns the loss of a single license plate at 7:00 p.m. in Ghent, NY. The license plate is numbered "2A2314" and is a 2010 New York Plate, The individual lines of the message conform to rules as follows:

   a. Line 1 contains the CDC of the originating agency ("KO" for SP, Claverack) and the function code for the computer of "RG" which directs the computer to store the data in its memory bank and is the same for all File 16's. "QL" and "QJ" are the CDC's for the New York State Department of Motor Vehicles and the Communications Headquarters of the State Police, both at Albany.

   b. Line 2 is the same as both prior message examples.

   c. Line 3 is the same as both prior message examples, i.e. shows the destination of the message.

   d. Line 4 is blank, same as prior message example.

   e. Line 5 is same as in a File 1 message, showing the license plate in order of plate number, state of issue and year of issue. The periods indicated in the example must be used in all messages. The example shows one lost or stolen plate. If both plates had been lost or stolen, Line 5 would be: "2A2314.NY.10..2.".

   f. Line 6 shows date lost or stolen, same as Line 8 of a File 1 message.

   g. Line 7 shows the NCIC Code of the originating agency, same as Line 9 of a File 1 message.

   h. Line 8 shows the CDC of the originating agency and its message number, same as Line 10 of a File 1 message.

   i. Line 9 carries any pertinent information desired on the lost or stolen plates, usually in briefest form, as not over 11 characters will be included in the computer memory bank.

   j. Second line below body is authority and sender, same as any other message.

   k. Third line below body is NCIC Code for originating agency, same as any other message, and is same as in Line 7 of the example.

D. PUNCTUATION

In sending messages, the usual punctuation marks cannot be used. Instead of commas, colons, semi-colons and periods, a dash must be used, except in File 1 message lines 5, 6, 7, 8, 9 and 10 and File 16 message lines 5, 6, 7 and 8. The reason for use of periods in File 1 and File 16 messages is that the data they contain on the indicated lines must be fed into the computer in specific segments and the segments must be separated and indicated by periods. If a necessary character is missing from any one of the segments, a period must be put in its place in the message.

NUMBERS IN MESSAGES

All numbers used in teletype messages must be in numerals (e.g., 1, 2, 10, etc.) and not spelled out (e.g. "one," "two," "ten," etc.) except that decimals and fractions must be spelled out in words (e.g. "one-half," "ten and sixteen hundredths," etc., instead of "1/2," "10 16/100," etc.

F. ADDED INFORMATION, CORRECTION, REPLY, CANCELLATION

Every message except an original message must show in Line 2, as in the first message example herein, whether it is an "Added Information," "Correction," "Reply" or a "Cancellation." The proper designation, of course, is determined by the purpose or nature of the message.

G. CODE SIGNALS

A Code Signal is a number which, when included on Line 3 of a message ("CODE 77" in the first example prior), directs certain specific handling of the message by addressees. More than one code signal may be used in a message. Approved code signals and their meanings may be found in the COPS Manual.

H. FIFTH LINE, OTHER THAN ORIGINAL MESSAGES

The fifth line of all messages other than original messages is the reference line. The reference line shall show: (1) whether the message relates to a prior message from the sending station ("REF," or "VOID" on cancellations), or from another station ("MESA"); (2) the message number of the original message; (3) the date of the original message; (4) whether the original message was sent direct ("DCT") or to all points ("APB"); and (5) the subject of the original message, including the name of persons first listed on the fifth line of the original message (if any such listing in the original).

1. The license plate number of any stolen motor vehicle, motorcycle, trailer or lost or stolen plate must be on line five of any message relating to stolen vehicles or lost or stolen plates ("File 1" or "File 16" messages).

I. BODY OF MESSAGE

The body of every message should be as brief as possible. All messages are required to be clear and accurate. Telegraph style must be used in messages, leaving out all connecting words and other words not essential to clarity.

CONTENT

1. The first word in the body of every original message should where possible, indicate the purpose of the message, e.g., "STOLEN," "WANTED," "BURGLARY," "RECOVERED," etc. This rule does not apply to File 1 or File 16 messages.

2. The crime involved must be specified by name in all original messages relating to crimes. The pertinent section of the Penal Law, Criminal Procedure Law, etc., may be added for clarity where deemed necessary.

3. Where the bare name of the crime is not sufficiently descriptive, a brief notation of what the crime involved may be added, e.g., "CRIMINALLY NEGLIGENT HOMICIDE-HUNTING."

4. Messages concerning persons wanted or missing should list the persons' full names or brief descriptions, if names are unknown (e.g., "unknown white male," "unknown colored female"), and the license plate number of any vehicle in their possession, on the fifth line of the message.

5. Stolen motor vehicle, trailer or motorcycle ("File 1") messages must carry the license plate number as the first item on line five in all such messages.

6. The license number shall be shown on the fifth line of all messages dealing with vehicles used in or connected with a crime.
7. The plate number of lost or stolen license plates must be shown as the first item on the fifth line of all messages dealing with such plates ("File 16" messages).

The time and place of the crime must always be set out in an original message. They should be set out in the first part of the message.

Information in the body of a message shall be set out in the following sequence, when applicable:

SEQUENCE

1. Name of subject (unless listed above the body of the message on the fifth line of an original message or in the reference line of any other message).
2. Name and brief facts of crime.
3. Time and place of crime.
4. Warrant data, whether will extradite.
5. Description of persons, with items of description set out in the following order:
   Racial description (White, Colored, American
   Indian, Chinese, etc.);
   Sex, age, height, weight, color hair and eyes;
   Complexion, build;
   Clothing, marks and scars, peculiarities;
   Addresses, occupation, relatives.
   EXAMPLE:
   "W-F-28-5-5-120 LIGHT BRN HAIR-BRN EYES-FAIR
   COMP-MED BLD-BLUE PLAID KERCHIEF ON HEAD-BLK
   TOPCOAT-DK GREEN DRESS-BLK LOW HEEL SHOES-BLK
   BAG OVER SHOULDER-NO MARKS OR SCARS-UNDER
   MENTAL STRAIN-RESIDES 1 MAIN STREET-COHOES
   NY-UNEMPLOYED-MOTHER MRS JOHN R. DOE-SAME
   ADDRESS"
6. Description of Motor Vehicles, with items of description set out in the following order: License plate number, motor number and/or vehicle serial or identification number, year, make, model, color, distinguishing marks.
7. Description of Property, with items of description set out in the following order: Name, make, model, serial number, color, material, size, peculiarities and markings.
   EXAMPLES:
   TYPEWRITER-ROYAL PORTABLE-SER 1J4813996-GREEN PLASTIC
   FRAME-CHEMICAL SYMBOLS ON KEYBOARD-NO CASE
   WRISTWATCH-WALTHAM-SPRITE-SER UNK-WHITE GOLD-SMALL
   BAGUETTE DIAMONDS EACH SIDE-BRAIDED NARROW YELLOW GOLD
   WRIST BAND-ENGRAVED ON BACK CASE-TO JANE WITH LOVE

J. AUTHORITY FOR MESSAGES

Every message must show the rank and surname of the police member authorizing and responsible for the message (and his department if different from the department sending the message). "Authority" is shown by typing at left margin, on the second line below the body of the message, the abbreviation "AUTH" followed by the rank and name of authorizing officer.

K.   FILE CLASSIFICATION CHART

The following File Classification Chart is required to be posted at every teletype-writer location associated with the basic system. This chart must be rigidly adhered to and the proper File Classification Number placed on every message. The File Classification Number assigned an original message must be used on all subsequent messages pertaining to and sent in connection with the same case. The File Classification number is used for message filing.

FILE CLASSIFICATION CHART

FILE	CLASSIFICATION
1	STOLEN MOTOR VEHICLES AND MOTORCYCLES
2	MOTOR VEHICLES - INFORMATION REQUESTS
3	EMERGENCY REPORTS TO DIVISION HEADQUARTERS
4	HIT AND RUN DRIVER
5	PERSONS - WANTED OR ESCAPED
6	PERSONS - MISSING
7	BURGLARY
8	ROBBERY AND HOLD UP
9	PROPERTY - LOST OR MISSING
10	PROPERTY - STOLEN (LARCENY)
11	ASSAULT
12	HOMICIDE
13	GENERAL POLICE INFORMATION
14	ORDERS AND ADMINISTRATIVE MESSAGES
15	REQUESTS FOR INFORMATION (MISC.)
16	LOST OR STOLEN LICENSE PLATES
20	CRIMINAL INVESTIGATIONS (BCI ONLY)
24	LEGAL BULLETINS AND OPINIONS
25	MISCELLANEOUS MESSAGES
26	TROUBLE REPORTS
27	WEATHER BUREAU FALLOUT DATA
28	ROAD CONDITIONS AND WEATHER REPORTS
44	TEST MESSAGES

DESCRIPTION

FILE 1: Use for all messages reporting stolen motor vehicles, trailers or motorcycles. In some agencies associated with the basic system, outside New York, stolen car messages are filed by license number and in others by motor, serial or identification number. It is thus necessary that all cancellations of File 1 messages list not only the license number but also the motor, serial or identification number, exactly as set out in the original message. The license plate number of the stolen vehicle must always be the first item on line five of any File 1 message except cancellations.

FILE 2: Use only for messages involving requests for motor vehicle, trailer, motorcycle or drivers' license information either from outside New York or from the New York State Department of Motor Vehicles. Whenever possible, File 2 messages must include the subject's full name, including middle name or initial and his address and date of birth.

1.   Where a message is sent to the New York State Department of Motor Vehicles concerning only a check of a name, the message should be directed to one of

three sections of that Department, depending on the first letter of the subject's last name, as follows:

"TO DMV SEC 1" (for A through G)

"TO DMV SEC 2" (for H through O)

"TO DMV SEC 3" (for P through Z)

2. Whenever a license plate number check is desired, the direction should be merely "TO DMV."

3. Department of Motor Vehicles conviction records are maintained on electronic data processing equipment and it takes several days to furnish complete information, as the data tapes are not updated every day, but at stated intervals. Accurate and prompt service can only be provided if the Department is given accurate and complete information. The subject's name, date of birth, sex and license identification number must be furnished exactly as they appear on the person's operator's or chauffeur's license.

4. The following information should be considered as a guide to requesting information from the New York State Department of Motor Vehicles files to avoid unnecessary work and delayed communications:

   a. Where only the previous record for Driving While Intoxicated or while Ability is Impaired is required, do not request complete record of all convictions.

   b. Where only data on previous suspension or revocation of license are wanted, do not request complete record of all convictions.

   c. Where only convictions in past 18 months are wanted, so specify.

   d. In requesting check on nonresidents, specify that the subject is a nonresident, and pinpointing information desired. DMV maintains a file specifically showing speeding convictions and all vehicle and traffic misdemeanors involving nonresidents arrested in New York.

5. The electronic data processing includes only moving violations, vehicle and traffic misdemeanors and suspension and revocation data. Equipment violations, overload violations and non-moving violations (other than misdemeanors) are not included.

6. Where a complete accident and conviction record (known as a "safety record") is desired on a driver, the message should be sent promptly after the driver's arrest since the limitations of the electronic data processing will delay the reply. The request should specify "COMPUTER ABSTRACT REQUIRED."

Photostats from Department of Motor Vehicles: When photostats of drivers' licenses or any records are desired from the Department of Motor Vehicles, they should be requested directly of the Department by mail and no teletype message should be sent requesting photostats.

FILE 3: This classification is only used by the Few York State Police.

FILE 4: This classification is solely for hit-and-run (leaving the scene of accident) motor vehicle or motorcycle violations. Original messages must always include as much information as possible pertinent to the wanted motor vehicle and driver. File 4 classification applies whether the hit-and-run involves property damage, personal injury or both.

FILE 5: Use for messages concerning crimes other than assaults, burglaries, homicides and robberies (which are File 11, File 7, File 12 and File 8 respectively). File 5 should also be used for messages requesting arrest or announcing that persons are wanted and subject to arrest, including escapees from prisons, jails and mental institutions. File 5 sconcerning escapees from mental institutions should be restricted to New York only, unless the authorities of the institution specifically desire dissemination outside New York. All File 5 original messages on persons wanted must begin the body of the message with "WANTED," followed by the name of the crime or other item justifying the arrest.

FILE 6:   Do not use for persons wanted for a crime. Use only in cases of persons missing over 24 hours, except no waiting period is required in case of young children, females 18 years of age and under, mentally incompetent persons or persons known to have been operating a motor vehicle. All File 6 messages must include the time or approximate time the subject left home and must indicate that either the sending authorities or the family or parents will promptly assume the duty of returning children, youths and mentally incompetent persons when located. If the missing person was known to be using a motor vehicle, the license plate number should be included in the message.

FILE 7:   Use specifically for burglary. Do not include any larceny without burglary. File 7 original messages must state the type of building burglarized, methods of entry, and complete description of property taken and persons wanted.

FILE 8:   Use for all robbery. Messages must adequately describe property taken and persons wanted.

FILE 9:   Use for all messages relating to property which has been lost or is missing, except motor vehicle license plates (which are classified in File 16). Stolen property cannot be the subject of a File 9 message, nor any property which has been the subject of a crime. Original messages must adequately describe the property involved.

FILE 10: Use for all messages dealing with stolen property or property which has been the subject of any larceny. This includes aircraft and boats (but not motor vehicles, trailers, motorcycles or vehicle license plates, as these are File 1 and File 16, respectively). Property involved must be adequately described. Long lists of unidentifiable property have little value and should not be sent.

FILE 11:   Use only for assault cases. (Motor vehicle hit-and-run cases are not included in File 11 but are classified in File 4).

FILE 12:   All messages concerning homicides must be classified in File 12, including all criminal negligence homicides, whether vehicle or other.

FILE 13:   Messages are to be classified in File 13 when they do not relate to a specific crime or arrest request in other file classifications and are of interest to police generally or in a special area. They may be sent direct to one or more stations or as all points bulletin as the facts indicate. File 13 messages would include reports of confidence games, notice that specific persons have been apprehended who may be wanted by other departments and their modus operandi (specifying distinctive or unusual features thereof). File 13's would also include notice that specific property has been recovered (including adequate description) and general police warnings. In all instances where a person is arrested for a serious crime, his name, aliases, description and fingerprint analysis or classification should be sent as an all points bulletin under File 13 for the information of all departments on the basic system.

FILE 14:   This classification is only used by the New York State Police.

FILE 15: Use on messages requesting information from special files, arrest or criminal records, firearms records, dog licenses, ear tags, birth, marriage and death records, aircraft license data, lost, missing or overdue aircraft and other types of information.

FILE 16: Use only for messages dealing with motor vehicle or motorcycle license plates, whether lost or stolen. List plate numbers at beginning of 5th message line. The plate number must always be the first item on the fifth line of any File 16 message.

FILE 20: This classification is only used by the New York State Police.

FILE 24: Use on all messages concerning notice of new laws, legal opinions, legal bulletins and inquiries concerning laws or legal opinions. It is largely used by the New York State Police but may be used by any agency.

FILE 25: Use for all messages not dealing with crime and which do not fall within any file classification previously set out. It would include messages concerning notification of relatives of persons who have been killed. No messages may be sent under a File 25 classification in criminal cases.

FILE 26: Any report of trouble on the basic system or with a teletypewriter installation should be File Classification 26.

FILE 27: This classification is used solely for official fallout data.

FILE 28: This is used for road condition and weather reports.

FILE 44: Used for test messages.

L.   DATA AVAILABLE ON PERSONS OR PROPERTY

The COPS computer is located at Communications Headquarters, New York State Police, Albany. On receipt of properly coded messages, it stores in its memory banks for later search all File 1 and File 16 message data on stolen motor vehicles, trailers, motorcycles and lost or stolen license plates. It also stores data as to vehicles used in commission of a crime and as to lost or stolen vehicle parts (by identification or serial number). Data on vehicles are stored by both license plate number and vehicle identification number ("VIN").

In addition, Communications Headquarters, State Police, Albany, maintains manual record files on stolen property and guns and on lost property. These will be automatically checked on receipt of messages concerning recovered property or guns.

The National Crime Information Center (NCIC) at Washington, DC, stores in its computers information on stolen vehicles and license plates, stolen or missing property and guns and on persons wanted for felonies or missing. Data on property is stored in the NCIC computers for individual items valued at $500 or more, or on loot from a single "job" worth $2,000.00 or more.

The New York State Identification and Intelligence System (NYSIIS) maintains files on persons wanted or missing covering New York. NYSIIS may be checked directly for wanted or missing persons data, by teletype message, or otherwise, such as direct telephone inquiry.

M.   COMPARISON OF NCIC, NYSIIS, COPS DATA

The NCIC computer in Washington, DC, stores data received from the continental United States, including, of course, data from New York. Its "wanted" data cover the whole country. The same is true of its stolen car, stolen property or other banks of data. NYSIIS files cover only "wanted" or "missing" from New York state.

The COPS computer at Communications Headquarters, State Police, Albany, also stores only New York data. This includes New York vehicles or plates stolen anywhere and any vehicles or plates stolen in New York.

N.   ENTERING DATA AND MAKING INQUIRIES

The COPS computer file on lost or stolen license plates and vehicle identification numbers and license plates is made up of data from File 1 and File 16 messages which automatically go into the computer when the proper function code is stated in Line 1 of the message. If the message's data meet the criteria required for entry into the NCIC computer in Washington, DC, the message is also automatically switched to the NCIC computer by the COPS computer.

Wanted data on persons should be forwarded to NYSIIS in accordance with the instructions pertaining thereto, as well as by appropriately coded message to NCIC, Washington, DC.

In checking on whether a "want" is outstanding for an individual, an inquiry should be sent to the NCIC Computer in Washington, DC. If a negative reply is received, inquiry will then be made automatically, by the State Police, by *"hot line"* telephone to NYSIIS at Albany, and the inquiring agency will be automatically informed of the result of the NYSIIS inquiry.

The COPS computer and the basic system are directly connected with the NCIC computers in Washington, DC. This *"interface"* makes all the information stored in the NCIC computers automatically available to those making inquiries on the basic system. Inquiries to NCIC and COPS can be made from any teletype machine on the basic system. If a *"no record"* reply is received by an inquirer, from the COPS computer in Albany, on a license plate or *"VIN"* inquiry, the inquiry is automatically routed to the NCIC computers in Washington. A reply will be sent from NCIC within approximately two minutes.

O.   MESSAGE RECORD SHEET

Each teletypewriter control point must list and periodically check status of all teletype messages originating in its area which are subject to cancellation. A form similar to the one shown should be used by other stations. Messages should not be entered on the form until they are ready for filing on the fourth day after their receipt.

1.   Each teletype installation is expected to use the form to list in numerical order all messages originating at the installation. Messages which are subject to future cancellation should be checked at least once each month, to keep all files clear of inactive messages.

2.   In Column 2, *"origin,"* designate for each message the agency originating the message.

3.   Sample form:

HASKINS POLICE DEPARTMENT
TELETYPE MESSAGE NUMBER AND
CANCELLATION RECORD

MSG. #	ORIGIN	FILE	DATE	SUMMARY	CANCEL MSG. #
1	Haskins	4	4-15-08	Hit-Run A/A	
2	"	5	4-15-08	John Jones,Petit Larc.36	
3	"	11	4-16-08	Assault Case	
4	Lake Como	6	4-16-08	Leo Moran, Missing	

P. CANCELLATIONS AND CORRECTIONS

A cancellation is advice that a prior message is no longer valid and that no further action is to be taken in respect to the prior message. A correction amends a previous message. Stations are responsible for promptly sending all necessary full or part cancellations and all corrections. Failure to cancel or correct a message or part of a message may result in serious harm when police action is taken on the basis of a message which should have previously been cancelled or corrected and was not. The responsibility for any such occurrence will be placed squarely on the offending department and its responsible personnel.

ANSWER SHEET

EST NO. _____ PART _____ TITLE OF POSITION _____
(AS GIVEN IN EXAMINATION ANNOUNCEMENT - INCLUDE OPTION. IF ANY)

LACE OF EXAMINATION _____ DATE _____
(CITY OR TOWN)   (STATE)

RATING

USE THE SPECIAL PENCIL.   MAKE GLOSSY BLACK MARKS.

	A B C D E		A B C D E		A B C D E		A B C D E		A B C D E
1		26		51		76		101	
2		27		52		77		102	
3		28		53		78		103	
4		29		54		79		104	
5		30		55		80		105	
6		31		56		81		106	
7		32		57		82		107	
8		33		58		83		108	
9		34		59		84		109	
10		35		60		85		110	

Make only ONE mark for each answer.   Additional and stray marks may be counted as mistakes.   In making corrections, erase errors COMPLETELY.

	A B C D E		A B C D E		A B C D E		A B C D E		A B C D E
11		36		61		86		111	
12		37		62		87		112	
13		38		63		88		113	
14		39		64		89		114	
15		40		65		90		115	
16		41		66		91		116	
17		42		67		92		117	
18		43		68		93		118	
19		44		69		94		119	
20		45		70		95		120	
21		46		71		96		121	
22		47		72		97		122	
23		48		73		98		123	
24		49		74		99		124	
25		50		75		100		125	

ANSWER SHEET

TEST NO. ____________ PART ______ TITLE OF POSITION ______________________________
(AS GIVEN IN EXAMINATION ANNOUNCEMENT - INCLUDE OPTION, IF ANY)

PLACE OF EXAMINATION ______________________________ ______________ DATE ______________
(CITY OR TOWN) (STATE)

RATING

USE THE SPECIAL PENCIL. MAKE GLOSSY BLACK MARKS.

1 A B C D E	26 A B C D E	51 A B C D E	76 A B C D E	101 A B C D E
2 A B C D E	27 A B C D E	52 A B C D E	77 A B C D E	102 A B C D E
3 A B C D E	28 A B C D E	53 A B C D E	78 A B C D E	103 A B C D E
4 A B C D E	29 A B C D E	54 A B C D E	79 A B C D E	104 A B C D E
5 A B C D E	30 A B C D E	55 A B C D E	80 A B C D E	105 A B C D E
6 A B C D E	31 A B C D E	56 A B C D E	81 A B C D E	106 A B C D E
7 A B C D E	32 A B C D E	57 A B C D E	82 A B C D E	107 A B C D E
8 A B C D E	33 A B C D E	58 A B C D E	83 A B C D E	108 A B C D E
9 A B C D E	34 A B C D E	59 A B C D E	84 A B C D E	109 A B C D E
10 A B C D E	35 A B C D E	60 A B C D E	85 A B C D E	110 A B C D E

Make only ONE mark for each answer. Additional and stray marks may be counted as mistakes. In making corrections, erase errors COMPLETELY.

11 A B C D E	36 A B C D E	61 A B C D E	86 A B C D E	111 A B C D E
12 A B C D E	37 A B C D E	62 A B C D E	87 A B C D E	112 A B C D E
13 A B C D E	38 A B C D E	63 A B C D E	88 A B C D E	113 A B C D E
14 A B C D E	39 A B C D E	64 A B C D E	89 A B C D E	114 A B C D E
15 A B C D E	40 A B C D E	65 A B C D E	90 A B C D E	115 A B C D E
16 A B C D E	41 A B C D E	66 A B C D E	91 A B C D E	116 A B C D E
17 A B C D E	42 A B C D E	67 A B C D E	92 A B C D E	117 A B C D E
18 A B C D E	43 A B C D E	68 A B C D E	93 A B C D E	118 A B C D E
19 A B C D E	44 A B C D E	69 A B C D E	94 A B C D E	119 A B C D E
20 A B C D E	45 A B C D E	70 A B C D E	95 A B C D E	120 A B C D E
21 A B C D E	46 A B C D E	71 A B C D E	96 A B C D E	121 A B C D E
22 A B C D E	47 A B C D E	72 A B C D E	97 A B C D E	122 A B C D E
23 A B C D E	48 A B C D E	73 A B C D E	98 A B C D E	123 A B C D E
24 A B C D E	49 A B C D E	74 A B C D E	99 A B C D E	124 A B C D E
25 A B C D E	50 A B C D E	75 A B C D E	100 A B C D E	125 A B C D E